Legacy of a False Promise

Legacy of a False Promise

A Daughter's Reckoning

MARGARET FUCHS SINGER

The University of Alabama Press

Tuscaloosa

Library of Congress Cataloging-in-Publication Data

Singer, Margaret Fuchs.
    Legacy of a false promise : a daughter's reckoning /
Margaret Fuchs Singer.
         p.   cm.
    Includes bibliographical references and index.
    ISBN 978-0-8173-1674-7 (cloth : alk. paper) 1. Fuchs,
Herbert, 1905–1988. 2. Fuchs, Frances Rice, 1907–1996.
3. Singer, Margaret Fuchs—Childhood and youth. 4. Singer,
Margaret Fuchs—Family. 5. Parent and child—United
States—Case studies. 6. Communists—United States—
Biography. 7. Anti-communist movements—United States—
History—20th century. 8. United States. Congress. House.
Committee on Un-American Activities. 9. United States—
Politics and government—1953–1961. 10. Washington
(D.C.)—Biography. I. Title.
    E743.5.F83S54 2009
    973.92092—dc22
    [B]
                                            2009010160

This memoir is dedicated to my parents
Herbert and Frances Fuchs
and to their grandchildren

[I]t will do no good to search for villains or heroes or saints or devils because there were none; there were only victims.

—Dalton Trumbo, referring to the McCarthy Era, as he accepted an award from the Screenwriters Guild in 1970

Contents

Illustrations

Acknowledgments

I can't think of any project that has been more meaningful to me than the writing of this personal story. It has been a journey of discovery, a working-through, a healing, and an opportunity for creative expression. Many people have accompanied me along the way, some contributing information, some offering writing suggestions, others lending a listening ear. I am grateful to all of you for your patience and support.

To extended family and old friends who helped me fill the gaps in my memory and knowledge, thank you: Devin Bent, Rose Marien Black, George and Eva Brecher, Vernon Fox, Richard Fuchs, Louise Hollander, Jim Lichtenberg, Helen Mandelbaum, Louise Casgrain Balboni, Phyllis Fahrney Raynor, Sandy Weitzman, and Dana Willens. You have helped me relive difficult childhood memories and see them in a new light.

I have been fortunate to find several other important people from my parents' past who were willing to tell me what they remembered. The unique perspectives of Fred Griffith, Gene Higgins, Howard Jenkins, and Harry Magdoff have added significantly to my sense of the meaning behind the facts. Their contributions to my story have been invaluable.

The writings of Hope Hale Davis, John Earl Haynes, Ann Kimmage, Bob Lamphere, Victor Navasky, Linn Shapiro, Alan Wald, and Allen Weinstein have contributed greatly to the world's understanding of the history of the American Left. I appreciate that they all took time from their busy schedules to share with me their knowledge and points of view.

By encouraging me to join an Eastern Michigan University workshop for teachers in the summer of 1996, Barbara Stark-Nemon inspired me to start writing; that was the beginning of a great adventure, which I have shared with her along the way. I have been spurred on, also, by my family and countless other friends. Thanks to Ruth Bardenstein, Joan Boonin, Nancy Brickman, Audrey Curtis, Jane and David Eger, Julie Fuchs, Peter Fuchs, Donna Gotlib, Mary and John Higgins, Kate Jenkins, Martha Kransdorf, Pam and Steve Landau, Ann Langford-Fuchs, Alice Meisels, Meira Miller, Karin Schneider, Dan Singer, Ilana Singer, David Wegman, Judy Weinblatt, Chane Yachness, and Simone Yehuda for your steadfast encouragement.

I am very grateful to Dan Waterman, acquisitions editor for humanities at The University of Alabama Press, for his support of this project through its many stages at the press: the peer reviews, the board approvals, and numerous revisions. Dan's respectful and patient approach to our work made it fun and rewarding. Thanks also to the press's project manager, Joanna Jacobs, and copy editor Lady Smith for their work with the manuscript during its final stages of editing and production.

For several years, I have shared drafts of my manuscript with Brenda Meisels and Susan Morales, my writing group. Their enthusiasm and critical feedback have been special gifts. I have learned so much while working with you, Brenda and Susan, and I treasure your friendship and our writing partnership.

To Aniko Bahr, who believed in me and traveled long distances to help me begin the editing process, thank you from the bottom of my heart. Your life-giving energy and remarkable skills are an inspiration.

And special thanks to Phyllis Ziman Tobin, to whom I owe a tremendous debt of gratitude. You know what you did.

I would have been unable to make this journey without the loving support of my husband, Michael Singer, who made it possible for me to devote myself to this undertaking by offering his emotional sustenance, psychological insights, and writing advice at every turn. Words cannot express my love and appreciation.

Prologue

I begin the journey after my parents' deaths; it would have been impossible while they were living. I sit on a granite boulder overlooking the Deer Isle Thorofare in Stonington, Maine, where the Penobscot and Jericho bays meet. In this familiar spot, a hint of balsam in the air, I remember my father and mother, Herbert and Frances Rice Fuchs.

In the summer of 1972, almost two decades after the crisis, my parents purchased a summer home here, to share with their children and grandchildren. This is their most tangible legacy, this homestead, which for over three decades has served as a retreat for our family and friends.

But my parents' legacy is a complicated, many-faceted one. Today, looking back, I am filled with memories of a traumatic time: the day I first learned, at age thirteen, that my parents were former Communists. That trauma and the events that followed it dominate my thoughts, and I wish to tell my children, Ilana and Daniel, about that experience. I want to let them know what I remember as a teenager in Washington, D.C., in the 1950s and what I have learned about my parents—two assimilated Jews, bright, idealistic intellectuals, who joined the Communist Party in the mid-'30s, became disillusioned and quit in the mid-'40s, and then faced the most terrible moral dilemma of their lives: how to respond to the demand to testify before the House Un-American Activities Committee in 1955. These were good people, caught up in a powerfully hopeful—then later, horribly destructive—period in our country's history. Their story is a human one, reminiscent of others of that time.

With this journey, I honor my parents' memory. Their story is unique because of their positions and associates in the U.S. government, their HUAC experience, the political climate in which they were living, and of course their own peculiar temperaments. But I'm getting ahead of myself. . .

The horrors of the McCarthy Era impacted people from many different walks of life—union members, teachers, actors, government workers, performers, writers, and scientists. Different also were the time frames and the social milieus in which their individual experiences took place. But no matter what the nature of their jobs and their personal struggles, many HUAC witnesses were parents, too, and the pain of those times deeply affected their children. I was one of those children.

Legacy of a False Promise

I

Moral Dilemma

1

The Family Secret

Early June 1955; Washington, D.C.

I'm not sure when I first heard the pacing overhead that evening. Did my mother call my attention to it—the insistent, even rhythm of my father's footsteps back and forth, back and forth across the length of their bedroom floor?

"Your father needs to speak to you and Peter during dinner," my mother told me as she darted down the hall to the kitchen, two full grocery bags heavy in her arms. A familiar, dull anxiety ran through me; Dad's pacing meant trouble.

My father, a fifty-year-old, slightly built man with a prominent nose and thinning brown hair, was brilliant, intense, and gentle, a man familiar with anxiety himself. And depression. Not infrequently, he would withdraw from us, perhaps to mull over his lectures at the American University Washington College of Law; or maybe, for all I knew, he withdrew because of something we had done to cause him displeasure. My constant uncertainty about the reason for his unhappiness and my fear that I might be the cause often disturbed my sense of well-being and promoted in me an extreme sensitivity to other people's moods.

The house was silent that evening but for the sounds of my father's pacing and the commonplace bang of cabinet doors opening and closing in the kitchen as my mother emptied the grocery bags and prepared dinner. From where I sat doing homework, I could see her face, tight and drawn.

Peter, my sixteen-year-old brother, burst through the front door at 5:55, flung his taut, athletic body toward the dining room table, and verbally assaulted our mother before the meal began with a question sure to annoy. "What's for dessert?" he demanded, the door slamming behind him. Mom responded with impatience. "If I've told you once, I've told you a thousand times," she scolded. "If you're going to live in this house you'll learn to come in quietly." Without a word Peter turned, bolted from the room, and took off up the stairs, leaving a trail of clothes and books behind him.

At 6:05, the four of us sat down at the old pine dining table, handmade by Dad when he and Mom were first married and money was tight. Drawn to the aroma of lamb chops and spinach soufflé, we began our meal as my father started to speak.

"I have something I need to tell you," my father began. He looked away for a minute, tapping his fingers lightly on the table as if trying to gather his thoughts. Then he faced us again, his eyes intense with pain. "I don't really know where to start," he said. "In the late '30s and early '40s, your mother and I were members of the Communist Party. In a few days I expect to be served with a subpoena to appear before HUAC, the House Un-American Activities Committee; there may be publicity. I don't know what will happen, and I must ask you *not* to discuss this with *anyone*." For a few moments no one said a word; I could feel my heart racing, perspiration dampening my shirt.

I cannot speak for my brother, but my father might as well have told us that he and my mother were convicted felons. Or terminally ill. I knew little, then, about Communism, or Communism's troubled place in our nation's history, past or present. My parents, usually open to sharing ideas and analyzing important issues with us, were afraid to discuss it; my teachers did not teach it; and I, at thirteen, was not a reader. What I had learned about Communism I had learned from the media, which reflected our government's conviction that Communists were the ultimate enemy of the American people, an evil threat to the free world, a force determined to infiltrate our cities and take over the minds and the lives of innocent Americans, just like me.

One night several months earlier, while watching a TV newscast, I heard the anchorman announce that some "Communists presently held in American jails have offered to leave the United States if freed." In a moment of daring, I imagined, *What would happen if I pretended, for just ten minutes, to be a Communist myself? No one would ever know my secret.* That had been make-believe, a flight of imagination into a forbidden world; this was real. What would happen to us? I wondered. Would my parents go to jail? Who would take care of my brother and me?

"Why, Dad? Why did you do it?" I asked, my words filling the awkward silence. My father took a drink of water from the tall glass before him and started again. Slowly, patiently, he explained his motives for joining the Communist Party. He spoke about his desire to be part of a movement that promised positive changes in society, his need to be active in the fight against unfair labor practices and social injustice. "We never thought we were doing anything wrong," he said. "We certainly had no thoughts of overthrowing the government. We were idealistic then. And we were also naive."

As I listened my stomach tightened, queasiness taking over where hunger had been. I put down my fork and pushed my plate away.

At first, my father explained, idealism had sustained them along with the stimulating discussions and political action. But after a while it had become clear that the Party required close ties to the Soviet government, which was no longer our ally. In his government job at the National Labor Relations Board, my father found that being a Party member meant more and more secrecy and dishonesty, and the goals of the Party leadership became progressively more distant from his own.

My parents now felt they had made a mistake by following that path, that hidden life, my father said. They left the Party in 1946 and, gradually, severed all ties to people and organizations associated with it. This had been difficult; it had isolated them. It had meant ending relationships with many special people, some of whom I remembered, including my father's youngest brother, my Uncle Vernon.

I searched my mother's face for comfort. All of her attention was focused on my father's words, as if to emphasize their gravity. I looked at Pete. Next to me and across from Dad, he sat transfixed.

"When I go before the House committee," my father said, "I'm going to face the most difficult decision of my life. Because I feel I made a mistake, I have the need to acknowledge my error publicly. I want to speak about myself and everything I did. But I'm unwilling to implicate others, my friends and associates in the Party." Dad paused to let his words sink in.

We listened intently as my father began again. He shared with us his fear that the House committee might not let him speak exclusively about himself. If that were to happen, he explained, he would risk contempt of Congress, risk being sent to prison.[1] His options in that situation would be either to invoke the Fifth Amendment and exercise his right to say nothing on the grounds that it might incriminate him or to talk about it all, *everything* and *everybody*. There would be no middle ground. Many people, some who never even joined the Party, were losing their jobs, he told us; some were in jail.

I felt myself drawn into my father's anguish as he went on describing this torturous dilemma and his wish to go on with his life and teaching with a clear conscience. He let us know that, in his view, "taking the Fifth" implied one had something to hide and meant not taking responsibility for one's decisions and actions. Furthermore, he told us, he was not technically at risk of incriminating himself, since the statute of limitations had run out. For him, "taking the Fifth" was not an acceptable course of action. There appeared to be no way out.

Finally my father ran out of explanations. My mother rose to clear the table.

"Listen," my father said, as he handed her his plate, "I know this is hard for both of you. I'm sorry. I can only hope you'll try to understand."

Peter and I left the table and walked together through the living room and up the stairs to the second floor. Stopping as we reached the landing, he turned toward me. "Things seem clearer to me now," he said. "Remember when we were in Maine two summers ago? Remember when Mom and Dad, for no reason at all, canceled our plans to see a play in Blue Hill? It was so unlike them not to tell us why. Now I see there had to have been old friends at that show, people from the past, people they did not want to see."

Without waiting for a response, Peter turned, entered his bedroom, and closed the door. How I wished he would stay and talk just a little longer—keep me company in my confusion and despair. He didn't. Frightened and alone, I went into my room and shut the door.

There were my drawings, my favorite dolls, my photo albums. They seemed unfamiliar to me now, as if I had walked into the room of a stranger. I could hear the muffled voices from Peter's radio next door and, outside my window, I could see the muted blue light of dusk.

It would be forty years before my brother and I would again broach the subject of our parents' troubles.

2

Paranoia

"I don't know what will happen, and I must ask you *not* to discuss this with *anyone.*"

My father's words of caution had the impact and finality of a judge's gavel cementing a verdict—topic of discussion closed, off-limits outside this house. At first I was puzzled by the gravity of my parents' warnings, but I soon learned that, in anticipation of testimony that could lead to contempt of Congress, my parents feared for our future. Whatever we knew and revealed to someone outside our home could later be used against us in the passionately American, conservative, and often anti-Semitic environment in which we lived. I never did feel at home in this community where my parents' liberal views stood out as strange, where houses a block from ours were closed to Jews, and where jeering boys called me "Jew girl" as I walked home from school. I always knew I was different. My family was different; we were outsiders.

My father often told a story that perfectly highlighted this difference for me. My family had lived in Denver, Colorado, during World War II. When we returned to D.C. in late 1945, my parents put a down payment on a house that would be their home for the next forty years. The house, located on an unpretentious block in the lovely northwest section of Washington called Palisades, was just off MacArthur Boulevard and within walking distance of the historic Chesapeake and Ohio Canal and the lush green, rocky-cliffed banks of the Potomac River. One Sunday morning, Dad took Peter to see the new house. Pete was excited, but his anticipation turned to apprehension when he got out of the car and saw our neighbor-to-be, Charles Lippert, a middle-aged post office worker, storm out of his house and call out to them.

"What religion are you?" Mr. Lippert demanded.

"That's none of your Goddamn business," my father said. Mr. Lippert retreated into his house.

Directing Peter to get back into the car and wait, Dad marched across the street and up the walkway to Mr. Lippert's front door; he knocked impatiently. Mr. Lippert opened the door. His wife, Georgia, stood by his side.

"I want you to invite me inside," my father insisted. "I have something to say to you."

"Well, all right, come in."

"I see you're wearing a Masonic pin on your lapel," my father said. "I thought the Masons believed in the brotherhood of man. That was no way to greet a new neighbor. I think you owe me an apology."

"You're probably right," Mr. Lippert acknowledged, halfheartedly. "It's just that I've invested a lot of money in this property, you see, and Jews throw chicken bones out their windows!"

Many evenings early in the spring of '55, my parents had walked together up our street, 49th Street, past the large, stately homes to Battery Kemble, the Civil War fort, now a park, a mile away. I learned later that on those troubled walks, my parents discussed plans for our care and safekeeping in the event of his—or their—imprisonment. With no extended family and few close friends to count on, my parents were forced to face this crisis alone.

In the days that followed my father's revelation, I drifted through my everyday life in a gloom-filled cloud, attending school as usual, pretending all was well. Within me, fear, shame, and isolation drained my energies. Avoiding my friends after school, I walked alone to the bus stop at 35th Street and Reservoir Road, determined to reach home as soon as possible, where I could be by myself. Many nights I cried myself to sleep while my mother stood by, concerned but unable to help. I wanted my mother to calm me: to sit at the side of my bed, put her arms around me, and stroke my hair as I tried to get to sleep. I wanted her to tell me that she loved me and that everything would be all right. But though I knew she cared, my mother could not offer me the reassurance I so desperately needed.

There was one exception to the strict injunction against speaking to others about our threatening circumstances and uncertain fate. One friend, Frances Lichtenberg, my mother's best friend and a liberal former Socialist herself, could be trusted with our confidences. My mother, recognizing my extreme isolation, gave me permission to talk with Fran if I chose to do so.

Frances and Henry Lichtenberg were my parents' closest friends, the people they trusted with our care during family emergencies, a couple that understood and sympathized with their political past. Henry, a serious, distinguished-looking, gray-haired man in his early fifties, was the youngest of twelve children born to Orthodox Jewish immigrants who had come to New York from Russia and settled on the Lower East Side. A well-established pediatrician and founder of the ground-breaking Group Health Association, an early model of organized socialized medicine in Washington, Henry had a charismatic personality and a reputation for being a great doctor. Years later, anticipating his imminent death from cancer, Henry would memorialize this greatness by posing for a sculpted portrait bust which he bequeathed to his family, lest they ever forget him.

Frances, his wife, was several years his junior. After a few years at home with her children, Jimmy and Louise, who were near me in age and more like cousins than friends, Fran established herself as a tutor of hearing-impaired children in a nearby public school system. Tall and elegant, she wore her short, natural, yet smartly coiffed gray hair pulled behind her ears, framing her handsome face. Fran was a passionate, energetic, and intelligent woman who could be warm and exuberant, a charming hostess. It was Henry, however, who dominated the Lichtenberg household, and Fran deeply resented his controlling nature and having to live in the shadow of his success. Frequently her frustration and anger poured out in uncontrolled rage, usually aimed at one of her own children, but sometimes spilling over to one of the many kids who gathered regularly to play at the Lichtenberg home. Any one of us who inadvertently said or did the wrong thing or who was in the wrong place at the wrong time could experience Fran's rage. We were all afraid of Fran; her outbursts were venomous and unpredictable.

One late afternoon, when I was alone at home gossiping on my parents' bedroom telephone with my school friend Louise Casgrain, I heard a knock on the front door.

"Hang on a second," I told Louise. "I'll be right back."

Eager to return to my call as quickly as possible, I ran downstairs and pulled open the door. Fran Lichtenberg stood before me, smiling. She greeted me warmly. She had come to drop off a book for my mother. Seeing her standing there, I completely forgot about my friend Louise, our conversation, and the phone left off the hook. I forgot also, in this time of intense isolation and fear, about my usual caution when in Fran's company. Only my urgent need to confide in someone, to share my fears with a person who might understand and comfort me, mattered to me now.

"Please come in," I said. She stepped inside and I closed the door behind her. She held the book out to me and I looked at it for a moment before taking it from her. I hesitated, searching for the words I wanted to say.

"Peggy?" she asked. "What is it? What's wrong?"

"Fran, do you have a few minutes to talk to me?"

Sitting beside me on the long, walnut-framed sofa, the soft, beige cushions propped up behind us, Fran, no longer the punitive authority figure I had come to know, became a sympathetic, consoling supporter. She spoke with me for more than an hour. Patiently, she described the political climate of the 1930s in New York when thousands of young people—many of them Jews with a family history of oppression and persecution—were drawn to groups and organizations dedicated to the cause of working people around the world. These young people saw the experiment in socialism and communism as a symbol of hope for the future, she told me. The way she spoke, from personal experience and with a touch of nostalgia, made me believe that what she said was true. Her eyes were kind and her simple explanations soothing.

Finally, it was time for Fran to go. Her family was waiting for her at home; it was dinnertime. Rising together, we walked to the door. I thanked her for taking time with me, said goodbye, and shut the door behind her. Suddenly I panicked. Remembering the phone off the hook, I bolted upstairs into my parents' bedroom and grabbed the receiver. By now the phone was dead, Louise no longer on the line. My parents' warnings rang in my ears—warnings as to the danger of disclosure. Might Louise have overheard my conversation with Fran? By neglecting to hang up the telephone before answering the door, had I put my family at risk? I was terrified. By the time my parents and my brother arrived home ten or fifteen minutes later, I was hysterical, inconsolable.

"What if Louise could hear me?" I raved. "I left the phone off the hook and I know she could hear me!"

"Don't worry," my mother tried to assure me. "There's no way you could be heard over the wire, all the way down to the living room. Weren't you speaking in a normal voice?"

Utterly shaken, convinced I had endangered my family and myself, I cried as if my whole world could come to an end. Mom and Dad had warned me that my words had the power to send them to prison. Now they tried to calm my fears, but it was no use.

After much discussion, Peter had an idea. "Let me run to the drugstore," he suggested. "I'll call home to prove to you that Louise couldn't have heard your conversation in the living room."

And so he did. Peter called; I answered the phone upstairs in my parents' bedroom; Mom and Dad spoke in normal conversational tones in the living room. Only after Peter *swore* he could not hear our parents' conversation—only then could I be consoled.

3

The Subpoena

During those difficult days after my father's revelation but before we could be sure of its consequences, my father's time was filled with the agonizing business of preparing for his probable Committee appearance. He struggled to find an attorney, finally consulting Edward Bennett Williams, a professor of criminal law at Georgetown University, considered by many to be the best trial lawyer in the country.[1] Dad met with American University president Hurst R. Anderson and the chairman of the Board of Trustees, Judge Robert V. Fletcher. Deferentially, he prepared them for the possibility of publicity and assured them that he had not been a Communist during his six years in their employ.[2] He attempted to get ready for the inevitable arrival of the dreaded subpoena.

Dad and I grew much closer during the days and weeks that followed. Gone was the sense of distance that usually divided us. No longer did his preoccupation with work or private thoughts leave him buried in a book, too busy to be bothered with my childish concerns. Now, suddenly he needed to talk and he sought my company. Often we sat together in our living room, Dad in his favorite overstuffed, yellow leather chair, I curled up in the antique French Provincial love seat across from him, the familiar, steady strokes of my grandmother Nona's brass mantelpiece clock ticking quietly in the background. I became his confidante, as he puffed gently on his Dunhill pipe or munched on a square of Baker's sweet cooking chocolate, remembering, reminiscing, reliving his life before I knew him.

During those talks, I learned about Dad's early years growing up in the Washington Heights section of Manhattan, the gifted oldest of three sons, his parents nonobservant Jews who had immigrated to America from Vienna in the 1890s. I had not known my father's parents, who died when I was very young and from whom Dad had long been estranged. During my time with my father, I learned about his three years at the academically rigorous Townsend Harris High School, his intellectual and political awakening in the stimulating environment of the City College of New York, and his early unsuccessful marriage to Rita Goldsmith, with whom he had had a stillborn son and for whom he maintained a deep fondness throughout his life. I learned about his law school career at New York University, where he and Rita first met and where they befriended Frances Rice, my mother, also a student there. My mother was then a plain, bookish young woman with large dark eyes who seemed to be drawn to the couple's charm and spirit. She had remained friendly with them after graduation when my father opened a small law practice with my grandfather on East 86th Street in Yorkville.

Dad described the 1920s as a wild and frenetic time. His marriage to Rita had been a stormy union characterized by reckless abandon and punctuated with discord—speakeasy drinking, partying, and bickering. Finally, recognizing its hopelessness, my father had been the one to call off the marriage. One night, after a particularly rowdy, rancorous evening, my father told Rita he thought there was no hope for resolving their difficulties. Grief-stricken, but proud that he had finally faced the truth, he made a dramatic exit from their apartment, tripping at the landing and falling on his face.

Despite the turbulent marriage, my father had thoroughly enjoyed the excitement of New York City, his friends, the social scene. But his love of ideas, his keen analytic mind, and his need to do something meaningful in life joined with his lack of maturity and sense of malaise to make him restless. It was time for something new.

What my father did not discuss with me then were the facts surrounding his decision to join the Communist Party. I learned about this later, from his HUAC hearing testimony, from newspaper and magazine articles, from the Federal Bureau of Investigation files accessed through the Freedom of Information Act, and from my father's personal records of the period. These sources told me that my father joined the Communist Party in November 1934 at the urging of a friend, a New York City cab driver and member of the taxi drivers' union. This friend interested him in Marxist ideas and ultimately convinced him that if he was serious about his "liberal proclivities," and if he wanted to make things happen, "the thing to do was to join the Communist Party, which was serious about bringing about the desired ends . . . [of] social reform, opposition to fascism, fighting against unemployment and bigotry [and] supporting the rights of labor and minorities."[3] I learned that as a new member of the Communist Party Unit, Section 4, New York, my father signed a membership card under the name Herbert Hacker, Hacker being his mother's maiden name.

In the fall of 1936, several years after his divorce, an intriguing opportunity presented itself. While working at the firm of Rosenberg, Goldmark and Colin, Dad got the word from a colleague that a man named Max Lowenthal was tak-

My mother and father sometime in the 1930s.

ing on staff for a Senate subcommittee later to be known as the Wheeler Committee. Dad was ready to leave New York, and the Senate job promised intellectual stimulation, career growth possibilities, and the chance to be closer to his new love interest, Frances Rice. Frances was living in D.C. by then and was working in a cutting-edge job at the Bureau of Labor Statistics. My mother and father were married by the justice of the peace on April 26, 1937. She had suggested to him that she thought "it was time." My mother and father would remain in D.C. for most of their fifty years of marriage.

On June 6, 1955, during one of our long afternoons, the piercing ring of the doorbell interrupted my father and me. It was I who walked to the door and opened it.

"Mr. Herbert Fuchs?"

The hulking stranger standing before me was ruddy-faced and imposing. My father rose from his chair and moved toward the door.

"I am Herbert Fuchs."

The stranger spoke again, his voice and his awkward stance acknowledging the intrusive nature of his mission.

"I'm here to serve you with this subpoena to appear before the House Committee on Un-American Activities, at ten o'clock on Monday, June 13," the man stated, shifting his weight uncomfortably from side to side. "Room 226, Old House Office Building. Do you have any questions? . . . I . . . I'm sorry to disturb you, I . . ."

My father reached for the subpoena and tossed it on the small, carved wooden table by the door. Speaking through clenched teeth—his words a mixture of rage, fear, and disdain—he responded to the messenger, cutting him off in mid-sentence. "I must ask you to leave my house," my father hissed, "immediately."

4

The Word Is Out

An American University part-time law teacher has testified to the House Committee on Un-American Activities that he was a member of three different underground Communist cells in the Federal Government in the 1930's and 40's.
    —Washington Star, *July 10, 1955*

Before my father was called to testify, I had been looking forward to a quiet and leisurely summer. I loved the fact that being thirteen meant more freedom to come and go independently and for some months now my parents had allowed me, with a couple of friends, to take the MacArthur Boulevard D-4 bus along Reservoir Road, through Georgetown, downtown into the heart of Washington. We liked to hang out at the "five-and-dime," Woolworth's, where we bought cosmetics and took pictures in the instant photo booth; I can still recall the enticing scent of my favorite "Powder Pink" lipstick. At Bakers shoe store I bought my first real pair of heels, the most beautiful shoes I'd ever seen—delicate black leather, low-heeled pumps with a thin thread of leather lacing woven along the outside. A highlight of our trips downtown was shopping at "Woodies," Woodward and Lothrop's department store, where for weeks I admired an elegant taffeta party dress, in a size seven. I was drawn to its tiny black and white checks, its satiny finish and simple lines. On each successive shopping trip, I tried on this special dress. When it finally went on sale, I watched the price drop, hoping that eventually I could afford to buy it. It never happened.

Friday nights, our crowd gathered in someone's basement for a party; I wore my new heels. We never tired of dancing to the 45–r.p.m. recordings of the Platters, Johnny Mathis, or Fats Domino, and I could count on dancing with at least one of my numerous crushes. Our infatuations were the focus of the group's attention during the days before and after each event.

Once summer vacation began, my friend Sandy Weitzman and I enrolled at

American University for a beginning typing class that met three mornings a week. Afternoons we often swam at the university swimming pool. Bill Fuhrman also swam at A.U. that summer. I knew Bill from the Gordon Junior High School orchestra, in which he played first flute, masterfully—I loved to listen to him breeze through the "Flight of the Bumble Bee"—and where Becky Mills and I shared second flute.[1] My infatuation with Bill was deep and long-standing. At fourteen, he was handsome, silent, and a little bit sad. I wished I could have gotten up the nerve to say hello to Bill and maybe even talk at the pool, but that was not to be.

My brother, Peter, worked as a lifeguard at a neighborhood swimming pool. He kept to the fringe of our family life that summer of '55. He came home for meals and slept there but otherwise seldom involved himself with us. He kept away to express his growing independence and probably also to stay clear of our family's difficulties. Competent in many of the ways our father was not, Pete excelled in physical activities. He was an accomplished horseman, sailor, and athlete, and by sixteen was driving and repairing cars. The rest of us were in awe of his skills. We idealized him, convinced he could accomplish superhuman tasks. I longed for my brother's acceptance, longed to have a relationship with him, but he never seemed to pay me any mind.

Inspired by nostalgia for a 1928 Model A Ford he once owned, Dad found one when vacationing in Maine and bought it for Pete, who now drove it everywhere. One afternoon after work, Pete came upon a couple of fire engines approaching Hardy Elementary School in Foxhall Village. He followed them to the school where he saw two city policemen, each holding one end of a rope stretched across the playground, trying, so far unsuccessfully, to corral some mules that had recently escaped from their stables down by the C & O Canal. Usually, on weekends, these mules were engaged in pulling the canal barge and on some weekdays they guided a sickle-bar mower that cut the grass along MacArthur Boulevard. But on this day, the mules had made their way the three miles or so to Hardy's playground. Upset by the actions of their would-be captors, the mules had gone wild. Peter to the rescue! Dressed in his usual attire—bathing trunks, glasses, and high-top sneakers (no shirt)—he used his considerable skill and experience with horses to calm the mules and help assist in their capture. The next day, a *Washington Daily News* story and photo recorded the dramatic event for posterity.

As always, Dad had looked forward to the start of the summer law school term. Having discovered his talent and penchant for teaching, he had finally found his professional niche.

My father standing next to the family's Model A Ford, August 1953.

Often, in the evening, I would accompany Mom when she drove to the Washington College of Law, on the corner of 20th and G streets, to pick up Dad after class. We were always punctual; my father did not tolerate lateness.

"Be quiet when Dad gets in the car," my mother instructed as we waited for the class to let out. "Let him talk; don't interrupt. You know how excited he gets."

How well I remember my father bursting through the massive front door of the college, bounding down the stairs to meet us.

"The kids were really 'on' tonight!" I remember him saying after a particularly exciting session. "Everyone was involved. They're really catching on; the discussion was great. I love it!"

While my father effused, exuding the energy and exhilaration of a contestant fresh off the field of an athletic victory, my mother, a law school graduate herself, listened and asked questions. An emotional support and intellectual partner, she indulged my father, encouraging him to review and critique the night's exchanges, as I sat quietly in the back seat listening but not understanding.

I don't remember the content of those postclass conversations—international law, tax law, labor law, they were all his areas of expertise—but I remember the intensity of feeling. My father's words reflected his deep commitment to his students and to the teaching process. He loved the exchange of ideas; he loved building a case; he patiently developed concepts which he convincingly explained, and his students responded.

Any hope I harbored that we, as a family, had returned to lives of normalcy following my father's June testimony, which we hoped would put the matter to rest, ended on Saturday, July 9. That evening, my father received a phone call from Edgar Prina, a reporter from the *Washington Star*, asking for comment on a story that had been leaked to him. Prina's source divulged that my father had testified before members of the House Un-American Activities Committee and that he had agreed, finally, to discuss fully his Communist activities while working for the government between 1936 and 1946. The story was true.

The next day after breakfast, my father washed the dishes while my mother drove down 49th Street to the MacArthur Drug Store to look for the Prina article in the morning edition of the *Star*, the conservative newspaper to which my parents did *not* subscribe. When Mom returned, she carried the paper to the kitchen and read the article aloud to my father, who breathed a sigh of resignation. My father's testimony before a subcommittee of the House Un-American Activities Committee had taken place in closed session with the express understanding that there would be no publicity.[2] Someone from HUAC or from the American University Board of Trustees executive committee had leaked the story to the press.

"Now the word is out," my father said, his voice trembling. "We will have to face the consequences."

My mother handed me the paper. "You need to read this," she said. The article's provocative language jumped out at me: "Former Red ties . . . three different underground Communist cells . . . covert Red apparatus . . . confessed former courier for a prewar Soviet spy ring." How would I ever show my face again in public? How would I go on?

My plan that steamy summer morning had been to drive to Aberdeen, Maryland, with Louise Casgrain's parents to visit her at a summer camp on the Susquehanna River. I had looked forward to seeing Louise. She was my close friend, and in spite of several years' difference in our ages, we relied on our daily contact for personal support and a connection with the events of our social group. Now I didn't want to go.

Looking up from the paper, I addressed my parents. "I will not be going to visit Louise today," I said. "There's no way I can go."

"What's that?" my mother asked.

"I'm not going to leave the house; I can't show my face. The Casgrains won't want me to drive with them." I realized at that moment how little I knew about my friend's parents.

A. U. Law School Teacher Tells of Former Red Ties

By L. EDGAR PRINA

An American University part-time law teacher has testified to the House Committee on Un-American Activities that he was a member of three different underground Communist cells in the Federal Government in the 1930's and 40's.

He is Herbert Fuchs, a part-time faculty member of the Washington Law School. He lives at 2220 Forty-ninth street N.W. and nas a private law office in the Dupont Circle Building.

Mr. Fuchs made his statement to the House Committee in closed session. He testified that he joined the Communist Party in New York in 1934 and quit it here in the late 40's.

The committee is expected to call Mr. Fuchs soon for questioning in a public hearing.

The Star has been informed that Mr. Fuchs, while willing to talk freely about his own affiliation with the Communist Party, has steadfastly refused to identify other members of the underground cells. He refused, yesterday, to comment to newsmen on the matter in any way.

He told the committee he joined the first such covert Red apparatus upon his coming to Washington in 1936 to take a post with the special Senate committee investigating the Nation's railroads—a group then headed by Senator Burton K. Wheeler, Democrat of Montana.

Mr. Fuchs testified that the cell was composed entirely of staff members of the Wheeler committee—himself and three others.

A couple of years later, according to his testimony, Mr. Fuchs took a post with the National Labor Relations Board and joined the Communist underground unit there.

At the beginning of World War II, the witness related, he transferred to the War Labor Board. He was sent to Denver and there joined a third Red unit, composed of employes of the board.

When he returned to the NLRB in 1946 he rejoined the Communist cell there, Mr. Fuchs told the committee. When he left the Government some time later, he held the position of solicitor of the NLRB.

The committee has been anxious to find out whether Mr. Fuchs can shed any light on the Red underground cell identified by Whittaker Chambers, confessed former courier for a prewar Soviet spy ring in Washington.

Mr. Chambers has charged that Nathan Witt, one-time secretary to the National Labor Relations board, was a member of this group, along with several other Government lawyers including Alger Hiss, Lee Pressman and John Abt.

Washington Star article by Edgar Prina on July 10, 1955, marking the beginning of two years of publicity about my father's case.

When the Casgrains arrived, my mother walked to their car and invited them into the house. "Peggy is not comfortable driving with you this morning," she explained, "until you've read this article that just appeared in today's *Star*." Mrs. Casgrain read the article and passed it to her husband. Her response was a surprise. "This is not a problem," she said, smiling. "I used to tell my friends in college that if I ever had a child who didn't grow up to become a Socialist, I'd have to disown her." I agreed to accompany the Casgrains to Aberdeen. We made the trip in silence.

Which friends would remain friends? I wondered. Which friends would be able to accept my parents' past and withstand the pressure, or instinct, to turn away from me?

Following this publicity, the amorphous threats to our sense of comfort and security increased. There were the crank callers, some who rang and hung up, others who stayed on the line to harass us: "Shame on you, Herbert," one anonymous caller scolded. "Why are you such a bad Jew?" For some time there had been the intrusive FBI surveillance. We knew that our phone had been tapped, and sometimes we would see the same parked car on MacArthur Boulevard, always the same two men inside, hats pulled down, newspapers hiding their faces, watching the movements of our family, friends, and associates as we went about the business of our daily lives.

I was frightened when, in more than one phone conversation, my most outspoken friend, Rose Marien, brazenly addressed the agents monitoring our calls directly: "You must be bored," she suggested between giggles. "Want to hear who's going steady?" With a provocative you-can't-do-anything-to-me attitude, she regaled them with a list of the latest of our friends' heartthrobs, heartbreaks, and reconciliations.

And, most disturbing of all, there were the neighbor-to-neighbor calls cautioning the parents of our friends not to let their sons and daughters associate any longer with "those Fuchs children."

"I was not permitted to hang out with you," Phyllis Fahrney explained to me four decades later. "I was not allowed to go to your house. I was hurt that my parents made that rule which I did not understand and, if you recall, I sometimes disobeyed them."[3] I remember that afternoon in the hellish summer of 1955 when Phyllis told me why her parents were trying to end our friendship; I was ashamed and confused. "If the Communists take over our country," Phyllis's parents had warned her, "they will have the rest of us doing all their work. They will dictate to us what we will do, and we will have to obey them; we will be mowing *their* lawns."

The events that followed the publication of Prina's article in the *Star* left me disheartened and alone. Dull gray replaced the vivid colors of my former life. I worried that my friends would abandon me; some of them did. I feared for my own and my family's future. During those days, I rallied what energy I could to hide my despair and appear as normal as possible. Anxious days gave way to sleepless nights.

5

The Demand for a Public Accounting

By the early 1950s, nearly all of America's radicals had been identified by the FBI. But the Inquisition demanded a public accounting. Witnesses before the investigating committees were expected not only to repent their past heresies but to name their former comrades. The pressure to collaborate was enormous. The full weight of government and society hung by a thread over each reluctant individual. One's livelihood depended on one's willingness to inform; and many times, so did the avoidance of a prison sentence. Federal agents were known to threaten the uncooperative with internment in the newly established camps, with the removal of their children, with the deportation of aging relatives. It was a seductive whisper: repent, ask forgiveness, give a few names. Of course, those named would in turn suffer. But might they not anyway? Hadn't they already been identified? Could anyone know for sure?

—Griffin Fariello, *Red Scare: Memories of the American Inquisition*

Monday, July 11, 1955—another scorching summer day, the perfect embodiment of Washington's reputation for insufferable July heat and humidity. This, we hoped, was to be the last day of an eleven-day heat wave; temperatures might ease, the weather bureau speculated, "on the wings of a cool air mass." As if the sultry air and high temperatures were not enough to frazzle the nerves of Washingtonians, four hundred thousand residents were stranded by a D.C. Transit strike which had tied up public transportation in the city since the first of the month.

On this day, in an editorial in the *Washington Post* entitled "Threat of Universal Death," several renowned scientists, following the lead of the recently deceased Albert Einstein, warned the governments of the world that they must "choose between the renunciation of war and the end of the human race." On this morning, also, a *Post* article reported that President Dwight D. Eisenhower—by now steadily gaining in popularity as the nation's economy improved and the 1956 national election approached—took his seven-year-old grandson, David, on a personal tour of the Civil War battleground at Gettysburg. And, in the local news, the paper told of a residential neighborhood's dismay over the escape of an ocelot from a pet shop on Wisconsin Avenue.

At noon, Sandy Weitzman and I stepped out of our typing class into the blinding midday sunlight. As our eyes adjusted to the glare, we walked to the edge of the campus and waited at the designated place on Nebraska Avenue where Sandy's father was to pick us up, take us to lunch, and later drop us off to swim at the A.U. swimming pool.

Sandy's father, Ellis Weitzman, a balding middle-aged man with glasses, was a psychology professor at American University who had recently suffered a major heart attack. A native of the Deep South, Dr. Weitzman and his wife, Ann, who was born in the Ukraine, had come to D.C. with Sandy and her younger brother, Warren, at the end of the Second World War, hoping to escape the prejudice and isolation they had both experienced as Jews in the inhospitable settings of their younger years. Sandy's parents gave the impression of having suffered deeply. They were strict with Sandy, and I often felt tension when visiting their home.

As a young teenager, Sandy had an alluring, mysterious, natural beauty. She was always a bit cautious; her lovely ash blond hair and soulful light brown eyes blended so as to render her at the same time reserved and sophisticated. The boys in our crowd were crazy about Sandy, always reaching out to her yet never really making a connection. I was in awe of her, longed for her affection, and was honored that she considered me a friend.

When, finally, Sandy's father approached us in his two-tone Oldsmobile sedan, he pulled up to the curb, got out of his car, and walked toward us. His arm outstretched, he handed me a sheet of paper and began to speak.

"You'll be interested in this memo I found in my office mailbox," he said. "It's a statement written by the university president, and it concerns your father."

Dr. Weitzman's face bore the pained expression of a reluctant messenger. Clearly distressed, he did not explain the nature of his discomfort. Sandy and I stood awkwardly together, leaning against the car as I took the memo from her father and read:

> To: The American University Faculty and Staff
> From: Hurst R. Anderson, President
> Subject: Statement by the President on the article concerning Mr. Herbert Fuchs appearing on the front page of the Sunday Star, July 10, 1955
> As the President of an educational institution, I have a strong convic-

tion that a member of the Communist party should not be employed in any capacity in an American educational institution, or once employed, should, upon adequate evidence of his current party membership, be released of his responsibility. I would never recommend for appointment such a person, and if I were to discover one on a faculty over which I preside, I should recommend his immediate discharge.

The question raised as to Mr. Herbert Fuchs' case is: was he a party member or worker when employed by The American University or/and is he now a party member or worker? From the information at my disposal at this date he was not in any way related to the Communist party when employed by this University, nor since has he been a member or worker of the Communist party.

He is known in our Washington College of Law as an intelligent, loyal, and devoted teacher. He made a serious mistake in the past, which he has recognized and declared. The American University therefore would support his right as a citizen to pursue his chosen professional activities. To take any other position at this time would be beneath the dignity of the institution with a Christian relationship and commitments.

Hurst R. Anderson[1]

What would this mean to our family? I asked myself. Might the future look brighter for us now? I folded the memo into my pocket and, not knowing what to say to Sandy and her father, retreated to the backseat of his waiting sedan.

Much to my disappointment and Sandy's, Dr. Weitzman never drove me again after that day, "because of poor health," he said. The car pool ended, and so too, for the most part, did my friendship with Sandy.

Looking back, I realize it's impossible for me to separate my memory of the events of those days from the memory of my father's reaction to them, since I was so closely identified with him. Vacillating between feelings of hopeless despair—the threat of "ruin"—and trusting optimism, my father sometimes allowed himself to believe that everything would turn out all right. He thought that if he were honest and sincere and willing to take responsibility for his past actions, he could expect to be exonerated. In spite of my all-too-frequent sense of impending doom, this too is what *I* thought, what I hoped.

It had been President Anderson himself who called my father to tell him about the university's statement of support. My father's personal journal recalls that conversation and his emotional reaction to it:

> Hurst called me
>
> Read me statement
>
> Said [Board of Trustees chairman Robert V.] Fletcher approved . . .
>
> I asked him if he had *read* the newspaper (with its statement about my re-fusal). He said yes. He said the statement was conditional only on the truth of the information referred to as being in possession of the University at that time.
>
> I wept. He said what else could a person with his convictions do.[2]

American University, referring to Christian tradition with its commitment to a belief in "repentance, conversion and forgiveness," had made a decision to maintain my father on its law school faculty. Now, we dared to hope that my father might be free of his past, free to begin a new life.

Our optimism was short-lived.

During the two days following the *Star* article and the university's statement of support, a flurry of activity developed behind the scenes with the purpose of pressuring my father to cooperate fully with HUAC—*to name names.*

HUAC, under the chairmanship of Democratic Congressman Francis Walter from Pennsylvania, considered the potential value of my father's testimony in its probe into Communist infiltration in government. Here then was their latest witness—the cooperative, yet still reticent law school professor, whose testimony could lead to a new investigation, perhaps "the biggest of its kind since the Elizabeth Bentley and Whittaker Chambers disclosures in the late 1940s."[3] This important witness could reveal as-yet-undisclosed information about people and activities in "secret cells" in the Wheeler Committee, the National Labor Relations Board (NLRB), and the National War Labor Board (NWLB) between 1936 and 1946. After all, hadn't the witness himself admitted to having been a group organizer and active Party leader in each of these settings? The Committee's task at hand? To solicit the support of the university and others and *get the professor to talk.* Should he continue to refuse to testify regarding people he knew as Communists in the government, at his next scheduled appearance on July 15, the Committee would have no choice, it concluded, but to cite him for contempt of Congress.[4] Pressure must be brought to bear.

Chairman Walter began his pressure campaign by contacting A.U. President Anderson and board chairman Fletcher. Impressing upon them the urgency of their cooperation in this matter, Walter shared with them information about my father, including details about several government loyalty investigations conducted as far back as 1941[5] and as recently as 1948.[6] My father had lied about his membership in the Communist Party and had minimized his affiliation with organizations considered to be subversive. No action was taken against him as a result of those investigations. Walter told Anderson and Fletcher that my father had associated with several individuals identified as members of a "spy ring" in the late 1930s or early '40s. Finally, he revealed that a current FBI probe was being conducted under the auspices of the McCarran Act.[7] Congressman Walter appealed to the two men to do whatever was necessary to "get Fuchs to cooperate."

Meanwhile, a second member of the Committee contacted the FBI Washington Field Office to request information that could "corroborate Fuchs' testimony." Did the FBI have the name of an informant, he asked, "who could place Fuchs in the Communist Party?" Citing the "confidential character" of the files, the Field Office refused to provide this information at that time.[8] Later, however, according to my father's FBI file, the Bureau did agree to review files of individuals alleged to have been "connected with the National Labor Relations Board (NLRB) or concerning whom Fuchs gave information" and to prepare "brief summaries indicating Communist past membership and public informants who could testify to such membership."[9]

In fact, the FBI *did* have a confidential informant, who, in early 1954, had identified my father as a former member of a secret CP apparatus in Washington between 1939 and 1942. This informant's testimony had led to the latest FBI investigation. Interviewed on three separate occasions in 1954 by agents of the Washington Field Office, my father declined to discuss any Communist Party involvement, though it was evident to him at that time that the Field Office had extensive information about him and his associates in the government. It was not until he was approached to testify before HUAC that my father agreed to provide information to the FBI, but only about *his own* Communist activities.

Over the next several months, my father and mother met many times with the two FBI agents from the Washington Field Office who had been assigned to interview them. The two young agents conducted themselves in an intelligent and respectful manner toward my parents, in contrast to some representatives of the Committee on the Hill, and ultimately they and my parents developed a fondness for each another. At one point in their relationship, my mother, who by then had become a special educator, responded to a crisis in the family of one of the agents by finding help for his child. My parents stayed in touch with these two agents for many years.

By July 13 and 14, the flurry of efforts behind the scenes to convince my father to testify fully had become a storm. The secretary of the Senate, a protégé of majority leader Lyndon B. Johnson, contacted L. B. Nichols of the FBI Field Office to inform the FBI that he and other alumni from the A.U. law school "had formed a committee in an attempt to persuade Fuchs to reveal everything to the FBI and to [HUAC] concerning his past activities and associates."[10]

My memory is of people pouring into our house, some coming alone, some in groups—colleagues from the law school, students,[11] members of the law school administration, FBI agents. Some were doing the university's bidding, others were fulfilling their patriotic duty as they saw it, while yet others were really concerned about the welfare of my father and his family.

The colleagues who visited, expressing their own and others' support, hinted at "a bad situation at school": a negative letter to the president from two unhappy students, complaints from a disgruntled professor who felt "uninformed about the Fuchs matter," a nervous dean.[12]

I stood at the front door observing my father stirred by the force of these strangers' words. Much as a Jew sits shivah, mourning the loss of a dear one,[13] my father sat in his yellow leather chair receiving visitors. In his usual quiet, gracious manner, he listened as each person leaned toward him to speak. He was already mourning life as he had known it, for no course of action felt right to him now, and he faced giving up a part of himself.

I heard the sympathetic yet insistent tones of each visitor's voice, along with my father's quiet response. In each case the message was the same: "Please, we beg you, please, Herb, for your own sake, the sake of your family and for the school, testify fully. This is your duty to *present* as opposed to *past* associates. Come clean; your students need you. Come all the way home." My father was deeply affected by what he called in his journal this "very touching" appeal. Attorney Edward Bennett Williams was certain that "[i]t's the only thing to do."[14]

Finally, on July 15, Chairman Walter offered my father a deal. In return for testifying fully, the Committee would assure the following:

- My mother would not be called to testify.
- There would be no public hearing, no publicity.
- HUAC would use its influence, if needed, to assure my father's continued employment at A.U.[15]

It was a seductive whisper.

II

BETRAYALS

6

Catch-22

Can it be that to live lives of moral equilibrium our values must never be tested, for when we adhere to them we destroy what we cherish (as happened to some of the uncooperative witnesses who were blacklisted) yet when we abandon them we destroy our sense of self (as happened to some of the informers)?
— Victor Navasky, *Naming Names*

By Friday, July 15, the date of my father's next scheduled appearance before the Committee, the pain of the past week's events had driven me more deeply into isolation. I retreated to my bedroom for comfort. A small room with space for only a bed, a bookshelf, and a simple wooden desk, my bedroom offered a quiet refuge, a place away from the relentless drama playing out in the living room below. Alone for hours at a time, I soothed myself by sewing (a tailored gray and yellow silk sheath dress with a coat to match) and painting with oils (a portrait of my mother, a still life of tulips, teenagers on the dance floor). I listened to my favorite radio station, WEAM, enjoying the hit parade and passively registering the news of the day (plans for an impending summit in Geneva, an appellate court decision ending segregation on city buses in the South). I could be most helpful to my family, it seemed, if I took care of myself and stayed occupied and out of the way. Though lonely, I took pride in the knowledge that by keeping in the background, I could avoid adding stress to my parents' challenging state of affairs. My greatest comfort was food. Each evening I treated myself to a big bowl of chocolate ice cream, topped with a generous dollop of Hershey's syrup.

It had been eight months since the day my father had firmly stated his unwillingness to acknowledge his Communist Party membership. At that time, on an afternoon when no one else was at home, he faced the two young FBI agents interviewing him in our living room, and, stressing his "complete loyalty to the United

States and its democratic institutions," he agreed to speak only "hypothetically" about his "left-wing activities."[1] When challenged by the agents to implicate former colleagues, he had responded to their questions by asserting that it would be morally repugnant for him to furnish information concerning people who were his friends and associates—lawyers, economists, and their spouses whom he assumed to have been divorced from left-wing activities, as he had, for many years. As the agents listened patiently, my father insisted he would rather go to jail than cause harm to his former associates, harm such as loss of job or reputation. He said he "would do almost anything rather than inform on others and would almost consider suicide rather than face the ordeal of living with [him]self after having informed on others."[2]

Then, in June, confronted with a HUAC subpoena and the knowledge that the FBI already had extensive information about his activities as a Communist, my father finally agreed to speak more candidly to the agents from the FBI and to testify about himself before HUAC, rather than take the Fifth Amendment. Also pushing him to testify were his strong need to rid himself of the past he had rejected and his conviction that current Communist Party membership, in the light of what was now known, was a threat to the internal security of our country.[3] "Perhaps naively, I decided to testify fully and completely about my own past Communist Party activities, hoping to persuade the Committee [HUAC] of my good faith and to dissuade it from pressing me for the names of others. In doing so, I stripped myself of the right to resort to 'Constitutional immunity' [the Fifth Amendment], as well I knew."[4]

HUAC members, reminding him that by testifying in executive session about his *own* activities he had waived his right to immunity, insisted that he was obliged to respond fully to all questions. My father politely refused, citing his moral constraint.

"Congressman Velde," my father later wrote, "saw fit to observe that he was convinced that I was 'sincere' in saying that it would hurt my conscience to name my former associates, but that I must." Furthermore, "[i]t would be a mistake," the congressman said, "to conclude that HUAC already had all the names."[5]

Now, in July, no longer having the option to plead the Fifth and with mounting pressure to testify completely, my parents were forced to face the full impact of their no-win situation. My father's gamble had failed; his next course of action had become less clear. So little time left; no turning back.

Early on the morning of July 15, Fran Lichtenberg phoned my father and offered to come over to lend support during the last few hours of his preparation for the

2 p.m. hearing. When she arrived, she found him deep in thought, intense and preoccupied. She had come to listen and to assure him that he was not alone.

I'll never know for sure my father's thoughts during those last decisive hours. Without being in his shoes, it's impossible to know, impossible to judge. I can only imagine his thoughts and the content of his conversation with Fran that morning:

> How desperately I need to own my mistake, distance myself from the Communist Party and put my past behind me . . . If only it were possible to accomplish this and still protect old friends . . . If only I could do this without jeopardizing our family's future.
>
> It's been years since I've seen those friends, friends like John and Peggy Porter. Peggy Porter and I shared an office at the NLRB, and we named our Peggy after her . . . And the Kurasches, Marty and Lillian. These were loyal Americans, and I'm certain they too have left the Party, now that Soviet dominance is so clear.
>
> I admire those who would willingly go to jail, remaining silent to defend their values. But is silence the right path for me? I'm afraid my silence would support the cause I have left behind, a cause to which I am emphatically opposed. I know I must be clear and explicit about my opposition.
>
> How best can I counter the accusations, open and unspoken, the dark damning brush strokes of those who would wish to cast doubt on my character? What will I have to do to prove my loyalty to the university, to democratic ideals, and to my country?
>
> Ed Williams is advising me to go ahead. If there were any way to avoid this thing, any way for me to succeed by testifying only about myself, with his wide influence he would certainly have found it.
>
> Chairman Walter promised no publicity if I cooperate. "There's no purpose in publicity," he said, and, if I testify fully, the Committee has agreed not to call Frances.
>
> What would it mean to our family if I'm cited for contempt and go to jail? What if Frances is also cited—which she will surely be if she too refuses to cooperate? A jail sentence—for how long? What will happen to the children then? Both of us without work, both of us in jail. . .
>
> Shall I agree to testify, or shall I resign myself to serving a prison term?[6]

Later on that morning of July 15, the decision made, Chairman Walter canceled the planned public hearing. *My father had agreed to cooperate.* In executive session that afternoon, conducted in the Committee's offices, my father would speak about people known to him to have been members of the Communist Party at the Wheeler Committee, the NLRB, and the War Labor Board in Denver.

Back then I felt I understood the basic facts of my father's consequential decision to talk. Consciously, I bought the logic of his thinking without question, as if it were the obvious, natural result of weighing and resolving conflicting factors. I trusted my father completely, never doubting his ability to make an informed and ethical choice. I had never had any reason to doubt him, and my loyalty to him and my mother was absolute. While my father's debilitating pain and remorse over his decision to name names overcame him immediately and lasted until his dying days, I had no understanding at the time of the deeper implications of his decision—the issues of betrayal surrounding the act of informing. In fact, I went into denial.

7

About-face

An urgent call summoned my father to A.U. president Hurst Anderson's office at 10 the next morning, Saturday, July 16, where an icy cold reception from the president and Chairman Fletcher awaited him. Refusing to shake hands and seething with hostility, Mr. Fletcher launched into a scorching diatribe.[1]

"It's clear," he said, "that you are not the sort of man we wish to have on our faculty. We've been stupid to have implied support and continued employment to a man such as yourself—a Communist, a plotter, an atheist, a subject of Moscow!"

"What you say is untrue," my father said. "I am none of those things."[2]

"I respect you for trying to defend yourself," Chairman Fletcher continued, "but there's no question of our position. You will request an immediate leave of absence. You have until Monday to submit it. If you do not do so by then, you will be suspended immediately."

"This is betrayal," my father said. "What about your statement of support—the memo sent to the entire faculty expressing the responsibility of a Christian institution to allow a man to acknowledge his mistake and pursue his chosen profession? You described me then as an 'intelligent, loyal, and devoted teacher.' Suddenly, you go back on your word?"

"I believe you have misconstrued the meaning of the statement we posted last week," said Anderson. "Our decision to maintain your employment was based on *all* the circumstances. I did not understand that you had been working for the government."

"President Anderson," my father said firmly, "do you not remember my asking you whether you had in fact *read* the article that appeared in the *Star* last Sunday which clearly stated the facts of my case and discussed my refusal at that time to testify about people other than myself? Do you not remember my asking if Chairman Fletcher concurred with your statement of support?"

"I do remember those things," Anderson admitted. "But I was mistaken. How do we know that you are not still a member of the Communist Party? Your stu-

Sunday 7/10 –

Nothing in early edition.

Found it in later.

Called Doc – out
Called Dave – he sorry. Said Hurst kept him
posted. Apologized about recent argument.

Hurst called me.
Read me statement
Said Fletcher approved (Quey – did Fletcher
meet?)

I asked him if he had read the newspaper
(with its statement about my refusal)
He said yes. He said the statement was con-
ditional only on the truth of the information
referred to as being in possession of the University at that time.

I wept – He said what else could
a person with of his convictions do.

Entry in my father's journal describing the phone call of support from American University president Hurst Anderson after the first publicity about the case, July 10, 1955.

dents don't even know where you stand. You are not the kind of person we want teaching in our law school. You are an atheist; this is a Methodist university, and I question whether you are able to cooperate in the achievement of the university's Christian objectives."

"There really is no more to discuss," Fletcher insisted. "You have until Monday to request a temporary leave of absence pending a decision by the Board of Trustees on the renewal of your contract. Your leave will be with pay. Dean Bookstaver will reassign your classes. This is final."

My father retreated from the room in a daze. Since President Anderson's earlier statement of support and his reassuring phone call, my parents had not questioned the backing of the university. My father's decision to talk had not been based on a fear of reprisal. Before he had agreed to testify fully he had been assured that the university community would stand behind him; since then, they had encouraged him to cooperate with the Committee, and he had done so. Their sudden reversal was devastating. My father drove home from the campus dejected and despairing—in his words, "sunk."

Calls informing colleagues of the university's sudden about-face produced surprise and disbelief. An increasingly nervous Dean Dave Bookstaver complained of a kangaroo court and threatened to resign from his position at A.U.'s law school. Professors Ed "Doc" Mooers, chairman of the Faculty Relationships Committee, and Ross Netherton expressed bewilderment. What could have happened to produce this change of mind? Students Gene Higgins and Norman Cournoyer remained optimistic, citing support of the law student fraternity, the Oliver Wendell Holmes chapter of Sigma Nu Phi, which had expressed support for my father in a letter addressed to President Anderson, a letter that described my father's service to the university as characterized by "a depth of understanding and unusual patience."[3] Higgins and Cournoyer were hopeful that in time the board would override the administration's action, especially as it was their understanding that Professor Fuchs had been held in such high regard as to have been considered to replace Dean Bookstaver upon his resignation in a couple of months.[4]

Attorney Ed Williams was appalled. "I have only one question," he said to my father. "Did you cooperate? Yes? Then I tell you they can't do it."[5]

My parents resigned themselves to a long and very rough time ahead; their "troubles," as they called them, showed no sign of letting up. Suffering deeply from a critical blow to his self-esteem, my father fought his impulse to withdraw completely. When a few families reacted to the media coverage by reaching out, my parents responded, recognizing the danger of distancing themselves from human contact.

Among them was the Bent family, to whom my parents turned for support. Donn Bent, a charming retired naval officer, worked as a lawyer for the Tariff Commission. Donn and his wife, Gail, had been my father's colleagues at the NLRB before the war. While Gail's principled liberalism caused her to take issue with my father's decision to cooperate, Donn was less judgmental and more sympathetic to my parents' dilemma in these difficult circumstances. In the end, the Bents' ongoing support reflected their fondness and respect for my parents, which had built over time.

The Bents' younger son, Devin, was my special friend. Handsome, with dark eyes and hair, Devin was more than a year older than I and had been the "love of my life" since the first moment I saw him in our second/third-grade classroom at Francis Scott Key Elementary School. He was the new boy in the class, and I remember his plaid flannel shirt—a MacPherson tartan—and his shy but confident manner of speaking.

On the night after my father's testimony in full, the Bents invited us to their house for the evening. Visits to the Bents in their three-story home nestled in the trees on the banks of the Potomac had become a favorite social outing for me, as it meant I would have the entire evening to spend with Devin, my friend and secret crush. On this night, as usual, we climbed the staircase leading to his tiny second-floor bedroom. Dev stretched out on his bed facing me, his head blocking the view of the thick trees that grew on the steep slope behind the house; I sat in a wooden chair across from him. We spent little time talking about our social life—our usual topic of conversation—and spoke instead about my family's difficulties. To my amazement, Devin had an extensive understanding of the historical facts influencing my parents' entry into the Communist Party. He talked at length about the conditions and events leading up to the Great Depression and the response of liberals and others who were determined to improve the plight of the poor.

The National Labor Relations Board, Devin explained, provided a way for our parents to help rebuild the country by helping implement the Wagner Act (the National Labor Relations Act),[6] guaranteeing the rights of workers to organize and bargain collectively.

Where did Devin learn all this? I wondered, appreciative of his willingness to explain what he knew. Devin was supportive, patient, and sympathetic, and I felt less alone.

A week later, my father received an envelope addressed to him in care of American University. Inside was an article published by the *Chicago Tribune* reporting my father's decision to testify in full; so much for "no publicity." The headline read, "New Evidence of Red Cells in Capital Bared: Probers Expect Public Hearing Sensations," and the article reported that "secret testimony of a sensational nature had been taken" and that due to the "new revelations" a "scheduled open hearing for testimony by Herbert Fuchs" had been canceled. In the sender's own hand, written in the column, were the epithets *"worm,"* *"Judas!"* and *"Weakling!"*[7]

8

Awaiting the Board's Decision

Forced to request a temporary leave of absence from the university, my father found himself with time on his hands. This meant he could chauffer me around and even chaperone my social engagements. He accompanied me to one small party at The Sycamore Island Club, an informal retreat to which the Bents belonged, on a tiny island in the Potomac accessed from MacArthur Boulevard, where we swam, picnicked, and played pool. Thick, verdant trees and bushes hung over the craggy riverbank. As we dove off the rocks on this hot weekday afternoon, my friends and I felt we had the whole river to ourselves. My father, though preoccupied, was mellow and unobtrusive; he sat down with a book in a comfortable chair and left us alone. I was relieved to have my friends to distract me from our family's problems.

I remember a Sunday trip with my parents to the beach on Chesapeake Bay, a rare but cherished treat. I was thrilled that Devin and Louise Casgrain had accepted my invitation to come along. Soothed by the heat of the August sun, I allowed my body to relax into the warmth of the powder-white sand. It was fun chatting with my friends and cooling off in the bay. Just being around Devin made me happy. Suddenly, about an hour into this lovely, refreshing afternoon, my pleasure drained away; my spirits sank. My two friends had drifted together onto a single blanket. Arms entwined, they left me a third wheel.

At home, burrowed into his pine-paneled basement study, Dad began the long wait for the decision of the board. Slowly, thoughtfully, he launched a concerted campaign to influence his chances for a positive outcome.[1] My mother, steady and supportive, worked as a teacher during the day, and in the evening handled all the household chores. My brother and I were expected to take care of ourselves.

My father met on July 19 with Dave Bookstaver, the anxious and tormented dean of the law school. Troubled by conflicting calls for action, the dean seemed the more needy of the two, seeking reassurance from my father to assuage the guilt and fear that the situation had elicited in him. My father also spoke by phone with his colleague Doc Mooers, who suggested he contact Methodist bishop Garfield Bromley Oxnam, currently a member of the A.U. Board of Trustees. Bishop Oxnam was known to be a champion of liberal causes and a staunch critic of McCarthyism and the House Committee on Un-American Activities.

The next day, Dad met with his attorney, Ed Williams, who derided the action of Fletcher and Anderson. By now, Williams insisted, the university should have known that Chairman Walter and the FBI had become thoroughly convinced of my father's clean break from the Party in 1946. Perhaps he, Williams, could influence his friends on the board. He would try.

The reputation of HUAC had suffered since the 1954 censure of Joseph McCarthy by the Senate. Its current chairman, Francis Walter, hungered for the kind of publicity that could rekindle interest and put the work of the Committee back on the map. Grabbing at the opportunity my father's testimony offered, Chairman Walter announced on August 15 "an investigation of Communist infiltration into Government circles" to take place at the start of the coming year.[2] Many newspapers, including the *Washington Star,* misrepresented his remarks and implied that at this time Communists *still* held positions in the federal government and continued to participate in "current Red Cells" in government agencies. Banner headlines deliberately omitted Walter's statement that the inquiry centered on the 1940s.[3]

At this point in my life, my interest in the newspaper was limited to back-to-school fashion. When classes began again at Gordon Junior High in the fall, my recently established clothing allowance served a double purpose. My mother thought I should learn what things cost, how to budget, how to plan. It was time, also, for the family to cut back, to conserve resources in the face of my father's rocky employment status. I willingly accepted the challenge and was happy with the results. I bought five nifty outfits, mix-and-match skirts and sweater sets, and a new pair of penny loafers. Shopping at Lerner's department store instead of the more expensive Woodies helped to stretch the money.

Normally I loved the starting-over feeling of September: spotless three-ring binders; shiny pens and pencils; a brand new wardrobe; and an opportunity to get, and stay, on top of class assignments. Typically I would not sustain that excitement past the first week, when notebooks began losing their crisp appearance and the novelty of fresh subject matter wore thin. Now, my anticipation didn't even make it through the first day.

This term, my classmates from last year's Latin course and I would join with the brightest Latin-bound kids in a new section, "9-7." Along with Latin, we would

Washington Post cartoon reflecting HUAC's diminishing reputation after the Senate censure of Senator Joseph McCarthy.

study world history, beginning algebra, English, and science. I would miss Devin, Louise Casgrain, Jim Lichtenberg, Bill Fuhrman, and the others in our crowd who had gone on to Western High School, but I was comfortable with the prospect of ninth grade with my eighth-grade friends.

Dad drove me to school that first day. I sought out my friend Rose and caught up with her just moments before we all made our way to the auditorium. Mr. J. Dallas Shirley, our stern and officious principal, welcomed the assembly of excited and fidgety adolescents to the new school year. One by one, my friends left the auditorium, called to the 9-7 homeroom of our Latin teacher, Mrs. Clapper.

I remained sitting in my seat after all my friends were gone. Hey, what's going on? I wondered. Did they forget me? Finally my name was called: "Peggy Fuchs. You will report to 9-6." It made no sense whatsoever. I knew no one in that class. Why were they separating me from my friends?

Later, Rosie tried to reassure me. "I know it's a mistake," she said. "Tomorrow, go see Miss Baines; she'll straighten the whole thing out. And oh, wait till you see the boy I sat next to in homeroom this morning. His name is Van, and *is he cute!* Wait till you meet him!"

Miss Baines was our school counselor. I found her in her office first thing the next morning, shuffling papers and trying to restore order to her desk.

"How can I help you?" she asked routinely as she offered me a seat. "What seems to be the problem?"

A homely, matronly lady, Miss Baines had been at Gordon for more years than one would care to count. She was the stereotypical spinster schoolteacher, but without the warmth that often accompanies old-fashioned firmness and decorum. And she was strange! Who could ever forget her bizarre instructions to a cafeteria full of junior high students taking a standardized reading test. Miss Baines spoke in gerunds: "Walking quietly into the cafeteria," she would command. "Sitting down in a seat in front of a test booklet, being sure to leave the booklet closed until instructed otherwise. Waiting until the signal is given to begin. Remaining silent for the entire testing period."

Not known for her empathy, compassion, or ability to connect with students, Miss Baines responded to my questions regarding my assignment to 9-6 as if, by ignoring the issue, she could will it away.

"I'm sure you'll be just fine, dear," she said in a patronizing tone that reflected her irritation and her wish not to be bothered. "You'll get used to 9-6 in no time at all," she said. "Go back to class. I'll give you a pass."

I regretted having gone to her office and felt a kind of powerlessness that I would experience again and again during those days. Exiled in my own familiar school, separated from the emotional support of my friends, I felt humiliated and lonely. It seemed that every aspect of my life had been disrupted. I found the situation intolerable; I wanted to disappear.

Fortunately, my Latin teacher saved me. Mrs. Clapper requested that my home-room be changed, insisting that I was in the wrong Latin class. The request was honored; I would be with my friends after all. By the end of the week, my crisis had passed. That feeling of humiliation, however, would remain for a long time, a parallel to my father's state of mind.

Dad's struggle continued throughout September. In a conversation with Hurst Anderson, my father learned that when President Anderson wrote that the university would support his right to "pursue his chosen professional activities," Anderson had meant "pursue retooling." Further, Anderson complained that the ensuing publicity "would do the university irreparable damage" and that he "could not allow the perception that the university was condoning communism."[4]

The September 12 faculty meeting to discuss the "Fuchs situation" was canceled. None of the law school faculty was available. Ed Mooers cited "business involving his wife and his maid"; Jack Myers, "two cars needing inspection"; Roy Franchino, "a writing deadline." Everyone was confused and scared. Do we really have enough information to tackle this problem? they asked themselves. Whose responsibility is this anyway? Is this problem for the faculty to consider, or should it be referred to the Faculty Relationships Committee?[5]

The next day at 10 a.m., the executive committee of the university's Board of Trustees finally met. Though permitted to bring legal counsel, my father, after consulting with Ed Williams, had declined to do so. There had been no need to bring counsel, they decided, because there was no legal issue involved: no charges had been made. Rather, my father expected this to be an exploratory meeting to be followed by either a lifting of the suspension or further inquiry by formal hearing. He and Williams wanted to avoid antagonizing the university.[6] Unfortunately, the two of them underestimated the adamantly negative position of Anderson and Fletcher and their influence on the board.

My father made a brief appearance to respond to questions put to him by individual members of the committee. While speaking, he was interrupted repeatedly by Mr. Fletcher, who was in the chair.[7] President Anderson had already presented his version of the facts of the case, and after my father was dismissed, the president led a brief discussion with members of the committee. This was not, in fact, an official hearing, although later the university chose to refer to it as such; at no time were formal charges presented with an opportunity for a statement in response.

Dean Bookstaver appeared before the committee to put into the record my father's history of service as a member of the faculty and to remind the committee of the position of the Association of American Law Schools (AALS) on the dismissal or disciplining of law teachers. The dean told the committee that my father had "performed all of the duties both scholastic and otherwise assigned to him competently and without criticism; that he was an able and proficient teacher; that he enjoyed excellent personal relationships with faculty, students and staff; and that no political slanting had ever been reported with respect to his classroom work or other relationships." The dean reiterated the AALS policy that "the only basis for the dismissal of a teacher rested upon a finding of [present] unfitness to continue in an academic post." When asked about the attitude of the students toward Professor Fuchs, Dean Bookstaver expressed his belief that the student body was "generally sympathetic," exhibiting "a willingness to have him continue to teach them." Concerning the position of the faculty, the dean reported that the staff members "deemed it inappropriate for them to take any position in the matter without being requested to do so by the Committee."

As to his own recommendation, the dean proposed that my father be retained as a teacher for the balance of his term because the university had a contract with him "which ought to be honored if at all possible," and, in the dean's opinion, nothing about the present situation suggested that serious consequences would result from keeping him on. On the contrary, Dean Bookstaver described my father as "a mild and inoffensive man whose classroom ability and decorum earned him the high regard of his students," a man who, he believed, "represented no such present danger as merited exclusion from the classroom," a man who "understood and appreciated his duties and responsibilities as a lawyer and law teacher." When asked by one committee member how he justified a recommendation for retention of an atheist and a perjurer, the dean said he "did not know that Professor Fuchs was an atheist, and rather doubted it." With respect to the issue of perjury (a serious issue for him), the dean felt that because of Professor Fuchs's "record of service with us . . . he might be forgiven that to the extent of being permitted to finish out his contract."[8]

President Anderson warned the committee, erroneously, that my father would be entitled to tenure at the end of the 1955–56 school year, after which it would be difficult, if not impossible, to remove him. In fact, A.U. required seven years of teaching before a professor could be considered for tenure; my father would not have completed that minimum for another two years. This error, if that's what it was, had a profound effect on the outcome of these deliberations. On the advice of President Anderson, the executive committee voted to relieve my father of his teaching duties, and to not renew his contract in 1956.

Bishop Oxnam, my father's hope for a strong supportive voice, did not attend the meeting; he was out of the country on that day. The vote of the executive committee was: two to discharge, four to suspend until June 1956, and one lone vote, attorney John Laskey, to retain.[9]

Anxious days and weeks ensued. Unwilling to accept defeat, my father's efforts on his own behalf intensified following the demoralizing action of the executive committee of the board. My mother was his constant support; every question was discussed with her, every decision shared. Both of my parents were determined to persevere, but it was my mother who remained characteristically unflustered.

Calls to and from the various players helped my father keep the ball in the air; he spoke individually to members of the faculty, to Anderson, to Ed Williams. Williams was encouraging. He had seen Laskey, who assured him that the executive committee's action was "only a recommendation." He had contacted Murray Marder of the *Post,* who was interested in doing a story and perhaps an editorial. In his effort to seek support, Williams had contacted someone at Georgetown University. Should it not work out at A.U., suggested Williams, Georgetown was prepared to consider my father for a position on its law school staff. "There is a sentiment to do the right thing," Williams said.

Ed Williams had also spoken with Thomas W. Beale Jr., chief clerk of the HUAC staff, the person who had earlier proclaimed the university's intention to continue employment if my father cooperated. Chairman Walter and his staff were angry, Beale reported, about the action of the executive board. In fact, in a letter to the university challenging their decision, Walter appealed to them to reconsider: "I respectfully request that you take another look at this matter in order to determine whether or not the recent action was in the best interests of the United States." Believing the university had gone back on an understanding it had with HUAC, Walter was bitter and indignant. Beale told Williams, "Chairman Walter says, if necessary, he'll hire Fuchs *himself.*" My father considered HUAC "a dubious ally." While he welcomed the support of his "right to teach," he shared "the university's shock at any attempt by the House Committee to dictate its personnel policy."[10]

An article appearing in the *Post* on September 22 by Murray Marder made mention of the university's earlier statement of support for my father. In the article, Marder quoted an A.U. official who asserted that there had been "'no repudiation of any kind in this case . . . [but rather] more mature judgment after a careful study.'" Marder's review of the case offered my father an opportunity to comment in response:

> The action of the trustees committee is a very disappointing repudiation of President Anderson's splendid statement of July 10, especially in light of the part played by the university in persuading me to cooperate with the House Committee.
>
> My dismissal serves no useful purpose. . . . It denies the doctrine of conversion and forgiveness . . . and it deprives the law school of an instructor described by the president as intelligent, loyal and devoted.
>
> Coming at this time . . . it marks an unfounded fear of publicity and can please no group in American life other than possibly the Communist Party. I trust the action will be promptly reviewed and rescinded.[11]

The next day, the *New York Times* announced my father's intention to "fight the ouster move." This day also brought a new twist to the arguments in my father's defense. The *Washington Post,* the *New York Times,* the *Washington Evening Star,* and the *Daily News* all ran stories highlighting the outrage of HUAC member Representative Gordon H. Scherer, who claimed that my father was being punished by A.U., under the influence of anti-HUAC board member Bishop Oxnam, for cooperating with the House committee.[12]

Concerned that the firing "would be a serious blow to future investigations," Congressman Scherer pointed out the contrast between the action of A.U. and the retention by Harvard University of Professor Wendell H. Furry. Professor Furry first admitted he had been a Communist but then enlisted the Fifth Amendment when asked to name associates in the Party. Scherer argued that "Furry was one of the most contemptuous witnesses I ever saw but Harvard kept him on. But Fuchs . . . sought to atone for his past actions by furnishing information on the Communist conspiracy and now 'faces loss of his post.'"[13]

Hoping to get support in his attempt to influence members of the board, my fa-

ther contacted Bishop Oxnam and met with him twice in October. Dad described
Bishop Oxnam as "a wonderful man," and characterized the two meetings as cor-
dial. The bishop was sympathetic but not optimistic. He indicated that he knew
the FBI and HUAC reports on my father were "favorable" but that backing from
other board members was minimal and weak. Bishop Oxnam wondered out loud
if Dad's colleagues had abandoned him. He advised my father to appear before
the full board to plead his case.[14] In spite of his sympathy for my father's cause
and contrary to the assumption of Congressman Scherer, the bishop decided to
stay out of the dispute. Perhaps because he concluded this was a losing battle, or
maybe because he felt it was inappropriate, for some other reason, to try to affect
the outcome of this case, Bishop Oxnam did not attempt to sway the vote of the
board.[15] This was a devastating disappointment to my father, a terrible blow to his
dwindling sense of optimism.

It became clear to my father that the administration of the university had completely washed its hands of him. Sadly, also, his colleagues on the faculty of the
law school were thoroughly intimidated and were unwilling to speak out in his
defense.[16] Having been unsuccessful in his attempt to meet with the faculty as a
group, Dad had spoken to individual members and had submitted to Doc Mooers a
grievance and request for a formal hearing before the Faculty Relationships Committee. In response to my father's letter, Professor Mooers referred him *back* to
the law school faculty and/or the executive committee of the board—both known
to be unsupportive. My father called this the "brush-off letter." Jack Myers, who
was particularly worried about displeasing the administration, voiced his unwillingness to "pass upon the matter as a member of the law school"—even in defense of my father's performance as a teacher—unless specifically "required to do
so." Myers was now in line for the deanship. Only Roy Franchino, a non-tenured
member of the law school staff, could be counted on to be firmly in my father's
camp.[17]

Late in September, Dad wrote several pages of reflection in his personal journal. By now, though he had "hoped and dared" that his chosen course of action in
response to HUAC's demands would be successful, he could see that his strategy
hadn't worked. In his journal, he explained the reasons for his "most crucial
decision"—the decision not to take refuge in Constitutional immunity:[18]

> As a lawyer as well as Communist, I had known of the expedient avail-
> able to unwilling witnesses, to refuse to testify on the ground of possible

self-incrimination. As a Communist I had recognized the "necessity" of resorting to it and thus thwarting investigation at no risk of punishment. As a *former* Communist, too, I felt the unfairness of being asked to turn into an informer. Nothing is more repugnant to feelings than to name long gone associates in activities we commonly then believed to be hallowed, and to betray them into the hands of a Committee with a long history of indiscriminate and irresponsible sadism to individuals. As a law teacher I was not unaware of Dean Griswold's brilliant defense of resort to the Fifth Amendment.

But I knew that the immunity that was available to me did not belong to me. Since no criminal prosecution of me could be aided by my testimony, my acceptance of this shield would be something of a fraud. Even so, I might have been tempted to embrace the jail proof method of remaining silent if only to avoid personal betrayal of long-gone friends, but for one further and decisive fact.

The ordinary man, however clear or however confused on the issue of communism has three alternatives. He can fight communism, or help communism or for reasons of doubt about the relative values to our country of ruthless exposure of long past acts as against forgiveness and reacceptance of good men and women, *he can stay out of the argument*. Not so the former Communist like myself. The former Communist has only *two* choices. He can only fight or help communism! By pleading immunity he does the [latter]. He helps communism by making a show of resistance to constituted democratic authority (however vicious in its methods). His *purpose* may be merely to acquit a debt of honor. The *result* is that he has aligned himself in defiance with the group whose continued conspiratorial existence *depends* upon such shows of defiance.

Let me not seem glib! I *know* the arguments the other way: that tyranny must be resisted; that personal values are the indispensable foundation of any wholesome state. They are *very persuasive*. On balance, though, I ask myself: "Am I totally disillusioned with the democratic process?" "Do I perceive a situation in which revolution alone is appropriate?"—Obviously not! If the excesses of McCarthy and [former HUAC Chairman Harold] Velde are to be curbed, it must be by the Congress, and if the Congress fails to act, the people will change its composition. Implicitly, my experiences, even since my initial appearance before the Committee has [sic] NOT impaired my confidence with the democratic process.[19]

These were the reasons for my father's determination not to take the Fifth. Later, upon reflection, he questioned his decision, seeing it as a mistake that ultimately led to his current crisis.

This period was torture for me. I struggled to manage my sinking spirits. I couldn't put my finger on the problem. I couldn't find my rhythm, couldn't get comfortable with myself. Though I spent a lot of time arranging my hair and clothes, I couldn't get them right. Homework was impossible; I finished the minimum required assignments but never achieved a feeling of accomplishment, the satisfaction of a project well done or a concept mastered. A major frustration was my difficulty practicing the flute. I loved the flute and admired my teacher, an exceedingly tall and handsome man in his mid-twenties who played for the Washington National Symphony Orchestra. I desperately wanted to play well, to express myself through the beauty of the music. I just couldn't concentrate, couldn't focus long enough for the learning to take hold.

It was around this time that I began to go home, rather regularly, with my friend Rosie after school. We did our homework together and often I would spend the night and go off to school with her in the morning. For some reason, I could escape at Rosie's house, lose myself in the bosom of her strange family whom I'd known all my life. Their home was a little white house with green shutters that her father had built before the war on the other side of the trolley tracks on Sherrier Place.

It's hard to imagine two personalities more different than Rosie's mother, Ida, and her father, Henry. Ida, born into a religious Jewish family in Rochester, New York, had left home in her early twenties. Her family was not happy when she met and married Henry Marien, a handsome, introverted German Catholic printer from Indiana, twelve years her senior. Though Ida was always affectionate, accepting, and kind to me, she seemed frustrated and unhappy with her own life, and took her frustrations out on Rosie, with whom she was critical and overbearing. Ida was obsessed with other people's business and consumed with the neighborhood gossip, carrying on like a *yente*.[20] She worked as a secretary in a home for young unwed mothers. Their stories provided Ida with hours of human drama and intrigue—a substitute for excitement in her own life. Henry, on the other hand, was reclusive, self-involved, eccentric; he preferred to live in his own world of books and ideas. Happy when communing with nature, he tended to plants and animals in his garden and on their small "farm" in the nearby Virginia countryside.

Ida and Henry spent little time together other than at meals, which were often accompanied by a discordant verbal exchange.

"Henry, come to dinner," Ida would shriek. "Your chicken's getting cold!"

"For God's sake, Ida! Don't interrupt! I'm watching the evening news. Can't you remember one simple thing I tell you?"

Rosie was caught between her parents' incompatible worlds, torn apart by their antagonistic relationship. Nervous and self-effacing, she had a habit of twisting her hair between her fingers for comfort.

For Rosie, this home was unnerving and confusing; she struggled constantly for a sense of her own identity. But for me, somehow, her home was a source of comfort and stability, in spite of the disharmony—or maybe even because of it, as the constant bickering provided me with a welcome distraction from my own inner turmoil. Ida Marien's affection for me was unconditional; she made no demands. I was always welcome in her home where she offered me delicious home-cooked meals and a warm bed and safety. No need to try to appear brave or happy here. And my friend Rosie, whose suffering seemed at least equal to mine, was like a loyal sister with whom pretext and explanations were unnecessary.

It would be many years before I realized that the Marien family, too, had been victims of the relentless search for Communists and pro-Soviet Communist sympathizers in the U.S. government. Perhaps this fact accounted for their willingness to open their home to me. If that is the case, however, I was unaware of it at the time.

Despite his fear of impending defeat, my father was still determined to carry on. He would fight the decision of the executive committee of the board at the university. He would make every effort to clear his name. And finally, if he could not convince the board to reverse its position, he would do everything possible to find a new job in academia.

On October 29, twenty-six members of the full fifty-person American University Board of Trustees convened. The "Fuchs case" was one of a number of items on the agenda that day. The chairman read a letter of support for my father written by four part-time instructors on the law school staff. But because the messenger who brought the letter refused to give his name, the president brushed the letter aside, dismissing it as inapplicable.

That afternoon, the board voted unanimously to accept the recommendation of the executive committee that called for allowing my father's current contract to lapse, placing him on inactive status with pay until the end of the contract with no contract renewal for the following year.[21] The *Washington Star* quoted President Anderson as saying he "felt the university had made a 'very, very generous arrangement' for Mr. Fuchs by continuing his pay until next June 30. 'We intended no harm to him,' President Anderson said, 'he has a family to feed.'"[22]

9

Public Hearing, Private Coping

The HUAC hearings were degradation ceremonies. Their job was not to leg-islate or even to discover subversives (that had already been done by the in-telligence agencies and their informants) so much as it was to stigmatize.

For a degradation ceremony to work it needs a denouncer. And the most credible denouncer, with the most impeccable credentials, is the one who has been there himself. The ex-Communists constituted a steady sup-ply of denouncers.

A successful status-degradation ceremony must be fueled by moral in-dignation. The anti-Communist hysteria of the cold war provided an ideal environment.

—Victor Navasky, *Naming Names*

The A.U. Board of Trustees' decision sent my father into deep and "soul sear-ing anguish." He blamed himself for the problems that resulted from his deci-sion to respond fully to HUAC's demands. This is how he described his feelings of isolation and gloom: "All that stands between me and a long long isolation—as of a leper—from the society of my fellows is my own determination that I am a good man and [the isolation] *must not* happen, that staunch human love of a few friends, including students, and the very sound constructive extroversion of our children."[1]

In fact, the "few friends" were few indeed—the Lichtenbergs, the Bents, Gene and Helen Higgins, George and Ottie Brecher, and a few others whose affection for my parents transcended political considerations. These friends reached out; they phoned, dropped by, let us know they were there for us. Most knew nothing of my parents' former political lives; it had not been safe to discuss these things.

When my parents first made the break from their old crowd, they forfeited ac-cess to the Left. Now, no larger community stood in the wings, no group of like-minded fellow travelers to share their future as they slid into the abyss of uncertainty and possible obscurity.

There was no extended family close by—no brothers, sisters, aunts, or uncles, for whom blood was commensurate with loyalty. As my parents' isolation intensified and the new likelihood of a public hearing loomed ahead, my father took the unusual step of contacting his younger brother Walter in Yonkers, New York. I remember meeting Walter on only one or two earlier occasions, yet he came to Washington to visit my father the next weekend to lend emotional support to the older brother whose life and politics he did not share but whom he had always admired.

It was a measure of the depth of their distress that my parents began attending church with the Bents. As non-practicing Jews, my parents had refrained over the years from participating in any religious observance. The Bents' minister, Reverend Charles Calkins, was somehow able to offer words of comfort to my non-religious parents. I never did know what he said that touched them, that gave them solace. I do know that Reverend Calkins and his wife remained close to my parents throughout their ordeal, offering a spiritual connection that helped to ease their pain. And when, in 1964, my brother, Peter, completed a three-year stint as a commissioned officer in the Navy, it was Reverend Calkins who officiated at Pete's marriage to his high school sweetheart.

As to our "extroversion"? Extroversion, indeed. I wonder how my father would have defined that word. I guess life with two teenage kids is always busy and active, but I have never thought of us as extroverted, rather the opposite. Peter was quiet but popular, mainstream but by no means flashy. As an active Western High School senior, he played football, was a lieutenant in the R.O.T.C. cadet corps, was a member of the Debate Club and the Student Council, and had recently joined the Sigma Delta fraternity. Though he worried about the effect of our father's notoriety on his status with his fraternity brothers, Peter continued his everyday life much as before. "Under the circumstances," Western's principal, Irene Rice, said to Peter, "you seem to be handling your situation pretty well."

As for me, I was chronically anxious and insecure; my constant worry and raw vulnerability were without focus. There was so much going on that I did not understand, so much stress and tension in our home. My parents and my brother were inaccessible, preoccupied with their own thoughts and problems.

For a while, however, as the fall got under way, my life improved. I had a new boyfriend. Ben,[2] the son of one of my mother's colleagues, was new to our school.

I had met him in the summer and we had become friends; now we were "going to-gether." Ben was different from the other kids, kind of an odd man out. He was shy and rather sweet, in a rough sort of way. I found him intriguing. I was attracted to his sullen darkness; his tall, muscular body; and his bohemian lifestyle, which included hootenannies[3] and summer work camp. Most of all, I was drawn to his potent sexual energy and the sadness in his eyes. It seemed that, through his own pain from a difficult childhood, Ben could empathize with mine. The other kids didn't really like him very much, though they tolerated him and invited him to their parties. He was not cool or confident and didn't wear the latest styles. He was an outsider, but then, really, so was I.

Our crowd's parties were serious business. The lights were turned down. The music was slow. Couples paired off. Ben and I held each other close as we danced; we kissed but did not talk. I was intoxicated, aroused, in love with love. *I* had a boyfriend. I was one of the gang. Between dances, the girls gathered to take mea-sure of the scene; the boys chatted by the soda table. Later, at our slumber party, my friends and I worked over the night's events, talking until dawn and analyzing every interaction, every glance, every problem. We worried about our weight; fat was the kiss of death. We struggled to balance our awakening sexual desire with the spoken and unspoken rules we had come to know; we were confused. Going steady conveyed status. Necking was okay, even encouraged. Petting, caressing above or—more dangerously—below the waist, was not acceptable to the girls but was pursued by the boys. Nice girls did not "go all the way." Girls that did risked getting pregnant, having to choose between a shotgun wedding or being sent away to have their babies in disgrace. Nice girls waited to have sex until they were married.

At school I busied myself playing in the orchestra and singing soprano in the glee club chorus. The Gordon Fall Show in early November was a highlight of the year, and I had a small lead in the Fall Show operetta, *Sunbonnet Sue*.

One day, the principal called me into his office.

"We have a talent show coming up soon," Mr. Shirley said. "We need a few more people to perform, and I'd like you to prepare a flute solo."

"Thanks for asking me," I answered, "but I'm not interested in doing a solo for the show. I'm involved in other things."

Mr. Shirley didn't take "no" for an answer. "I'm expecting you to do it, Peggy," he said. "I'm counting on you."

I remember this as if it were happening today: A Handel sonata, that's what I practice for the show. My teacher has chosen it for me. He plays it through so I'll

know how it should sound; I want to play like he does. Every day I practice after
school. The first several measures go well. Ah, I can do this, I assure myself. No
problem. But then, after a few minutes, my mind begins to wander. I try again. Each
time I start, I delve further into the piece before I give up, but I *never master it*.

Finally, the day of the talent show arrives. I have not slept. Several kids perform before the master of ceremonies announces my solo. I walk on stage into
the blinding spotlight. I raise the flute to my lips and start to play, believing that
a miracle can make my fingers work for me. The first several measures go well,
as usual. And then I freeze. Waves of anxiety anesthetize my brain, erasing all
memory of the notes; my heart beats in my ears, my stomach knots. I start again.
Shrieking, disjointed sounds crash through the oppressive silence. Horrors! My
fingers are no longer part of me; they do their own thing. Everyone I know is in
the audience: my family, Ben and his family, all of my friends. Shame drowns me.
Looking directly into the spotlight, I contort my face in an anguished scowl and
I walk off stage, mortified. After the show, no one—no one from the audience,
not one of my friends or family—says an unkind word to me. Everyone acts as
if nothing has happened. Ben walks me to our car; we speak of other things. We
pretend. All the while, my shame and humiliation stick to me like a new layer of
permanent skin.

By December 5, the day HUAC investigator C. E. Owens arrived at our door, it
had become abundantly clear that Francis Walter would not make good on his
promise of no public testimony. Owens served my father with a subpoena to appear before the Committee at its December 13 public hearing. Disheartened, my
father went to the Hill the next day to remind Walter of his promises. "You got a
bum deal," Chairman Walter said. "I told them not to call you." He had been over-
ruled, he said, by his Committee colleagues.[4]

My parents were particularly upset that HUAC had contacted my mother to
appear as well. "Tell her to stay home," Walter told my father. "I'll take care of it."
On this issue, Walter successfully intervened. My mother did not testify.[5]

At noon on Sunday, December 11, Owens again visited our home, this time
with a plane ticket for my father. The hearing was to be held at the federal court-
house in Chicago.

My parents wanted to devote the day to preparing for my father's Committee
appearance. My mother arranged for me to spend the day with Ben and his family;
I was delighted. His mother's boyfriend, Ted, picked me up so that my parents
would be free to concentrate on their work.

It was a long drive to Ben's house, out MacArthur Boulevard, across the District line to Glen Echo, Maryland, right by the Glen Echo Amusement Park. I found it awkward driving with Ted. What was there to talk about with a forty-some-year-old, longhaired, bohemian bachelor? Whatever did we have in common? He was friendly enough, I guess; at least he tried to be.

"I think it's so nice that you and Ben are getting to know each other," he offered. "It's a great way for each of you to learn about the opposite sex."

Is this guy crazy? I asked myself, annoyed. I don't need to learn about boys, for God's sake. I know about boys.

Ted asked me questions about school and friends; I answered, self-consciously. I was relieved that my mother would pick me up later so I wouldn't have to put up with this awkward conversation on the way home.

As soon as we arrived at Ben's house, his mother and Ted took off somewhere, leaving Ben and me alone. His sister, Carol, was gone as well. I don't know where they all went, only that they left us to do as we pleased.

The house was worn and comfortable, like a favorite old shoe. Bits and pieces of things were piled up on top of other stuff, newspapers, books, blankets. Cigarette butts filled ashtrays everywhere; Ben's mother chain-smoked.

Ben led me into the small, cramped study off the front room, a tiny space lined with shelves that were bursting with books and records. Armed with a solid supply of snacks—potato chips and dip, nuts, and Canada Dry ginger ale—we sat down on the narrow sofa. Ben reached for a record from his large collection of 45s. He picked "Strange Fruit,"[6] the eerie, compelling protest song made famous by Billie Holiday, and placed it on the phonograph.

Outside the large bare windows, snowflakes fell in silent rhythm, a thick, white veil of dancing dotted Swiss. I welcomed our solitude; my senses were aroused.

Ben pulled a photo album from the shelf and showed me pictures from his work camp in Vermont, in particular, a photo of his summer girlfriend, Ellie, a fifteen-year-old exotic-looking, dark-haired girl with large breasts whose tight T-shirt and jeans (tighter yet) clung to her body like plastic wrap.

"We had lots of freedom at camp after our work detail," Ben explained, "lots of time to be together. I learned a lot from Ellie; she was older, you know, with lots of experience."

Putting his arms around me, Ben pulled me gently toward him and down against the sofa cushion. There was barely room for both of us, so he moved really close and coaxed our bodies toward the wall to make us fit. I let myself move with him, enjoying the strength of his embrace. Softly, he stroked my face, played with my hair, and then he kissed me, a full, firm, urgent kiss. My heart skipped several beats and propelled me out of myself and into a state of blissful empty-headedness. With my eyes closed, I followed his lead and returned his kiss, clearly conveying my pleasure.

Time went by. We lay together, kissing, touching. I wonder what he's thinking, I said to myself, too afraid to ask. I wonder if he likes this as much as I do. I drifted into a trance, as if floating down a river. I listened; the house was still. I opened my eyes and saw the snow, a thick, white wall sheltering us from the outside world. We moved, just slightly, to rearrange ourselves. I smiled, contented, and he smiled back. I felt accepted, cared for.

We stayed there for several hours, pausing only to get food, go to the bathroom, or find music. Ben was strong and intense but surprisingly sensitive; we seemed tuned to one another. I could stay like this forever, I thought.

And then . . . it all fell apart. Slowly, almost imperceptibly, he slid his hand inside my flannel shirt and covered my breast. Panic and dread invaded my reverie. Damn, I thought, knowing I'd have to stop him. Why does he have to do this and ruin everything?

I don't remember much about the rest of the afternoon, only that the spell was lifted. We stayed together on the sofa a while longer; then again he cupped his hand over my breast and again I removed it.

We gave it up, played Scrabble, listened to music. The mood was gone and I was sure we'd never get it back. I knew I would not give in to him; the rules were too clear. I knew also that if I didn't, he would not stay around.

From my private suffering, I watched the next stage of my father's public humiliation. Neither my mother nor legal counsel would travel with Dad to Chicago. He made the trip accompanied only by his own shame and dread.

The public testimony would yield no new information; the Committee had heard it all before. Rather, its true purpose was the promise of fresh publicity for HUAC. By publicly degrading my father, the Committee would justify its own continued existence. And the more dramatic my father's humiliation, the greater the assurance that HUAC would survive.

Chairman Walter called the Committee[7] to order and began the hearing by explaining the responsibility of the House Committee on Un-American Activities:

The Congress of the United States has imposed upon this committee
the duty of investigating the extent, character, and objects of un-American

INVESTIGATION OF COMMUNIST INFILTRATION OF GOVERNMENT—PART 1

HEARING

BEFORE THE

COMMITTEE ON UN-AMERICAN ACTIVITIES
HOUSE OF REPRESENTATIVES

EIGHTY-FOURTH CONGRESS

FIRST SESSION

DECEMBER 13, 1955

Printed for the use of the Committee on Un-American Activities

(Index in Part 2 of this Series)

UNITED STATES
GOVERNMENT PRINTING OFFICE
WASHINGTON : 1956

70811

Cover of my father's HUAC hearing testimony, December 13, 1955.

propaganda activities in the United States. . . . In 1948, the Committee on Un-American Activities of the House of Representatives heard, for the first time, testimony of Communist cells within the Government.

Whittaker Chambers, a contact for Soviet espionage agents as early as 1933, . . . identified a number of Government employees being used by the Soviet Union as contacts who furnished the Communist conspiracy with information regarding the operations of our government. As a result of Chambers' testimony, Alger Hiss was convicted and sentenced to prison.

Subsequently, Elizabeth Bentley . . . revealed a second Soviet apparatus within the Government agencies, and as a result of her testimony, William Remington was convicted and sent to prison.

From the testimony of these two former contacts for the Soviet espionage network in the United States, it was quite apparent that other organized cells of Communists within the Government agencies existed. . . .

This committee has never relaxed for one moment in its efforts to determine if such cells did exist, who were the leaders, what were their objectives, and whether they are still operating. Our efforts have been rewarded, at least partially. The present investigation . . . is expected to reveal the former existence of at least 10 cells of organized, disciplined Communists, within several Government agencies and comprised wholly of Government employees. . . .

But to the witness who has once been a part of that alien conspiracy and who has seen the error of his ways and broken with the Communist Party, and is possessed of the fortitude to take the stand and relate his experiences and give the committee the benefit of his knowledge, the committee and the country owe a debt of gratitude. It is not an easy task to appear before a congressional committee and lay bare all of your shortcomings of years gone by. Such persons will be subjected to all the vituperations that can be heaped upon them by the well-organized smear bund of the Communist Party and its henchmen. To those witnesses who decide they will give us the benefit of their knowledge, I have this to say—you will have the heartfelt thanks of your fellow Americans and you will have made a worthy contribution to the cause of a free world.[8]

Frank S. Tavenner Jr., counsel for the Committee, called his first witness. My father was sworn in. Tavenner asked about his background and training and his recruitment into the Communist Party. In a manner both earnest and clear, my father discussed his earliest activities as a Communist in New York City, at first in a unit of taxicab drivers in the Party's Section 4 in Manhattan. In November of

1934, my father had been recruited by a close friend, a cab driver and member of the taxi drivers' union, who knew he was interested in studying Marxism and suggested to him that the Communist Party was the proper venue in which to fight against fascism and for the rights of labor and minorities. Dad was convinced. Using a pseudonym, he signed a membership card at that time.[9]

Later, he affiliated with another unit, which was organizing workers of the Consolidated Edison Corporation. Dad told the Committee, "our purpose was simply to get a union started, and to get some more Communists in there to help.[10]

Tavenner next asked about my father's work and associates at the Wheeler Committee, a subcommittee of the Senate Committee on Interstate and Foreign Commerce, where he had served as a staff attorney from July 1936 to October 1937. Dad had been directed by his Communist contact, Arthur Stein, to join with another member of the Wheeler staff to create a Communist group there. Tavenner asked for the names and professions of the people who were subsequently admitted into this group.

It was then that my father did what to him had been the unthinkable. He gave the names, one by one, of his colleagues in the group at the Wheeler Committee and described the role each person had played on the staff.

At one point in the hearing deliberations, Dad's testimony was interrupted by a burst of flashbulbs. Too late, the chairman reminded the press of the rules prohibiting their use of camera equipment while the hearing was in progress.[11] The damage had been done. The unauthorized AP and UP photos show my father sitting stiff and upright as he faces his inquisitors, a taut expression revealing his state of nervous resignation.

My father testified that in October of 1937 he was told that staff reductions at the Wheeler Committee were likely but that he could be easily "placed" elsewhere. By this point, the Congress, firmly committed to President Roosevelt and the New Deal, had undertaken the job of establishing a new national labor policy. The National Labor Relations Act (the Wagner Act) had come into law in May 1935, and a new agency, the National Labor Relations Board (NLRB), had been established to implement and enforce its policies. Dad was interested in working there.

An interview was arranged for him, and subsequently he left the Wheeler Committee to join the NLRB staff. Communist Party contact Arthur Stein told Dad to get in touch with three Communists already working at the board: Allan Rosenberg (no relation to Julius Rosenberg), Martin Kurasch, and Joseph Robison. Together, they formed a new secret Communist unit at the NLRB; my father was the group leader. In response to questioning, Dad listed all the people he had known as members of this group, seventeen in all. He spelled each name when requested to do so, identifying each person's profession, title, and role on the staff and any other government employment previously held.

Tavenner asked my father to describe the function and organization of the NLRB during his first employment there, from 1937 to 1942. Dad characterized the two-fold function of the board as the settlement of conflicts relating to union representation and the prevention of unfair labor practices on the part of employers. As an attorney in the Review Division, his job had been to analyze testimony and make recommendations for action to the board.

The Committee was eager to learn how members were recruited into the secret group. My father explained that Communist Party members watched out for like-minded people, worthy of recruitment into the Communist Party organization. When a Party member felt positively about a coworker, he suggested the name to his comrades. If the group approved the individual, the matter would go to "a higher authority," from whom the group would wait for "a favorable report back." Once that positive report was received, one or more members of the group would be permitted to speak with the prospective member and invite him to join the group. Recruiting was severely limited, however, because of firm restrictions inherent in the recruiting process and fear of exposure.[12] Government cells were secret; their existence was not known by rank-and-file members of the Communist Party.

Tavenner informed Committee members that some of the people named by my father had agreed to testify. Chairman Walter interrupted the proceedings to express his gratitude to these witnesses, "who have the courage to do what Professor Fuchs is doing now, . . . indicating to the scoffers that this was a serious thing, and that the American people are determined now to put the bright light of publicity on it . . . and prevent the same thing from happening here that has happened in many places in the world." He went on to comment on the action of A.U.: "I do not think the American University did a service to the work of this committee by putting Professor Fuchs in the position that he is now in. I think it was a very reprehensible thing to dismiss a man who has done what he has done, and who has made the great contribution he has made toward carrying out the work that the Congress has imposed upon this committee."[13]

When the questioning resumed, my father testified that in the fall of 1942, he left the NLRB. He had been approached by Allan Rosenberg (the same person who had helped him organize the Communist group at the board) about a job at the Board of Economic Warfare (BEW), where Rosenberg was currently employed. According to my father, Rosenberg was aware that he was interested in a change:

My father at the National Labor Relations Board, date unknown.

"It was a desire to get into something that was more directly and vitally connected with the war effort," my father said.

Tavenner wanted to know more about Rosenberg's invitation. "Was the suggestion made to you from any Communist Party source," Tavenner asked, "that you change your employment to something of greater importance during that general period?"

"No, it was not," my father testified. "There was a general restlessness among the employees of the board, characterized also by many who were not Communists to get into something that was closer to the civilian firing line."[14]

This series of questions was interrupted by Congressmen Ed Willis and Gordon Scherer, who placed two newspaper articles into the record that criticized American University for firing my father. The congressmen wanted to counter the impression that it was dangerous for ex-Communists to testify. Chairman Walter echoed his colleagues' concerns, placing in the record a letter he had written to Hurst Anderson voicing his displeasure with the university and requesting reconsideration of the Board of Trustees' decision to let my father go.

Scherer pursued this issue further:

> **Mr. Scherer:** Mr. Chairman, it seems to me that they praised this witness and said that they would keep him on at the institution immediately after he had refused to testify, when they perhaps should have condemned him and then after he does cooperate with the congressional committee they fire him. I am at a loss to understand the action on the part of the university. . . . I would say that the university didn't take the trouble to inquire of this committee as to what his testimony was, or whether Mr. Fuchs was a member of the Communist Party.
>
> **The Chairman:** You are mistaken there, because I told the president myself that he was not.

This exchange led Mr. Tavenner to ask my father the famous HUAC question:

> **Mr. Tavenner:** I have not asked you the question yet, but I think that I should now. Are you a member of the Communist Party?
> **Mr. Fuchs:** No, I am not.

Dad told the Committee he quit the Party in the middle of 1946; there was no question in his mind about the accuracy of this cutoff date. He had not yet become a member of the faculty of American University at that time; he was still employed by the NLRB.[15]

Tavenner returned to questioning my father regarding his employment at the Board of Economic Warfare, where his job dealt with how the United States was going to govern future territory regained from the enemy. Dad had not stayed long at the BEW; he felt his skills as a labor lawyer were not being used there. By the end of 1942, he changed jobs once again, this time returning to a position in his own field but in a war agency, the National War Labor Board (NWLB). Two months later, he was transferred to the board's newly established regional office in Denver, where he served as Disputes Director. In Denver, he formed a group with several people whom he had known previously as Communists in Washington. Again, he was their leader.

When questioned about his tenure at the NWLB, my father testified as to the names, occupations, and roles of the people in the Communist group there, some twelve in all. Of these twelve, seven were actually members of the staff at the board. Tavenner was anxious to know when each group member was recruited. My father answered as best he could remember.[16]

In anticipation of the expiration of the National War Labor Board at the end of the 1945 calendar year, Dad exercised reemployment rights with the NLRB and returned to Washington as Head Supervisor for Representation Cases. Finding his old Communist group still functioning there, he reaffiliated and attended a few meetings, but he was beginning to feel "a conflict of loyalties." This feeling was intensified, he explained, by the fact that he had been promoted to the position of Assistant General Counsel, a role he felt did not fit with remaining in the Party. By now, his membership in the Party was coming to a close.[17]

After a brief recess, Tavenner returned to questions about the Communist group at the NLRB. His interest was in the group's relationship to the "higher authority" of the Party organization, and his questions dealt primarily with my father's experience (as leader of that group) with his contact, known as "Mike." This was Victor Perlo,[18] an economist, employed at that time by the Brookings Institution. My father testified that when problems arose in the secret Communist group at the NLRB, he would consult with "Mike," or "The Chief," as Perlo was also known.[19]

Tavenner's next questions centered on the practice of government employees lying under oath, as my father had done.

> **Mr. Tavenner:** How does the Communist Party explain the action of its members . . . when seeking Government employment, to deceive the Government about their Communist Party membership?
>
> **Mr. Fuchs:** I certainly don't propose to tell you how the Communist

Party explains it, because I don't know how it explains it and I am not a spokesman for it. . . . I can't reconcile it and I can't condone it. . . . I can tell you what happened to me and what may have happened to some of the people around me without wanting to excuse it. . . . I could say to you very glibly that it was a part of the Communist doctrine that the ends justify the means, and that if your substantive purposes were good then any means you resorted to, to accomplish them were thereby sanctified. You are familiar with that. I think it is a very misguided notion, and it was one of the central theses of Communists. . . .

There was [sic] also aspects of the thing, the way it developed, that made us feel, or made me feel a little bit sore at being confronted with prohibitions where theretofore I hadn't been. I had come into the government lawfully, and I had been a Communist, and I had not disclosed it but I hadn't been asked. It was not unlawful for me to be a Communist in the first few years of my employment. It later became increasingly unlawful. I don't excuse what I did when I say to you that there was an element of resentment or an element that "they can't do that to me," and I am in this job and I have a right to it, and now they are just making it illegal. I just hope that no member of the committee will construe any of this as justification—it isn't. I don't mean it as justification.

Mr. Moulder: Was it your reasoning at that time?

Mr. Fuchs: Yes, sir, and when I think back, what do I really regret about all of this? What shames me?

It appears to me that the only thing that I was impelled to do that I can't stand behind is this deceit, this deceitfulness of which Mr. Tavenner has been talking. It was not good; it was bad. It troubles me very much. . . .

Retrospectively . . . it seems to me that there is an advantage to the Communists and this is the trap of communism in their own illegality, because as they are a conspiracy and secret, then every member is involved in a kind of trap, potentially a blackmail trap or perhaps only a trap with respect to his sentimental desire not to involve other people in trouble. As soon as he has engaged in one or more violations of the law, he is a hostage to this conspiracy to which he perhaps altruistically lent himself in the first instance. But I don't know if it is worth anything to the committee to hear these speculations and perhaps I should drop them.

Mr. Moulder: I think it is an explanation of your conduct, because as I understand you, you did not consider yourself involved in a conspiracy at that time.

Mr. Fuchs: Only to the extent, Mr. Moulder, that if a group denies its existence and lies about its identity, it is a conspiracy then.

Mr. Moulder: Was it a philosphy [*sic*] or did you feel yourself a member of a conspiracy to overthrow the Government by force and violence?

Mr. Fuchs: No, sir, that isn't the conspiracy I meant.

Mr. Moulder: Or to commit any act of disloyalty to the country?

Mr. Fuchs: No, you are making the distinction that I meant to make. I think not only of myself but all of the people I worked with as Communists and I don't think any of us ever willingly were disloyal to the United States, or would willingly bring any injury to our country.

Mr. Scherer: Eventually you got out of the Communist Party because you found that the objectives of the party were to do just those things that you say you did not do.

Mr. Fuchs: That is right, Mr. Scherer. I think everybody gets out at a different time and everyone thinks his time was the right one, and the right one came for me when the United States and Russia were at the parting of the ways and began to separate. Up to that time I had had no problem of loyalty. It just so happens I hadn't had. During the war period the Communist Party line and American policy were almost exactly identical in many areas, and certainly in the area in which I worked. I had no problem of loyalty then. But after the war with the breaking up of this alliance, it became evident that the two horses that I had been riding were now going in different directions, and I had to choose, and that is when I chose. . .

Mr. Scherer: There is no question in your mind, in view of what you have just said that the Communist Party is under the direction and control of a foreign power, that is, Soviet Russia?

Mr. Fuchs: This first broke through [to] me in the immediate postwar period, and now there are times people tell me when I should have been aware of that in 1939, and that a lot of people were. I was not. This struck me toward the close of World War II, not simply that the two foreign policies diverged, but also that the American (Communist) Party was being pushed around pretty obviously to a position of opposition which it had substantially abandoned during the war, you see, and I just couldn't take it.[20]

Tavenner asked my father if he had been acquainted with or had ever met Elizabeth Bentley. He had not.

> **Mr. Tavenner:** Elizabeth Bentley identified before this committee two groups of individuals who were referred to by her as espionage groups. One was the Nathan Gregory Silvermaster group, and the other the Victor Perlo group. She identified certain members of the Victor Perlo group and testified before this committee that that group through Victor Perlo delivered documents and information to her which she in turn delivered to Jacob Golos who was an espionage agent of the Soviet Union.
>
> Here are the names of the persons she identified as members of the Victor Perlo espionage group: Allan Rosenberg, the man that you were directed to contact to form this group in the NLRB; Donald Niven Wheeler; Charles Kramer, whose real name was Charles Krevitsky; Edward Fitzgerald; Harry Magdoff; and Harold Glasser. . . .
>
> Were you acquainted with these other people whose names I have mentioned? Let us take them individually. Donald Niven Wheeler.
>
> **Mr. Fuchs:** No.
>
> **Mr. Tavenner:** . . . Charles Kramer?
>
> **Mr. Fuchs:** I met him once or twice on an introduction-only basis.
>
> **Mr. Tavenner:** . . . Edward Fitzgerald?
>
> **Mr. Fuchs:** I knew him socially.
>
> **Mr. Tavenner:** Harry Magdoff?
>
> **Mr. Fuchs:** I knew him socially.
>
> **Mr. Tavenner:** Harold Glasser?
>
> **Mr. Fuchs:** I knew Glasser not as well as the other two, but casually.
>
> **Mr. Scherer:** Would you say, Professor, you did not know these latter individuals mentioned as members of the Communist Party?
>
> **Mr. Fuchs:** That is right, sir; I did not know.
>
> **Mr. Scherer:** When did you know these people socially?
>
> **Mr. Fuchs:** I don't know how long I knew Fitzgerald and Magdoff.
>
> **Mr. Scherer:** About when was it?
>
> **Mr. Fuchs:** It seems to me that I knew both of them at some time before and after my departure for Denver.
>
> **Mr. Tavenner:** Were you acquainted with Jacob Golos?
>
> **Mr. Fuchs:** No.
>
> **Mr. Tavenner:** During the period of your acquaintanceship with the indi-

viduals mentioned, including Allan Rosenberg, did you observe or learn of the furnishing of any information to either Victor Perlo or Elizabeth Bentley for transmission to any Communist Party sources?

Mr. Fuchs: No, sir.

Mr. Tavenner: Did you ever attend a Communist Party meeting at which any of the persons mentioned other than Allan Rosenberg was present?

Mr. Fuchs: No, sir.

Tavenner asked if there had been an effort on the part of anyone to secure information from my father regarding an action of the NLRB or any of its procedures. In response, my father alluded to an attempt, on the part of an acquaintance, to get advance information on a decision of the board: "This was an effort on the part of somebody to get some advance dope which was not proper for them to get, and there was nothing subversive about his getting it, but it would give him an advantage. He didn't get it, and I would like to spare him . . . The committee has the information." My father did not think this had anything to do with Communist Party activity. He asked, and was granted, permission not to testify about this incident publicly.[21]

The end of my father's testimony dealt with his departure from the Party and his reasons for leaving:

Mr. Tavenner: You have told us that you were through as a member of the Communist Party in 1946?

Mr. Fuchs: Yes, sir.

Mr. Tavenner: Did you give any official of the Communist Party notice of your withdrawal?

Mr. Fuchs: No.

Mr. Tavenner: Did you just quit?

Mr. Fuchs: I said I wasn't coming around any more. I didn't do it in any official way, and I didn't do it in writing. I stopped coming around.

Mr. Tavenner: After that time, did you engage in any Communist Party activities?

Mr. Fuchs: No, sir.

Mr. Tavenner: Were you solicited at any time after leaving the Communist Party to come back to it?

Mr. Fuchs: No, sir. I was not.

Mr. Tavenner: I would be glad to have you tell the committee any circumstances you desire regarding your withdrawal from the Communist Party; that is, what led up to your decision to leave the Communist Party, and any information which might be of assistance in determining and deciding what ultimately are the determining factors in a person deciding to leave the Communist Party.

Mr. Fuchs: I have already mentioned to the committee part of the reason. I quit because I felt [for] the first time in my Communist Party history a conflict of loyalties which would not permit me to remain a Communist. This was accentuated by the fact that right around that time I received a promotion in my agency to Assistant General Counsel. Again it all accumulated and made me feel it was inconsistent to accept that office and remain a Communist, so I stopped.

I don't think that I have anything more to add except to say that in retrospect, after 9 years of trying to live down this rather serious error, I would like to sum up what I don't like about communism as a way for people to operate, quite aside from the international question, because as I have tried to tell you gentlemen, the international issue didn't affect me until it caused me to drop out. It didn't affect me until 1945 and 1946.

The other things I regret are having lent myself to a movement that depends upon deceit as a way of influencing people. It depends upon the notion that if the objectives are noble, any means are justifiable, and it ends up inevitably by substituting some kind of a discipline or mass will for the individual conscience.

These are the things that in retrospect I deplore on my own behalf. I think that is all I have to say.[22]

At 4:35 p.m. the day's proceedings came to an end, and my father's day of testimony was complete. In closing, the Committee expressed its appreciation for my father's cooperation: "We all join together on this committee in highly commending you for your appearance and cooperation before the committee," Moulder said, "as well as your loyalty and patriotism as an American citizen."

The day's testimony made front-page news.

My father returned to Washington that evening to find the *Evening Star* headlines announcing,

16 NAMED AS REDS HERE IN 1936
8 Cells Listed by Fuchs, One in Senate Unit
Others Were Placed in Federal Agencies, Witness Testifies[23]

The next morning, the front page of the *Post* proclaimed,

45 AIDES OF OLD NLRB, OTHER AGENCIES
WERE REDS, FUCHS TELLS PROBE
Former Professor at American U. Makes Charge at Chicago Hearing[24]

and *The New York Times* reported,

34 EX-U.S. AIDES LINKED TO REDS OUSTED
PROFESSOR TESTIFIES
Employees of Two Labor Units Were in His Cell.[25]

Evening Star headline, December 13, 1955.

Washington Post front-page headline, December 14, 1955.

WEATHER FORECAST

Considerable cloudiness and not as cold tonight, low 32. Mostly cloudy and warmer tomorrow. (Full report on Page A-2.)

Temperatures Today
Midnight 26   8 a.m......26   2 p.m......39
4 a.m.....25   10 a.m.....32   3 p.m.....40
6 a.m.....24   Noon.....36   4 p.m.....39

The Eveni

WITH SUNDAY MORNING EDI

103d Year. No. 348.   Phone ST. 3-5000   WASHINGTON, D. C., WEDNESDAY, DECE

AU Pressured Into Firing Fuchs, Red Prober Says

Oxnam Denies Charge Made By Scherer

By L. EDGAR PRINA
Star Staff Correspondent

CHICAGO, Dec. 14. — Representative Scherer, Republican of Ohio, says he believes that American University dropped Prof. Herbert Fuchs, an admitted former Communist, from its law school because he co-operated with the House Committee on Un-American Activities.

Mr. Scherer made this charge last night after a day-long series

None Named by Fuchs Hold U. S. Jobs
Today,   Page A-8

of barbs directed at the university's action by other members of the committee during Mr. Fuchs' testimony on his 12 years in the Communist Party, 1934-46.

Mr. Scherer said he believed that "someone with considerable influence at the university prevailed upon" Dr. Hurst Anderson, the president, "to change his mind after he made that fine eulogy" of Mr. Fuchs following disclosure of the latter's appearance before the committee in executive session.

Refers to Oxnam Book

"The contents of a recent book entitled "I Protest," which is a violent attack on this committee, helps me reach these conclusions," he said.

The book was written by Bishop

FUCHS AT RED PROBE—Chicago.—Prof. Herbert Fuchs strikes a serious pose at the hearing of the House Committee on Un-American Activities.—AP Wirephoto.

Front-page article in the *Evening Star* with AP photo of my father, December 14, 1955.

I had been home alone the evening of my father's testimony, waiting for my parents to return from the airport after his flight from Chicago. It was from Walter Winchell's evening news report that I learned the highlights of my father's hearing. The force of Winchell's words went through me like the recoil of a rifle. I knew that this broadcast, delivered in Walter Winchell's familiar, rhythmic tone, would reach millions in the national radio audience that had come to rely on him for the significant news of the day.

After my parents returned home, I tossed and turned in the night, waiting for sleep to come, fantasy my only comfort. I felt desperate, not suicidal but without hope of ever again having a normal life. My parents were consumed with their own challenging reality; my brother was in a world of his own.

The ending of my relationship with Ben became the focus for all my grief and anxiety. I was devastated by the loss and cried myself to sleep for weeks. It was painful seeing him in class each day; the loneliness consumed me.

The Chicago degradation ceremony had accomplished its objective. The people my father named had become dehumanized, numbers on a list, "Reds."

Pushed into a corner by refusing to take the Fifth and wishing to live down what he considered his rather serious error, my father had agreed to testify. He had confessed his mistake. But the hearings had not, as Victor Navasky suggests in his 1980 book, "insulated him from direct contact with the moral dilemmas of betrayal."[26] On the contrary, the exposure of the public hearing and the ensuing publicity served only to seal his shame.

10

Cause Célèbre

Fighting the Blacklist

Considerable irony invests the McCarthy era dismissals within the academic community, for the nation's colleges and universities allegedly subscribed to the doctrines of academic freedom and to the notion that professors should not be punished for their political activities outside of class. But academia was not immune to McCarthyism.

—Ellen Schrecker, *The Age of McCarthyism: A Brief History with Documents*

An Underwood typewriter, a large hardwood desk, two sofa beds, and paintings from my parents' past—these simple furnishings became the backdrop for my father's battle to escape the blacklist. The small basement study had once been our playroom and later served as a site for slumber parties. Now my father transformed it into a serious place of business, equipped with the tools he needed to carry on his work. His challenge was to structure unstructured days, to stay positive and focused while riding an emotional roller coaster.[1]

One moment, good news—a *Post* editorial, for example, that encouraged him to hope that his prospects would improve: "Although Mr. Fuchs does not enjoy tenure, the American University has an obligation to avoid capricious or arbitrary conduct in regard to all its faculty members. This obligation grows out of its 'Christian relationship and commitments' and equally out of a regard for the principles of academic freedom which have at their core the concept that teachers should not be penalized on account of political associations and beliefs."[2]

Then, on the same day, grim reality—articles appearing in the *New York Herald Tribune*, *New York Times* and *Washington Post*, with bad news from the American University administration: "Hurst R. Anderson, president of American University, said today 'no pressure under Heaven' could force him to withdraw the dismissal of a professor who once belonged to three Communist cells in the government. . . . [A]ny relationship between the professor, Herbert Fuchs, and the university is 'undesirable.'"[3]

This is how it was in the fall of 1955, as my father hunkered down in our basement fighting for his survival. Dad knew that the university's fear of publicity had been a significant cause for his dismissal, but he seemed not to have fully comprehended the other factors at work against him: the administration's alarm over the fact that he had been a Communist Party member while working for the government, and that he had been a "cell" leader and had lied under oath about his membership; their doubt that he had left the Party in mid-1946; and his colleagues' unwillingness to provide needed support. Dad had no way of assessing the impact of Edward Bennett Williams's delay in getting to Anderson and Fletcher to emphasize evidence of my father's complete break from the Party. He had not yet questioned his decision (on the advice of Williams) to attend the executive committee meeting without counsel nor had he considered the possible effect of Chairman Fletcher's opposition to informing. Finally, from what I have gleaned, he had not yet wondered whether anti-Semitism might have contributed to his situation.[4]

My father did not know what the future would bring, only that he must persevere and ultimately triumph over his current crisis. Nor did the university know what was coming. A.U.'s administration and board of trustees were caught completely off guard by the barrage of letters, telegrams, articles, and editorials condemning the board's position. "Whatever merit A.U.'s decision might have had, it proved to be popular with almost no one," claimed an editorial in *Time* magazine, referring to the building storm of public protest.[5] The Fuchs case became a national cause célèbre.

The American Civil Liberties Union (ACLU) sent a telegram to A.U. president Anderson protesting the executive committee's move to drop my father from the law school faculty. The ACLU was "deeply disturbed" over the suspension and challenged the university for not "meeting standards of academic due process." The ACLU took issue too with Anderson's suggestion that my father's religious affiliation was "not in sympathy with the objectives" of the university. "Do you intend to let go of men who have taught well and conducted themselves irreproachably," the ACLU asked, "if they are agnostic, Jewish, Roman Catholic, or Presbyterian?"[6]

Also interested in my father's case was the Association of American Law Schools (AALS), whose Academic Freedom and Tenure Committee chairman wrote my father in October requesting permission to look into the facts of the case. The committee spent countless hours over the next two years gathering information, requesting clarification, and meeting with both sides of the conflict. My father maintained a correspondence with two successive chairmen, Professor Clark Byse of the University of Pennsylvania and, later, Dean Henry P. Brandis Jr. of Stanford Law School, a dialogue which included at least eighteen letters. On the basis of its findings, the AALS became convinced the university had acted improperly.[7]

In November, the executive director of the American Committee for Cultural Freedom (ACCF) also contacted my father to offer the backing of his organization of "anti-totalitarian" artists, writers, scholars, and scientists.[8] The ACCF conducted months of investigation. It followed up its pledge of support with a letter to every member of the A.U. Board of Trustees reviewing the case, reiterating its arguments in defense of my father, and urging the trustees to reconsider their action taken in September: "The action taken against Professor Fuchs raises a grave issue of public policy and academic freedom, namely: Are ex-Communist members of the academic community to be penalized when they fulfill their obligation to the community by testifying before Congressional investigating committees concerning their past activities?"[9]

Even the conservatives joined the fray. Intellectuals such as William F. Buckley Jr., editor of the *National Review,* who believed that the investigative committees were performing a valid and honorable service to our country, were critical of the university for firing a witness with a positive work history who had fully cooperated with HUAC. Buckley's brother-in-law L. Brent Bozell interviewed my father and President Anderson and drew highly critical conclusions about the way A.U. had handled the case.[10]

Anderson took grave exception to Bozell's article. In a follow-up letter, also published by the journal, he asked

1) Should the private church-related college or university have the right to choose its faculty in light of its stated objectives?
2) Should a congressional committee presume to suggest whom such a college or university should employ or not employ?

His answer to the first question, yes, to the second, no.[11]

I remember peering out the window of my parents' bedroom, watching Brent Bozell leave our house after coming to speak to my father. I remember his red hair

NATIONAL
REVIEW

20 Cents

January 25, 1956

A WEEKLY JOURNAL OF OPINION

The 'Times' Slays A Dragon

WM. F. BUCKLEY, JR.

The Firing of Herbert Fuchs

L. BRENT BOZELL

Mill's 'On Liberty' Reconsidered

RUSSELL KIRK

Articles and Reviews by . . . . RICHARD M. WEAVER
ROBERT PHELPS · ERIK VON KUEHNELT-LEDDIHN · FREDA UTLEY
JAMES BURNHAM · JONATHAN MITCHELL · SAM M. JONES

Cover of *National Review* with article defending my father in his battle with American University, January 25, 1956.

and how really young he looked. At the time, I didn't get the full meaning of his visit, but I understood he had taken on my father's cause and I hoped that he and others, who had come to my father's defense, would ultimately succeed in helping him.

My father appreciated the support of the lobbying groups. Each time they challenged the university's erroneous claims, each time they found substantiation for his own, he was encouraged. For two years, they reported the university's continued attempts to defend its position and asked him to explain conflicting factors. Their voluminous correspondence offered an opportunity for him to clarify his point of view, explain his actions, and, possibly, contribute to saving his reputation. It also gave him a chance to voice his indignation, as in the following passage from a letter to Dean Henry P. Brandis of the AALS concerning President Anderson's precipitous about-face:

> Where he first described me as "intelligent, loyal and devoted," he now says I am morally and intellectually unfit; Where he first said I had recognized and declared my past error, he now questions whether I have ever renounced communism; Where he first said that he had no evidence of continued party activity on my part, he now rejects compelling evidence that such activity ceased; Where he first respected my right "as a citizen," he now declares that the public interest requires my removal; Where he first invoked Christian commitments to forgiveness in my behalf, he now presents me as an irredeemable sinner, and atheist to boot.
>
> In presenting these new conclusions, Dr. Anderson (1) adduces [sic] no evidence in their support, (2) ignores objective evidence to the contrary, and (3) refuses to credit my own assertions solely because I admit that in the past I was a Communist and concealed the fact. In effect, he is saying "Once a Communist, always a Communist."[12]

Gratifying also were the prominent theologians and philosophers who wrote to President Anderson to voice their concerns, individuals such as Reinhold Niebuhr, vice president of the faculty of the Union Theological Seminary; John C. Bennett, professor of Christian Theology and Ethics at the same seminary; and Brand Blanshard, professor of Philosophy at Yale. Typical of their point of view was a letter Niebuhr sent to Anderson in March: "I would like to challenge this decision on moral grounds. If a man has been involved in the Communist conspiracy and has made a clean breast of it, is there any moral reason why an institution should dismiss him? It rather puts all repentant Communists in the category of martyrs, and it incidentally makes repentance a very hazardous adventure."[13]

My father was heartened as well by the widespread support expressed in editorials in the national press. These were all variations on the same few themes: failure to provide academic freedom and due process, public policy in relation to former Communist cooperative witnesses, and the role of repentance and forgiveness.[14]

But my father was, by nature, a very private man, and the constant limelight took its toll, especially as time went on and a positive outcome became less and less likely. Furthermore, he believed that publicity was the major contributor to his having become controversial in the first place, and, in the long run, he concluded it was of doubtful help to his cause later on. Then too, though most of the publicity was supportive of him, the few comments critical of his actions affected him deeply, as they almost always addressed moral issues about which he himself was profoundly conflicted. On this score, he could not win. While some (*Life,* the *National Review,* and certainly his detractors at the university) criticized him for not having spoken out sooner,[15] at least one person, Yale law professor Fred Rodell, in a letter to the ACCF, criticized my father for naming names, a tough reminder of his own feelings of guilt for having spoken out at all about his former friends and colleagues. The ACCF chose not to publicize this letter, though they passed it on for my father to read:

> There is not the slightedst [*sic*] doubt that Professor Fuchs got a raw deal and an unfair deal from American University. In a sense, I think he asked for it when he abandoned his original conscientious scruples against playing the conventional ex-Communist stool-pigeon. . . . Personally, I do not believe in legal confession-and-avoidance nor do I believe in religious confession-and-absolution. I think adults are—or ought to be—responsible for what they do and ought not be relieved of the consequences of their actions by the easy ritual of saying "I'm sorry." In short, I would have far more sympathy for Fuchs if he had displayed the courage and integrity required to refuse to name his former fellow-Communists. . . . If Fuchs is, as I gather he is, an able and honest teacher, it seems to me utterly irrelevant that he is an ex-Communist, a repentant ex-Communist, an atheist, an agnostic, or anything

else but an able and honest teacher. I agree completely with your Committee that he should be reinstated in his job. I disagree completely with most of the reasons stressed by your Committee—which have led to your campaign in his behalf.[16]

My father wrote an angry response to Professor Rodell in which he defended himself, claiming, "I am not a conventional stool pigeon . . . not a professional, anti-Communist," but rather a "coerced informer." In this angry, sometimes petulant letter, Dad reiterated his position on the Fifth Amendment and went on to play cynical word games with Rodell's critical remarks. Fortunately, he never mailed this letter:

I do not condemn those who use Constitutional Immunity as a shield to enable them to shield their former comrades. I could not follow that course

   1) because I was unwilling to pretend I ran a risk of prosecution and
   2) because I did not want to serve the purposes of the C.P. and
   3) because I did not wish, in the light of my past false denial about my pm
       [past membership] . . . to continue in an ambiguous and evasive role.

Moreover, I ended by refusing to defy Congress because I could not rationalize a right to do so. It is true that I took refuge in compliance with law and in the truth.

As I read your letter in its semantic fullness you hold that it was (noble but?) misguided to have joined the party; unheroic (because no longer safe) to quit; infamous (weaklings who confess and tell all) to admit; heroic (I would have more sympathy for Fuchs . . .) to defy. . . .

Finally, then, it is bad to have been a Communist, worse to have quit, and intolerable to have responded to questioning.

In short, you would have had more symp w. [sympathy with] me if I persisted in my misguidedness by frustrating the present misguided efforts of the legislature to investigate the misguidedness of my former misguided colleagues.[17]

As my father's exile grew longer, he spent most of his days corresponding with the lobbying groups and meeting with anyone who might lead him to a possible job. He contacted employment services, teachers' agencies, and lawyers' cooperatives. He applied for a loan to pay for Peter's freshman year at Union College the following fall; my mother's teacher's salary would leave many bills unpaid. Dad tried to keep his emotions in check. He was ashamed of his inability to provide for his family; he feared that his situation might not improve, and he felt the weight of his responsibility for his current predicament.

My father missed teaching, and so, when some of his former students asked him to conduct a seminar—to coach them in Contracts—he readily agreed, though he declined the fee they offered.[18] Then too, there was a need for his teaching skills closer to home. My classes at Gordon were challenging that year, and I was struggling with Latin translations. I went to Dad for help. He could translate passages without a dictionary, in spite of having been away from Latin for over thirty years. Hearing of his facility with the translations, my friends soon began to ask for help as well. Several boys called regularly, even Ben, who'd hardly spoken to me for months. Ben phoned Dad to say "thank you" and told him that Mrs. Clapper had praised him for his work. He said he would not have passed without Dad's help.[19]

In the spring, my father allowed himself to be distracted by the glorious weather and the allure of blossoming trees and flowers, the explosion of vibrant colors and smells that make Washington so special at that time of year. He always loved the cherry blossoms and made a point each year of driving the family to see them at the Tidal Basin—a profusion of pink and white against sky blue. Dad spent time in his garden weeding and caring for his roses, clematis, portulaca. In April he attended Gordon's Dogwood Festival, a seasonal celebration featuring singing, dancing, and acrobatics performed by students. For me, the highlight of the annual festival was the crowning of the Dogwood Festival queen, an event that fueled my fantasy. Along with hundreds of other girls, I longed to be chosen myself to wear the crown. Mary Jo Pyles was crowned queen that year. A terrific girl, smart, pretty, and popular, Jo Jo reigned with grace over her court of princesses.

It was around this time in the spring of 1956 that Judge Fletcher, American University Board of Trustees chairman, met with representatives from the ACLU and the ACCF. As a result of that meeting, the chairman agreed to take the matter of my father's dismissal to the members of the board one more time for reconsideration, warning, however, that "[i]f Fuchs is re-employed by the American University, I shall immediately resign as Chairman of its Board of Trustees." On April 22, the press reported that the university had "declined to consider a request that admitted former Communist Herbert Fuchs be continued on the law school faculty. 'The matter,' said Chairman Fletcher, 'is finally concluded.'"[20]

With A.U. a thing of the past and no good news from Georgetown or anywhere else for that matter, my father stepped up his letters of inquiry to other law schools. In early May, Dad began to keep track of rejection letters: five by May 10, two more by the twelfth, seventeen more by the twenty-fifth.

He stopped counting at forty-nine rejections and experienced more and more difficulty doing any work. He grieved all that he had lost; he missed teaching, contact with his students, even the colleagues who had let him down.

Meanwhile, the American Committee for Cultural Freedom had hired author James Rorty to write a report for the committee on the Fuchs case. This report again stressed the issues of academic freedom, the status of repentant former Communists, and the question of Christian morality. In his poignant summary, Rorty identified the essential consequence of blacklisting for its victims. After citing examples of my father's notable teaching record at A.U., "prompt promotions from Assistant to Associate to Full Professorship and four annual salary increases in five years," Rorty's bottom line read, "What is at stake here is on the one hand the moral responsibility of a Methodist supported University, and on the other the moral and economic survival of Fuchs, who, lacking some evidence of forgiveness, faces permanent exile from the academic world, and even to some degree moral exile from the community of free men."[21]

Unfortunately, the results of the combined pressure brought by the ACLU and the ACCF still fell short of the desired goal: to reestablish my father's eligibility for a law school faculty position. On June 5, 1956, the Association of American Law Schools' dean Henry Brandis and ACCF member Professor Charles Wright met at A.U. with Fletcher, Anderson, Bookstaver, and Jack Myers, who succeeded Bookstaver as dean. At the conclusion of that meeting, the university conceded only that 1) my father had not been teaching Communist doctrine, 2) he had not been a Communist since 1946, and 3) he was a good teacher. This was the limit of the university's willingness to yield.

And life went on. Amazing how it just went on and on, in spite of all that was happening. On June 13, at two o'clock in the afternoon, I graduated from Gordon Junior High. At six that evening, we attended Pete's graduation from Western. That night, the family celebrated these milestones with a couple of rounds of miniature golf and a party at the Bents' house. I had gone to the Gordon prom with an old friend, whose girlfriend was out of town. We had a terrific time, except for a rough moment at the end of the dance when Mr. Shirley lit into us for talking during the playing of the National Anthem. I was stunned by the force of his rebuke. (Might he have been singling me out?)

A few days later Mom, Dad, and I went out to Ben's house for a picnic. For six months, Ben had taken no notice of me; I'd gotten the cold shoulder. But on this day, to my surprise and intense pleasure, he was friendly and attentive. It was a crystal-clear early summer night, the air so perfectly balanced that the temperature was barely discernible. We feasted on picnic fare: hamburgers, hot dogs, potato salad.

"Wanna get out of here?" Ben asked, after the meal was over and our parents had fallen into boring adult conversation. "Wanna go over to Glen Echo?"

"Sure, okay," I answered, caught up short but wildly flattered by his attention.

Ben and I walked the several country blocks to Glen Echo Amusement Park, the old D.C. area landmark, replete with memories of magical afternoons. For many years, before the service was discontinued, my friends and I used to ride the trolley car along the river from our neighborhood to Glen Echo whenever we could. We spent long hours in the blistering sun, swimming among the throngs of people in the huge pool; riding on the roller coaster; driving and crashing the noisy bumper cars; and eating cotton candy, Cracker Jacks, and ice cream.

On those summer afternoons, the sun shone so brightly that its light reflected off everything metal and its heat shimmered along the roofs of the cars lined up in the massive parking lot. The air was alive with the carefree cries of swimmers and the cheerful music of the hand-painted Dentzel carousel. But on this night the park was closed, locked down tight; there had been a drowning two days before. The evening was beginning to cool. A sign warned intruders to "Keep Out."

Ben walked over to a small opening in the fence, crawled through the narrow space, and gestured for me to come. Fearful, but at the same time eager, I followed him. It was dusk by now, the evening light diffused as if covered by a thin film of gray netting. The deserted park was still, strange, and eerie. There were no crowds hurrying to their destinations, no shouts of abandon from the swimming pool, no shrieks of ecstatic terror from the roller coaster. The place was dead. I was excited to be there alone with Ben, but I was also apprehensive. *What will happen if we get caught in here?* I worried.

Ben led me to a park bench; we sat for a while. I took in the spooky ambiance. He leaned over to kiss me. I returned the kiss but I couldn't hold back the accumulated anguish of the last six months, and out of my mouth came the dumbest, most embarrassing thing I could possibly say to him:

"Why don't you like me anymore?" I sputtered. It was almost as if I had to ruin the moment, once and for all, rather than go on.

Unable to respond, Ben mumbled something inaudible, something that conveyed his dismay at hearing my question. He turned away.

I couldn't believe what I'd done. All I knew was that I managed to end the thing *again,* this time for good.

Each day, my father returned to his basement office and constructed lists of people to call, people to see, leads. In July, Donn Bent suggested he recontact HUAC chairman Francis Walter. "Might there be a job for you on the Hill?" Donn wondered.

"I'll be happy to look into this," Walter told my father when they met on July 10. "There's a possible Immigration assignment that might be of interest, for a foundation in New York—your own hours. . . . or maybe something at the Joint Commission on Government Security—purely a clock job. . . . There may be a role for you at Judiciary, Manny Celler's committee—something about bank mergers. I'll see what I can do. Call me in a day or so."[22]

On July 25, my father returned to the House, this time to meet with Walter and Representative Emanuel Celler, chairman of the Judiciary Committee of the House of Representatives. In this meeting, my father was offered a temporary position as a staff member on Celler's Anti-trust Subcommittee. Dad was deeply conflicted about taking this job. He did not like accepting help from HUAC, the committee he had described as having a "long history of indiscriminate and irresponsible sadism."[23] Despite his extreme discomfort, he felt he had no choice. This was the first break he had had in months; he accepted the position.

As it turned out, there was indeed a role for my father to fill on Celler's staff: as counsel, first on the Anti-trust Subcommittee and later on the subcommittee for Patents, Trademarks, and Copyrights. Dad's "temporary" job with Manny Celler would last until his retirement twenty years later.

In a final attempt to achieve justice, the Association of American Law Schools presented a report to the American Association of University Professors (AAUP), citing A.U.'s failure to provide academic due process in the case of Herbert Fuchs.[24] At their annual meeting in December, the AAUP recommended that the university be censured. Despite the report's conclusions, A.U. managed to avoid a formal vote of censure by immediately strengthening its bylaws to assure due process in the future.

In the end, all of this was too little, too late for my father. His battle with the university was irreversibly and unequivocally lost, and the emotional roller-coaster ride was over.

Case closed.

III

DISCOVERY

11

Breaking Away

When, as an adult, did my journey begin? When did I emerge from the cloud of denial that housed all memories and emotions relating to those teenage years?

Certainly the early denial was encouraged by my father, who forbade—not a word easily attributable to him—but, yes, forbade any discussion of "the troubles." Once, as a senior in high school, I wrote a short piece for an English class about the night I learned my parents had been Communists. The essay was devoid of emotion; frustrated and blocked, I just couldn't get the feelings out, but my teacher insisted I send it to a writing contest anyway. My father opposed my entering the competition and my mother had to call the teacher, explain Dad's misgivings, and request that the entry be withdrawn. Years later, still wary, he even objected to the placement of my wedding announcement in the local newspaper. "You can't do that," he insisted. "I must be sure that the next time my name appears in the paper, it will be in my obituary."

Later yet, when my mother decided that my nieces, Peter's daughters, were old enough to hear about their grandparents' political past, she asked my father's permission to talk to them about it. I remember my father's reluctance. Ultimately, my mother prevailed and spoke to her granddaughters, explaining my parents' involvement in the Communist Party and how the events of the 1950s unfolded.

Actually, in spite of the thousands of family conversations during the 1960s and '70s, when my father worked for Emanuel Celler's Judiciary Committee and had a front-row view, on a daily basis, of current events making history, I do not ever remember discussing those two difficult years with either one of my parents, nor with my brother. It seems we all put our thoughts and memories into storage.

So what was it in my personal evolution that allowed those memories to push themselves back into my consciousness?

In 1959 I went off to Colby College in Waterville, Maine. Anxious about leaving my parents and friends, I lay awake the last few nights at home wondering how I would survive the grief of separation. But my adjustment to the small, intimate New England college was effortless; I loved it there and made friends from day one.

One person in the Colby class of 1963 stood out among the others: Camilo Marquez; he was hard to miss. A token black student, he was tall and slim with intense hazel eyes. His friends nicknamed him "Teak" because of the color of his skin. He held his head high and walked with a grace and elegance that could sometimes make him appear arrogant or aloof. I wondered what it must be like for him, one of so few blacks on campus, whether he felt strange or alone.

Everyone seemed to like Teak, especially his brothers in the Jewish fraternity Tau Delta Phi, who took him in as if he were one of their own. If Teak felt ill at ease or out of place, no one knew. This was a young man with charm and a strong social consciousness who seemed, even back then, to be at home on this predominantly white campus. Teak and I became friends, and on my twenty-first birthday he was the only one of my college mates to send me a card.

My friendship with Teak intensified one afternoon in 1962, during a study break at the window of the Miller Library. For some reason, I told him that my father had been called before HUAC; intrigued, he asked thoughtful questions. It was as if for him, an upper-middle-class liberal black from Harlem, my family's experience gave me value and respectability. I felt flattered by Teak's attention and validated by his interest in my story.

I was a junior that semester, taking a class in American history. I was pleased with this course, as Professor David Bridgman chose to teach through trade books instead of a traditional history text. This approach was unusual in my experience at Colby, and I found it particularly motivating.

In his lectures, Professor Bridgman described the paranoia of the McCarthy Era. He spoke at length about the country's fear-based obsession with fallout shelters and air-raid drills, reminding us of the films we'd seen in the 'fifties advising citizens to stock shelters with food and supplies and teaching schoolchildren how to "duck and cover" under their desks.

It was also Professor Bridgman who brought a film about the McCarthy-Army hearings to our campus and encouraged us to see it. I went to the viewing with a few of my friends, guarding, as usual, my secret—that my father and mother had been Communists and that my father had been called to testify before HUAC. After the film, I recall having the strangest altered perception of reality: There's not a hint of anti-Communist sentiment expressed by anyone here, I noticed with surprise. There seemed no call for me to feel ashamed that my parents were active Party members. Here, everyone speaks instead of the horrible wrongs done to the victims of the McCarthy and congressional witch hunts. Cautiously, I related the basic facts of my father's HUAC experience to my friends. Instead of the familiar muted, but nevertheless obvious, disapproval or pity (the solicitous concern one might offer the child of parents who had committed a violent crime), my classmates treated me more like some kind of hero. Young America's perception of history was making one of its many revisionary twists and turns. For the first time, I was seeing my McCarthy Era experience from a dramatically different point of view.

Following graduation in June 1963, I moved to New York City to study for a master's in the education of the deaf at Columbia Teachers' College. Camilo (Teak used his given name by then) had settled in the City as well and worked for the Welfare Department, a caseworker in Lyndon Johnson's war on poverty. By the end of that year, our friendship had turned to courtship.

I was taken by Camilo's cool reserve; there was something exotic about him— that long, graceful body, the smooth tan skin, the way he sometimes hesitated before speaking. After a while, I won him over by lending a sympathetic ear to his tales of unrequited love. Ultimately, fondness and physical attraction brought us together as a couple in a comfortable connection rooted in common interests: good friends, great music, and a fascination for all things New York.

Camilo's West Indian parents, his grandparents, and other relatives all took me into their homes and into their lives. They treated me with respect and affection, and I quickly became part of their family. I established deep and loving relationships with his people. In the seven years I was with them, I never once experienced rejection from them based on race or any other aspect of my being.

I expected my father and mother to welcome Camilo into our family in much the same way his family had welcomed me. Surely, I thought, my parents would support my dating a black college mate with whom I had so much in common. I'd been taught liberal values the way others of my generation learned their catechism or their Bar Mitzvah readings. "We are liberals," my father had told me when I was eleven, explaining the difference between us and the conservatives. "Among other things," he had said, "we believe that all people should be treated equally no matter what the color of their skin."

There were certainly ways in which my father and mother had moved to the Right in the years since their ordeal, particularly where their personal values were

concerned. In 1963, for example, they joined a golf/country club, one that only recently had begun to admit Jews into its membership. I remember my shock that
they had come to consider this a natural thing to do. Then, too, in the 1960s and
'70s, I was surprised to witness their pleasure in attending lavish social events—
perks of Dad's job at the Judiciary Committee. But my parents were still solidly
liberal.

And so I was shocked and deeply hurt when my parents first voiced their opposition to my seeing Camilo. They simply did not approve but would not or could
not articulate their concerns.

My mother and father first met Camilo in July of 1964. I had brought him and
some other friends to see my parents off on a trip abroad on the *Queen Elizabeth II.*
Comfortable now with the material advantages of a good job on the Hill, my parents looked forward, unapologetically, to the comfort and luxury that the famous
cruise ship promised. This was to be their first trip to Europe together, and they
were in wonderful spirits. Mom and Dad were polite to Camilo that day but not
warm. In spite of their cool reception, he tried to reach out and engage them.
Pointing to the headlines in that day's press, which reported the signing of the
Civil Rights Act of 1964, Camilo made reference to the fact that Dad, in his position as a staff member of the Judiciary Committee of the House of Representatives, had had a role in the writing of the bill. Camilo congratulated my father on
a job well done.

The second meeting occurred a year later. Camilo and I had gone to D.C. to attend a civil rights march and arranged to stay with my parents. The weekend was a
strain for all, awkward and uptight. As we said goodbye that Sunday at Union Station, Camilo thanked my parents for an "exquisite" visit. This unfortunate word
choice, a gesture toward decorum, was his clumsy attempt to salvage a disaster.

It never occurred to me to end the relationship because my parents didn't approve; the idea never even entered my mind. And gradually, Camilo and I spent
more and more time together. He worked on his Ph.D. in economics at City College, and I taught classes at the School for Language and Hearing Impaired Children. We were both busy but reserved evenings and weekends for each other.

Though we lived in Manhattan, where an interracial couple was not the novelty it would have been in another American city, we were aware that many
people—maybe most—disapproved of our relationship. Sometimes, when I was
with people who weren't part of our crowd, I felt as if I was living a double life,

one with my white friends and colleagues on the Upper East Side and the other with Camilo. It made me uneasy.

Nevertheless, my not-quite-conventional life with him was full and exciting. We had good friends—white, black, and a few Latino—with whom we frequently got together for gourmet meals or parties.

My father had been afraid to participate in politics after his departure from the Communist Party because of the shame and trauma he had endured. Probably as a result of his reticence and my own disturbing memories of our family's ordeal, I was cautious about becoming politically active myself. Camilo became my mentor. He helped me to examine my views about the important issues facing our country. He challenged me to put my values into practice and to participate with him in local politics by joining the Reform Democratic Party in Manhattan. It felt good to be part of the action, to belong. Together, we attended meetings and rallies in support of civil rights and in protest of the war in Vietnam. We attended Black Power conferences where I was, at times, the only white person present. At these gatherings, I had the opportunity to confront my own racial prejudice and alter my perception of the meaning of the Black Power movement. Now, for the first time, I came to appreciate it as a campaign to promote black interests and self-esteem rather than a crusade against whites.

It was during this time that I became curious about my father's case and decided to read about it in *New York Times* articles of the period. As I scrolled through the microfiche, the stories brought back memories of events I had almost completely forgotten. But while my mind was now engaged, I was emotionally detached from the material, almost as if reading about strangers.

In March of 1968 New York senator Robert F. Kennedy threw his hat into the ring to run as a Democratic candidate for president. Many progressive Democrats in New York City joined his campaign with enthusiasm and hope for change. When, at a fund-raising dinner at the Tavern on the Green in May, I found myself shaking hands with RFK and his wife, Ethel, I realized I was living in the center of the modern world. Here I was, witness to a significant moment in history, no longer an outsider as I had felt in my childhood.

That same spring, I announced to my parents that Camilo and I had tentative plans to marry. My father shocked me by uttering a strange and uncharacteristically blunt directive. "Do not marry this man," he said. "Do not darken my door."

What was he really trying to say? "I forbid you to marry him"? "Don't bring this shame down upon me"? "Don't make the same mistake that I did—by bringing the problems of an unconventional life upon yourself"? I didn't know then; I still don't know. I remember only the strong racial overtones his words conveyed and my terrible pain upon hearing them.

Soon, for whatever reason—rebellion or anger, maybe both—this edict spurred me into action. I made up my mind to marry Camilo and to do it soon.

We were married on the twentieth of September in 1968, in the seven-room rent-controlled apartment on Riverside Drive that was to become our home for the duration of our two-year marriage. My father agreed to give me away.

The following year, Camilo was asked to run on the Reform Democratic ticket for the office of district leader in a neighborhood in Washington Heights. This was the same ticket that championed Hispanic Reform candidate Herman Badillo for mayor. Camilo's campaign pit him against the longtime incumbent Angelo Simonetti. Just blocks away from where my father was born more than a half century earlier, our team canvassed the largely Spanish-speaking neighborhood one apartment at a time. Though the campaign was not victorious, we made a great showing and succeeded in demonstrating to the people of this community that change from patronage politics was well within their reach.

On the outside, everything in our married life seemed just fine; Camilo and I got along well. But somewhere inside of me, there was an uneasy feeling. Something important was missing. I could not reach Camilo emotionally, no matter how hard I tried.

In the second year of our marriage, Camilo was drawn into the counterculture of parties and drugs that encircled us in the New York City scene. He began to look for other relationships. It became clear that he wanted to pursue a lifestyle far freer than the one to which I could comfortably subscribe. Though he felt a real affection for me, I could see that he did not want an intimate monogamous relationship. This was not okay with me. Still, it took almost a year for me to realize that it was time for me to go.

We stood on the roof of our apartment building in Harlem that Sunday afternoon, early in September 1970, hanging our laundry to dry. I had finally decided to leave him. A flood of tears blinded my view as I lifted each piece of clothing to the line. This was the worst moment of my life.

I wiped away my tears. I looked down to the street below, to the traffic on Riverside Drive, and wondered if I should jump, if I should end my life to kill the pain. It was then that I felt the full power of my will to live. I would leave him the next day. I would grieve for as long as it took. And someday I would finally be okay.

Even though it was I who initiated this drastic move, I felt abandoned and rejected by Camilo. Depressed and grief stricken, I cried for hours at a time, relieved (and frankly surprised) that I was able to stop crying long enough to go to work. A Colby friend invited me to move in with her until I felt whole enough to look for a place of my own. After several months the tears began to subside. Encouraged by my resilience, I began to move forward with my life, far stronger and more independent than before.

I have always thought that my choice to marry Camilo was an expression of my unsatisfied need to rebel against my parents. But now I can see that, as with all things, the reasons for this marriage were many and complex. Marrying Camilo was not simply a rebellious act. It was also the culmination of a long courtship based on genuine affection, a manifestation of my inability to ask for and expect what I needed for myself, and an attempt on my part to break through to this man who was emotionally distant, as I had tried to do before with my parents and my brother.

My marriage to Camilo caused a tectonic shift in my relationship to my parents. On the one hand, I was hugely disappointed that they were unable to practice the principle of racial equality that they had always held so dear and had inculcated in me. On the other hand, as a result of this seven-year relationship, and with the help of intensive therapy, I was finally able to separate emotionally from my mother and father and develop a sense of my own self.

Finally, looking back now, I see this marriage also as a positive expression of what I learned from my parents' early idealism about race—that people in an ideal world might live together in harmony and that all of us are equal regardless of the color of our skin and we should live our lives accordingly.

12

Red Diaper Babies

By the mid-1970s I had an independent life as a single woman living in Manhattan. I had benefited from several years of psychotherapy and matured since my divorce. No longer dependent on others for my sense of self-worth, I had learned to treasure living alone and had, at last, developed an adult relationship with both my parents, particularly my mother. I enjoyed a satisfying career, deep friendships, and the rich culture New York City had to offer.

On December 31, 1975, while visiting a friend in Ann Arbor, Michigan, I met Michael Singer, an Israeli-born psychologist. It was New Year's Eve, my birthday; it was love at first sight. This serious, well-grounded, sweet, and funny man delighted me. He captivated me with his tales of growing up in Israel. I loved his gentle voice and handsome bearded face. Within days, I knew I wanted to spend the rest of my life with him.

I left my job and friends in Manhattan to join Michael in Ann Arbor and take on the challenge of an administrative position at the Washtenaw County Intermediate School District, supervising programs for physically handicapped children. I was thirty-four years old, grown up enough, finally, to establish a mature relationship.

Michael and I were married on a bright summer afternoon in August 1977 at my family's summer home in Maine. Friends and relatives came from cities all across the country to join us in affirming our union. My parents were very fond of Michael, and my mother took great pride in finding a rabbi to marry us—someone religious enough for Michael's family, not too religious for ours. Rabbi Harold Blanck was a retired professor from the Union Theological Seminary whose blessing brought solemnity and wisdom to our bayside wedding. Though he'd met us only a few days earlier, his remarks captured the essence of our new commitment and our hopes for the future.

Michael and I made our permanent home in Ann Arbor and, in March of 1981, I gave birth to our first child, Ilana Michelle. An old soul, this strong, healthy baby with soft-brown eyes and porcelain skin was the daughter I had longed for. Wise,

My mother and father at my wedding to Michael Singer, Stonington, Maine, August 26, 1977.

affectionate, and always her own person, she brought great joy to Michael and me and to our families. Our son, Daniel, followed three years later; now our family was complete. Dan was a jolly baby, gentle and deeply thoughtful. Ilana treated her little brother with kindness; in turn, he looked up to her, devotedly. It was such fun for me to watch them interact—my greatest parenting pleasure.

When she was a young child, Ilana shared some precious time with my parents on vacations in Maine; these are special memories. But Daniel didn't get to know them. In fact, he and my father met only once, when Dad, living in a nursing home, was nearing the end of his life and Daniel was only ten months old. Though no words passed between them, Dad recognized early signs of baby Daniel's delicious sense of humor. "I like him," my father told me that day. "He's a very funny baby."

Sadly, my father's last years were marked by major decline due to Parkinson's disease. Gradually, he lost his sharp mind and physical strength and, in the end, did not recognize us. My father died in the spring of 1988; he was eighty-three.

Following my father's death, with a mature marriage, loving children, and a network of friends to support me, I felt ready to explore repressed feelings connected with my parents' troubles of the past. When I mentioned to a friend, David Wegman, that my vague curiosity about my father's HUAC history had become an active interest, he told me that Michael Meeropol had been his schoolmate at Swarthmore College in the 1960s. Michael was the older son of Julius and Ethel Rosenberg, Communists accused by the U.S. Government of passing secrets of the atomic bomb to the Russians. The Rosenbergs were convicted of conspiracy to commit espionage and ultimately were executed on June 19, 1953, following one of the most highly publicized and controversial trials in the history of our country.

I had known only a little about the Rosenberg case at the time of their execution, but I can remember my mother picking me up after school that day. Her voice sad and incredulous, she told me the Rosenbergs had been put to death. That was all she said, that they had been killed; she didn't seem to want to talk about it, but the gravity of this event was clear from her demeanor. I was eleven years old at the time.

The Rosenbergs' sons, Michael and Robbie, were the innocent victims of their parents' trial, incarceration, and execution. When, as my interest in my father's case intensified, I read the sons' accounts of their nightmare experiences, I found myself responding as if their ordeal were happening in some way to me: Michael's horror upon hearing of his mother's arrest, the insensitive treatment of the boys at the Hebrew Home for Children, the withdrawal of support from their maternal grandmother, whose words and actions let them know they were unwanted.[1] These descriptions brought back my own early fear of abandonment, as I'd spent many nights paralyzed by the fear of being separated from my parents. In a recurrent childhood nightmare, I was kidnapped, grabbed in the street by a stranger.

I never questioned that the Rosenbergs were innocent. Thus, at age fifty-four, when I read an article in the *Swarthmore College Bulletin* entitled "Shadows of an Execution,"[2] I expected—no, I *knew for sure*—that the article would confirm their innocence. I was terribly dismayed when I realized that there was credible evidence linking Julius Rosenberg's activities to the Soviet Union. This led me to read books that argued the case, pro and con.[3] Gradually my certainty evaporated. I became confused about the Rosenbergs. *Were they innocent or guilty? Of what?*

One day in the early 1990s, I was on my way to a school in Ann Arbor when I heard a National Public Radio interview with Carl Bernstein, the *Washington Post* reporter of Watergate fame. Bernstein was discussing his memoir about his personal experience as the son of left-wingers Alfred and Sylvia Bernstein. The interview grabbed my attention; I borrowed the book from the library and read it in one sitting.

For the younger Bernstein, the compelling question was whether or not his parents were ever card-carrying members of the Communist Party and what their relationship was to the Party's alleged goal of overthrowing the government. Ultimately Bernstein realized, as his father predicted he would, that the truth about his parents' Party membership contributed little to an understanding of their ideals, motivations, and actions. Bernstein learned that his parents had joined the movement because, in his father's words, "[t]here was a Depression, the threat of fascism." People did "certain things. . . . You joined the unions, you organized, you joined certain fronts—maybe even the Party eventually."[4]

Alfred and Sylvia Bernstein had committed their political energies to defending the rights of government workers who were "oppressed" because of what they believed. They had not been involved in any way with a movement to overthrow the United States Government. I found it ironic that Carl Bernstein, on the other hand, through his exposure of the Watergate scandal, had contributed dramatically to the demise of an American presidency.

Carl Bernstein is two years younger than I and was brought up, as I was, in Washington during the 1940s and '50s. Our parents had known each other and had had close friends in common. Reading about people whom I had known and places where I had played and socialized—the miniature golf course and Hot Shoppe on Wisconsin Avenue, the A.U. swimming pool, Glen Echo, Fletcher's boathouse—I was unprepared for the barrage of strong feelings that arose inside me. I identified with the shame and confusion Bernstein experienced as a child and also with the pride he finally felt as an adult.

But perhaps most poignant for me was his characterization of his father, a man of keen intellect, whose energies were focused on "matters of the mind," not the body, a man with "an innate sense of decency" who could often appear helpless or absentminded. As I read, I sympathized with Bernstein's resentment toward his father, who was often so preoccupied as to be emotionally unavailable to his children growing up. All of me resonated to the paradox expressed in these words: "Above all my father is a cautious man, a believer in weighing the consequences of behavior before choosing a course, or so he has always seemed to me. With the exception of that decision to join the Communist Party, I do not know of a single act in his adult life that might be characterized as reckless."[5]

I wept throughout this book. It struck a raw, vulnerable chord in me. It was then, about a year after my father's death, that I first experienced what would eventually become a ceaseless drive—the intense need to write my own story.

My deepening curiosity about my parents' political life intensified once more when I spoke about Carl Bernstein's book with my friend Miriam.[6] Though I'd known Miriam for some time, she surprised me with her extensive knowledge of the Progressive movement; in fact, I learned she was writing a book about a black-listed New York City schoolteacher. Miriam had a genuine red diaper baby[7] pedigree: her parents had been leftist activists in New York City, dedicated to union and neighborhood organizing. In the fifties, her mother left the family to go underground to London, fearing arrest for her Left political activities.

It was Miriam who introduced me to Kim Chernin's memoir, In My Mother's House.[8] When I read Chernin's account of her mother's tale of courage and sacrifice, I was riveted. Rose Chernin, a Russian émigré active in the Communist Party, had gone to prison for assisting foreign-born activists. As the author and her mother worked together on the book, recalling and relating their memories of the period, they mended their previously strained relationship and reached a new understanding.

Again, my reaction to this book was visceral. Kim Chernin's mother was a forceful woman who knew what she believed and was convinced that she was right. She acted on her beliefs and was so confident that she made it her business to let everyone else know exactly where they had gone wrong. Rose Chernin provided an example of clarity and purpose that was difficult, if not impossible, for her child to follow. I too was the daughter of such a woman.

It struck me that Kim Chernin, Miriam, and I had some unusual things in common. While all three of us had been blessed growing up with mothers who were competent, active role models, we were emotionally scarred as a result of our parents' shortcomings: notably their lack of parenting know-how and their pre-occupation with causes that took them away from home. All of us had suffered difficulties managing food and weight and had turned, as adults, to Judaism, the religious heritage our parents had left behind. Was there some connection among these seemingly unrelated factors? Were these three intellectual, high-powered, politically active mothers too busy when we were young to focus enough attention on us, to guide us and help us come to know our own power and worthiness? Did we suffer from a lack of affection that created an emptiness we tried to fill with food?

Of all the children of the Old Left, the one who touched me most was Ann Kim-mage, the daughter of journalist Abe Chapman, a highly valued Party member in the 1940s. In 1950, Chapman and his wife, Belle, both still active Communists, were sent by the Party underground to live in Prague. Ann, then eight, and her older sister accompanied them and were forced to deny their American past and establish a new identity. In her compelling memoir, Kimmage describes her suc-cessful assimilation into Czech Communist life. She tells of later being uprooted three more times, as the family moved to Russia, then to China, and finally, against her will, back to America.[9]

As I read Ann Kimmage's story, I wept for the young girl torn away from her life in New York, the only life she had known. I was horrified to think how dan-gerous it must have been for her in Czechoslovakia where, in her words, "oppo-nents of the government . . . and other 'traitors' disappeared in unmarked graves, work camps, or prisons."[10]

As I read I thought: What if, in the year 1950, my parents had maintained their strong views championing the Communist cause? What if they had not had a change of heart? I could have been the one sent away from my home to suffer the deep scars of separation from family and friends, forced to deny my early years and start a new life in a strange foreign land.

I was struck by the commonalities in the stories told by children of the Old Left. Many red diaper babies describe their Communist parents as intelligent, ideal-istic, hard working, and unquestioningly loyal to the cause. Most paint a picture of the threatening conditions of the times, the paranoia. But while some remember happy childhoods steeped in ideals, exciting political action, and rich cultural and community life, others describe early years fraught with neglect. Their Communist parents had placed a higher value on the political ideals of the Party than on the goals of family life.[11] Such contrasting experiences helped me to see the complexity of the movement that contributed so much to society, became so controversial, and had such a profound effect on its children.

Many of these stories, captured in the 1998 book *Red Diapers*,[12] reveal the effect of trauma on the children and the diversity of responses to their left-wing beginnings. As I read this anthology, I identified strongly with one parent-child dynamic observed by the editors: "Some parents, motivated by fear, wanted to protect their children by not burdening them with potentially harmful knowledge. . . . Often, parents held back information by a process that was itself laden with fear, confusion, and secrecy. . . . Picking up on the emotion without the content, their children felt anything but protected."[13]

During the period between 1946, when my parents quit the Party, and 1954–55 when my father was approached by the FBI and called to testify before HUAC, my parents tried to protect my brother and me from the knowledge of their reality. They sat alone, preoccupied by their secret. I can remember the atmosphere in our home at that time. The air was heavy with tension and stress. Tied in knots, I was emotionally constricted and ill at ease. I was desperate that my friends accept me and frequently had hurt feelings following a real or imagined slight. "You're too sensitive," I was often told.

Something was very wrong but I had no clue what it could be. Anxious and insecure, I felt frightened, like a child alone in a forest at night. While my father and mother were caring parents, neither one of them had any idea of the painful impact the family secret was having on their children.

There was wide disparity in the experiences of red diaper babies, and as adults many of them developed dramatically opposing views on the historical significance of American Communism. One thing is for sure: few, if any, view its significance casually. Decades after the death of McCarthy and long after the fall of the Iron Curtain, intense emotion and controversy continue to surround the subject. We are still debating. We cannot agree. We argue about who did what, when, and what it all means.

It is the intensity and personal significance of these opposing perspectives that make them so compelling. Ironically, this same deep personal meaning causes each side to view issues in black and white. The ongoing dialogue, fifty years after the events, is usually characterized by intolerance, misunderstanding, defensiveness, and denial. For me this has been frustrating; few of the people I've interviewed have demonstrated the kind of balance that I need to help me discern fact from hype. I think my father could have been helpful to me here.

Following my mother's death in 1996, I felt, in spite of my grief, finally free of constraints and inhibitions. It was time to tell my story. I participated in a writing workshop, and by the end of the summer I had written five chapters. Exhilarated by the emotional release, I read portions to Michael and some friends. Sensing this was an important healing process that would offer me a chance to work through a childhood trauma, they encouraged me to persevere.

The most daunting test of whether I could continue to write would come when I told my brother about the book. Peter and I had become good friends. We had visited one another for family events and holidays and successfully shared the maintenance and use of the homestead in Maine that our parents had left us. But, regarding my writing, I feared that Peter would strongly object, that he would be unhappy at the thought of my opening the door to forgotten events and feelings. "Why would you want to do this?" I imagined he would say. "Why don't you just leave well enough alone? Haven't we suffered enough?" Admonishing words such as these would have been sufficient to make me give up the project, even though nothing had ever seemed more important to me.

I've got to at least try, I thought. I owe myself that much.

And so, I called Peter and asked if I could read him the first chapter on the phone. My anxiety left me almost unable to speak but somehow I read it. I paused, waiting for his response.

"Wow!" he said. "That's really interesting!"

And then, "Wait a second. Is that what happened that night . . . ? Gee, I guess it did!"

We talked, and he made some very astute suggestions.

"No, Peggy, I'm not upset," he said. "I'll be interested to hear more."

13

"Fancy Naming a Baby 'Herbert'"

> *. . . in Ann Arbor lives another*
> *an unknown first cousin*
> *we were sentenced by Stalin*
> *shortly after our births*
> *to live the next fifty years*
> *in that strange gulag*
> *for golden, grieving souls*
> *who cannot connect*
> *from separate orbits in the Siberia of space*
> *over the fault line in Marxist dialectic*
> *that left one father quaking before HUAC*
> *and the other fighting a war on two fronts,*
> *family and politics . . .*
>
> —Portion of a poem by my cousin Dana Willens, written after we
> spoke for the first time, in October 1996

It took me five years to access my father's FBI file. I had read his HUAC testimony, his journal and correspondence, the American University archive files,
and more than seventy-five newspaper and magazine articles about his case; I
had interviewed family and friends. Still, there were unanswered questions. As
my journey began, it was hard for me to reconcile my image of the thoughtful,
cautious, and reflective man I knew with the younger man I was reading about,
a man identified with Communism and committed to its rigid code of behavior,
who was certain he was right. Where was my father coming from? What went on
in his early life that might help to explain his allegiance to this movement? Did
his views really change over time, or was he never completely convinced ideologically in the first place?

Deeply hidden within these questions was a small but nagging uncertainty. In their effort to protect former friends and colleagues, might my father and/or mother have concealed details about their own activities that could further implicate them? Might either of them have knowingly or unknowingly provided privileged information to the Party that was later passed on to the Soviets?

My father's parents, Alfred Fuchs and Paula Hacker, were born in Vienna, he in 1871, she in 1876. During a period of political liberalism, Vienna had become the center of a rich and varied culture in which enlightened Jews were allowed to take part in all aspects of the city's intellectual and artistic life. By the last quarter of the century, however, anti-Semitism was prevalent and growing. Jews met with discrimination in all areas of professional life.[1] Like many of their contemporaries, my father's family assimilated into the liberal German culture of the city as a path to acceptance. But as anti-Semitism became more and more virulent and living conditions for Jews in Vienna became intolerable, they made the decision to leave.

My paternal grandparents immigrated to America with their own respective families in the 1890s. They met in New York City and were married in 1898. Maintaining a sense of continuity with their roots by joining the *Gemeinshaft alt Vien* ("Community of Old Vienna") and shopping at Wertheimer's department store, Alfred and Paula Fuchs settled in Washington Heights. There, in an apartment on 184th Street, they raised three sons. My father, born Herbert Oscar Fuchs on September 20, 1905, was the oldest. "Fancy naming a baby 'Herbert,'" my father used to say.

The anti-Semitic milieu in which my grandparents grew up appears to have had a profound effect on them, not only on their families' decision to make their home in America, but also on my grandparents' ambivalent attitude toward Judaism and their limited identification as Jews. For the most part, my father's family rejected religion; in its place they embraced liberalism with its trust in reason and humanitarianism. At the same time, they maintained Jewish traditional values: learning as a priority, social consciousness, and the importance of living an ethical life. These values they passed on to their three sons. My father passed them on to my brother and me.

As a child, Dad excelled in his studies. My grandparents' deep commitment to education helped to make it possible for him to attend Townsend Harris Hall, a prestigious high school located on the campus of the City College of New York. By his own account, my father had a very high opinion of himself and his abilities. He was arrogant and conceited, "too big for my britches," he would later say.

He did not seem to have an adult role model worthy of his admiration, with whom he could identify.

Dad finished high school at age sixteen and went on to City College where he and other young, bright, mostly Jewish students from the City were introduced to the radical ideas of a group of brilliant, charismatic professors. In spite of their influence, my father's performance in college was lackluster. Even later, when he attended law school, his academic record reflected immaturity and lack of direction; at New York University Law School (where he received his J.D. in 1928), he received only Cs and C minuses in his classes.[2]

I asked my cousin Richard Fuchs, only son of Dad's middle brother, Walter, what he knew about our fathers' history. Richard remembered the apartment on 179th Street and Broadway, "over the Indian Walk Shoe Store," where my grandparents lived when he was growing up. Richard described this Washington Heights neighborhood as a community of German and Austrian immigrants: genteel, middle-class people who valued their connection to the German language and culture. Overlooking the Hudson and with a view of the George Washington Bridge, my grandparents' apartment was spacious, its long hallway stretching the length of a whole city block. There was a sewing room in back of the kitchen where as a little boy Richard was fascinated by the "real dumbwaiter." He told me about the parlor with its "old-fashioned Viennese Victorian rosewood furniture," and, best of all, he remembered our grandmother bringing out special treats, such as marzipan and rich chocolate Viennese pastries.

Though my grandfather was trained as a chemist in Austria, in the States he decided to study law. He attended NYU Law School and opened an office at 226 East 86th Street, in the German neighborhood known as Yorktown. My father joined him there for a brief period after law school. Apparently my grandfather was unable to earn his son's respect. Working there, my father once told me, was a frustrating experience, as he often had to bail his father out of trouble resulting from the older man's unwise financial decisions.

"Our grandfather," Richard recalled, "was a wild man. He had Albert Einstein hair and eyes and was crazy and excitable; he was always yelling. At the end of his life, he became senile and had to be hospitalized."

Grandma Fuchs was a "very proper Victorian lady," Richard said. Stiff and controlled, she spoke English with a slight German accent. She never failed to point out that she was "not German but Viennese," as if this somehow made her better than her neighbors. Our grandmother worked as a secretary for Julia Richman, the first woman superintendent of schools in New York City, for whom, later, a school in Manhattan was named. Richard remembered seeing a letter written by Julia Richman to our grandmother, thanking her for years of service.[3]

There was bad blood in my father's family of origin. I know very little about his relationship with his parents, but I remember that as an adult, he had an intense dislike for both of them. He seldom spoke of them and rarely visited their home after moving to Washington. I never knew my grandfather Alfred, who died in 1944, and only met Grandma Fuchs on one occasion, as a very young child. My memory is of waking up in her apartment in New York; it was time to eat and she used this as an opportunity to teach me that the word *breakfast* meant to break the fast. I was so impressed.

My father and his brothers, Walter and Vernon, were not friends. According to Richard, there was a nasty fight when they met the last time at my grandmother's funeral in 1947. As Richard tells it, Vernon verbally attacked my father. Were they fighting over dividing my grandparents' possessions or might they have been arguing politics? My parents had decided to leave the Communist Party by that time, while Vernon and his wife, Florence, also Party members, were still fiercely loyal to the cause. Richard wasn't sure, but he recalled his own father, Walter, siding with my dad. "He always did."

Dad left his parents' home that day never looking back. He took nothing to remind him of them except for a couple of old photos that his aunt gave to my mother as they were leaving. My parents never saw Vernon and Florence again. They met with Walter only once more, when he came to visit us at the time of the HUAC hearing fiasco. Richard and I became friends later, on our own initiative, as adults living in New York.

I have to wonder whether my father's lack of connection to family, community, and religion contributed to his need to belong, a need he may have tried to fill by joining the Communist Party and staying involved even after he realized that to do so had its obvious dangers.[4]

Even as a small child I was aware that my father had the gift of a brilliant mind. I saw that he had absolute power of concentration, was a very quick study, and was blessed with a wide range of intellectual interests, from literature and music to science and math. He read extensively (*The Complete Works of Proust* was a favorite), did double acrostics in his head, and solved brainteasers to entertain himself. Usually, when he was engaged in these activities I would see him become totally immersed, shutting out life around him. When I started dating, for example, my father would think nothing of greeting my date at the door with an invitation to help solve a *Scientific American* word problem. I remember my annoyance at being kept waiting while my date worked on a puzzle with Dad. It would never occur to my father that he should not engage my friends in this way, nor did it occur to me to complain.

Dad was reflective and creative in his ability to use his superior intellect. As a young adult, I remember listening, fascinated, as he explored an issue relating to his work on the Hill—the death penalty, for example. He showed me how he analyzed the issue, thoroughly exploring all of its conflicting points of view and developing arguments in support of all sides of the question. He showed me how he challenged those points of view opposed to his own, one by one, until he had successfully proven their fallacies.

My father's ability to understand and even empathize with the other person's point of view and then articulate positions on both sides of an issue helped to make him a talented problem-solver and mediator, as well as a competent trial lawyer, review attorney, union/company arbitrator, law professor, and, finally, congressional staff writer. From my father's example, I have developed a love of ideas and a need to search for the truth; I have been lucky that he's passed on some of his skills as well, problem solving and mediating in particular.

For most of his adulthood, Dad depended on the adoring attention of the favorite women in his life, women who particularly struck his fancy. One such woman was a young artist he met walking on the C & O Canal. "Excuse me, sir," the young woman had said to my father as she approached him walking on the towpath. "Would you mind walking with me? I think I'm being followed." My father and mother befriended the young woman and her husband, and she became my father's regular painting and walking companion during his last years. Another of his admirers was the wife of one of my mother's colleagues, an intriguing, intellectually gifted woman who doted on my father and shared literature and good talk with him over the years; they were devoted friends and he was there for her during her several hospitalizations for depression. My mother was not threatened by these friendships. She accepted, even encouraged them; they seemed to feed my father's ego, to satisfy some unfilled need and I think she felt they helped my father and her maintain a balance in their own relationship.

Dad was usually affectionate with me, but I think he saw me as just a sweet kid; he did not take me seriously or show much interest in my thoughts or activities. I was neither clever enough nor pretty enough to really capture his attention. It was not until I became his confidante, not until I began listening to him talk for hours during the time of his troubles, that I felt he took me seriously, and then only through my attentiveness to him. Sometimes, my father could be flip and biting with his quick and clever wit. On occasion, insensitive to my feelings, he would call me "Rat Nose," a term of endearment I'm sure he would say. He was not conscious of his words' stinging impact.

Over the years, Dad became more and more depressed, distant, preoccupied. Sometimes I would see him, propped up on pillows on his bed, obsessing about money—adding figures over and over in the notebook he kept at his bedside. In his mid-sixties, while still working on the Hill, he began to suffer symptoms of Parkinson's disease, which included increasing difficulty with short-term memory and proficiency with numbers. As time went on he lost sleep worrying about the impact of his failing memory on his ability to perform the duties of his job. One day, a young colleague confronted him: "It's time for you to leave," the colleague said, "and let someone else take over." My father retired in 1975 at the age of seventy.

Fast forward to 1996. My mother and father are gone. I am missing them. Writing is my form of grieving.

"How strange it is," I comment to Richard on the phone, shortly after my mother's death, "that we don't know our fathers' brother and his children. Why have we never connected with these people?"

"Our cousin Dana Willens is a New York City schoolteacher," Richard tells me. "I know someone who met her at a conference. If you want, I'll try to get her phone number. Whatta we have to lose?"

"Is Dana Willens there?" I ask, my stomach in my throat and my voice shaking.

"This is she."

"My name is Peggy Fuchs Singer. I'm your first cousin, the daughter of your uncle Herbert Fuchs."

"Oh."

"How do you do?" I say, not sure how to proceed. "I, um, hope your family is well . . . I called an old number I found for your father. There was no answer. Is he okay?"

"Yes. He is."

"I wanted to call to tell him that my mother, Frances, died in April."

"Oh dear."

"And then also, you see, I've begun to write a memoir and I wondered if your father could be of some help."

Pause.

Oh God! I think to myself. I've intruded on this woman. Now what? Why did I think she'd have any interest in talking to me?

"You know," I begin again nervously, "really, I don't understand how it could be that I never called you before. I'm a family-oriented person, a sociable person. I don't understand how it is that I never tried to get in touch with you before." I chatter on, fearing empty spaces and rejection.

"I have photos of you as a little girl," I say. "Do you at least know about me and my brother, Peter?"

"I know almost nothing," my cousin answers. "I vaguely know your names but did not know which brother was your father."

"I wonder about the cause of our parents' estrangement. What could have happened to brothers to separate them for life?"

"Do you mean the political abyss?" my cousin asks.

"I don't know."

"I'm glad you called," Dana says. "I'd like to talk some more. I'm really interested in pursuing this conversation."

We set up a time to speak at length; I hang up, euphoric. I have connected.[5]

In a conversation the following week, I learn a little about my cousin's life: her early years as a young radical, her activism in the sixties, her career as an assistant principal in a high school in Harlem, her two young-adult sons in college and graduate school, whom she has brought up as Jews in spite of her nonobservant background. I learn of her ultimate rejection of her parents' left-wing politics. Dana invites my family to visit her home during the Christmas break. She invites our cousin Richard and Joseph, his partner.

It seemed as if we drove for hours that day in late December 1996, through one ugly working-class New Jersey town after another, before we finally arrived at my cousin's home. The house and street seemed dark, even drab in the withholding winter light. What would these people be like? I wondered. Would we have things to talk about? I was conscious of Michael and our children, Ilana and Daniel, conscious of my gratitude for their patience. This was my thing, this "reunion," but I knew their support was total; their curiosity had been aroused. After all, as Dan said, "We know nothing about our family tree!"

"Stand against the wall as you come into the house," Dana's daughter-in-law warned, as my family and I went inside. "Hold very still and let the dog sniff you."

There we stood, lined up against the wall of the tiny front hall, restrained from moving a muscle as our hosts' small terrier, aptly named Thor, pulled against his owner's leash, releasing a ferocious growl from the depth of his throat and holding us at bay. Michael wrapped his arm around twelve-year-old Dan's shoulders, protecting him from the dog who seemed somehow drawn to him. Dan, forgetting the warning to stay still, moved his hand. Thor snarled and snapped, missing Dan's fingers by millimeters before rearing up on his hind legs as his owner yanked him away. Richard, never known for his subtlety, muttered something under his breath that only Lana and I could hear: "For God's sake," he muttered, "do something. For God's sake, kill the damn dog!"

Finally, Dana's husband, Len, removed Thor from our midst and took him to the basement to bark in solitude.

Dana's eyes danced with pleasure as she greeted us. She and I embraced. We hugged like long-lost friends, like soul mates, like twins separated at birth, like best-friend-sisters. I was struck by her beauty: her petite, toned body, her handsome face, her radiant smile. We bonded immediately, all the more for the time lost between us.

Cousins, husbands, partners hugged and shook hands, the joyful exchanges in sharp contrast to the dog's angry greeting. Dana's boys took us on a tour. They proudly displayed their father's photos hanging on the walls, majestic landscapes of favorite spots from summer trips out west.

Dana, Richard, and I, newly acquainted cousins, sat in the center of the room, our families surrounding us; Joseph took pictures. The conversation turned to a discussion of our lives. We had much in common: teaching careers in New York, civil rights marches, children's Bar and Bat Mitzvahs, an interest in writing, a love of opera. The talk was easy, relaxed, the excitement of discovery palpable. My cousins listened attentively as I talked about my book. Eventually, Dana began to tell us about her childhood. She talked about her parents' uncompromising love of Russia, their rigid commitment to Left politics (even after having been kicked out of the Party), and their lifelong hatred for everything American. She told us of her own early radical views and her ultimate disillusionment with them; she expressed understanding and sympathy for my father's crisis.

Then, with tears in her eyes, she described the years of psychological and physical abuse that she and her younger brother and sister endured at the hands of their parents. She remembered hiding with her siblings in a closet to avoid explosive verbal assaults and violent body blows. Her mother would egg her father on, Dana told us; she would goad him. "Watch out for their heads," her mother would say, as she encouraged her father to hit them.

By now there were tears in everyone's eyes.

Later, on reflection, I wondered how people who were such staunch champions of the rights of the oppressed could see fit to abuse their own children.

"When you call my parents," Dana had warned me in our first phone conversation, "don't tell them we've spoken. Needless to say, we are not on good terms."

When I called him late in October, my uncle Vernon seemed happy to hear from me. I told him about my search for information about my parents' early life, and he expressed willingness to talk but voiced concern that his memory would fail him. He claimed that his estrangement from my father was due to the distance between their homes in New Jersey and Washington. He said he had not known that my father "named names." Was this a memory lapse or an unwillingness to talk about this difficult subject, or both? Obviously uncomfortable, my uncle tried to bring the conversation to a close by offering to call me back sometime and taking my address and telephone number. When I sent my regards to his wife, Florence, he asked me if I would like to speak with her. I said I would.

"This is so long in coming," my aunt Florence said when she took the phone. "I've been married to Vernon fifty-eight years and in all that time his family has been so cold. When we married they sent no presents; there were no invitations to their homes, nothing. Your parents were cold, withholding people. Vernon tried to reach out but it was always one-sided, never reciprocated." My aunt's tone was stern, her message clear. It seemed to me she'd been waiting fifty years to unload her grievances against her husband's family. I was surprised when her words did not cause me pain. Instead, I experienced her diatribe as almost funny, a caricature.[6]

"I know a great deal about your parents," my aunt continued, "maybe as much as anyone. I could tell you many things but I don't want to upset you." I encouraged her to tell me what she knew.

"We are political animals," my aunt began. "Some people kept their idealism but left the Party; some people went to jail; people did different things. Some people rejected the Party outright; some named names. When the heat was on, your father sacrificed thirty-four families to save his own career. The story appeared in a magazine. When my daughter read it she was horrified. 'That can't be *my* uncle!' she said.

"Once we visited in D.C.," my aunt went on. "I remember you were a baby sitting on your mother's lap pulling at her nose and hair. She was trying to settle you down. I walked into the nursery and there was Peter in his crib. I had no children then but wanted them. I reached over to pick him up but your mother stopped me. In an icy voice she said, 'We really don't want him disturbed.'

"The real break in our relationship came," Florence told me, "when your parents quit the Party and refused to have anything to do with us anymore. Once, after that, we dropped in on them in D.C. We were on our way to other friends in a house called the Blair House of the Left, in Virginia. People who were victims of the HUAC investigations went there for support. Herbert told us, 'If you want to go there, you must go on a separate visit, separate from visiting us. We must not be seen together.' He drove us to the railroad station. That's how scared he was. It was a scary time."

Florence told me about her ill health. Now in her eighties, she suffered from Parkinson's and several other debilitating ailments. "My mind, I'm promised, will not go," she said, "because I am always using it. I write all the time. I write for the cause. If you'd like, I will send some of my work, after my next deadline passes.

"We would like it if you would come to visit us," she said, as the conversation came to a close, "although we are no longer able to drive guests around."[7]

I met my uncle Vernon in person in August of 1997, at his tiny apartment overlooking the beach in La Jolla, California. By now, his wife of almost sixty years had left him, claiming physical abuse as the reason she had to go. My aunt had taken most of their furniture; the apartment was almost totally bare.

Though grieving the end of his marriage, Vernon was happy to receive me and to see his daughters, son-in-law, and grandsons, who had brought me to him on this rare visit to his home. Even at age eighty-six, my uncle appeared strong and physically fit. He had been an accomplished athlete—an ice-skater and fencer—and still worked out three times a week.[8] There was something very familiar about this man, something about his appearance and voice. I felt as if I had met him before.

Dana and her younger sister, Toni, left to visit their mother, now in a nursing home. My uncle and I sat down to share photographs and stories; he was eager to reminisce. I reminded him of his father, he told me, as he became nostalgic and emotional, obviously moved by the attention I paid him.

I asked Vernon questions about his early years, his memories of my father, his move toward Communism. My grandparents encouraged their boys to do well in school. My father was "the smart one." Herbie, as his friends and family called him, earned the admiration of his younger brothers. He was, my uncle told me, "a role model." My father and his brothers attended P.S. 132 where, as the Jewish underdogs, they were regularly harassed by the Irish and Italian boys in the neighborhood. In retaliation for the constant taunting, the brothers threw horse manure at their adversaries. Eventually, because of the teasing, Vernon changed his name from Fuchs to Fox.

In his early twenties, Vernon worked as a runner for the stock market on Wall Street. In time, he learned to trade. It was there, after discovering how brokers manipulated the market, that he became disillusioned with the American financial establishment. He and Florence were already members of the Communist Party when they met while working for Warner Brothers in California. Fighting fascism was their shared goal. They had two things in common, union membership and an interest in acting, and they were married after knowing each other only three weeks.

My aunt and uncle were fervent supporters of the Soviet Union. During World War II, Vernon offered to fight for the Russian army. Though the Russian government declined his offer, he did receive an official letter of thanks. Vernon and Florence made three trips to Russia as guests of the government, the last in 1988; each time they found confirmation for their commitment. They never saw crime in Russia, my uncle told me. Education was free. Rent charges were made according to a person's ability to pay. Apartments were resold for "not one kopeck more than the buying price." Visits to synagogues revealed people praying. If a woman gave birth out of wedlock, the father was forced to support the child. This was the good life. Vernon wondered aloud whether some of his activities on behalf of the Russians could possibly be interpreted as "spying." He declined to explain what he meant.

For most of his working life, Vernon earned a living as an engineer at RCA. Florence was a writer for left-wing publications. In their spare time, my uncle and aunt fought for tenants' rights. Their photo albums and scrapbooks chronicle successful campaigns on behalf of renters, well into the 1980s.

Sometime in the 1950s, my aunt and uncle were expelled from the Communist Party; Vernon claims not to know the reason why but wondered if my father's testimony may have been a factor. Their expulsion did not deter them from their dedication to the Russians nor from their work on behalf of tenants.

After we had talked for several hours, Dana and Toni returned from visiting their mother. Now for the first time, seeing her as an almost total invalid, Dana could imagine an end to her power to hurt them. They joined our discussion.

Dana, who had never talked with her father about these things, asked him to tell us how he reconciled his dedication to Russia with what we know about the "monster" Stalin and the purges. Vernon's face tensed, reddened. "I don't know much about Stalin," my uncle said, "or purges." His stern tone and rigid facial expression made clear his intention to end this conversation.[9]

After Florence died in 2002, Vernon lived on alone and lonely in the small apartment overlooking the beautiful beach at La Jolla. His health was giving out, and it was the owner of his apartment house who drove him to regular doctor appointments. One day Vernon called his daughters, my cousins, to inform them that they were no longer in his will. This defender of tenants' rights, seeing fit to ignore the needs of his children and grandchildren one more time, had made the decision to leave his small estate to the landlord.

14

Secret Cells

I felt that this had been the most wonderful experience of my life, one of those rare moments when intellectual conviction is in complete harmony with feeling, when your reason approves of your euphoria, and your emotion is as a lover to your thought.
—Arthur Koestler, *Arrow in the Blue: An Autobiography,* referring to his first meeting with a Communist group

It's clear that my father's primary interest, at the time he joined the Communist Party, was in the field of labor. He joined the Party at a time when it played a dominant role in the growing labor movement. Then, too, since fascism was anathema to him, he welcomed the Party's new direction, moving away from its former exclusivist position in favor of a unified front against fascism. The new policy advocated building a coalition in which Communists would work together with other progressives—liberals, as well as the once-hated Socialists, to realize the goals of the New Deal.[1] The change of focus meant that Dad could now support the Party line, which he considered to be "a little to the left of the New Deal," while viewing its aims as essentially consistent with the basic objectives of President Franklin D. Roosevelt's administration. Dad was convinced the Party could be effective, particularly as a result of its discipline over its members. A person could feel good about doing something positive for society.[2]

In the summer of 1936, divorced from his first wife and frustrated with his dead-end law practice, Dad left New York. He had handed his Communist Party membership card over to the head of the New York Party and gathered the names of Party contacts in Washington, D.C. My father was one of thousands of well-educated professionals who poured into D.C. in the mid-1930s to fill positions in FDR's administration in newly established agencies dedicated to promoting Progressive causes. This was the opportunity he had hoped for: a chance to put his political views into action and use his legal skills to contribute to the country's social, political, and economic recovery. He was excited and eager.

Dad joined the staff of the Senate Wheeler Committee in July of 1936. At Arthur Stein's direction, he and economist James Gorham established a secret unit of Communists there. Wondering what transpired in those underground meetings, I returned to my father's testimony and his description of the groups in which he had been a member and leader. What did his HUAC testimony reveal about how the units functioned? How did group members relate to the Party leadership? And, most important to me, what was my father's role and how significant was it at that time?

In the mid-1930s the Communist leadership softened its stance toward the U.S. Government and other Western nations. If this temporary suspension of open hostilities toward the West was a calculated political move on the part of Communist Party leaders to further the goals of the Soviets, my father had not viewed it in that way. Rather, he had considered this change a reflection of a genuine coming together of mutual goals. My father did not see in his Party membership a conflict of loyalties or a threat to the United States but, instead, a way to participate in the nation's economic and social recovery. In 1955 he told the FBI the following:

> While the overall aim of the Communist Party may be to overthrow the government of the United States, at the time I was in the Party I did not believe this or take it seriously. Nothing in my work as a Communist was directed to that end. Communist theory teaches that capitalism must decay because it cannot solve its own problems of overproduction, and that this decay of capitalism will result in violence. The Communist Party, it is said, must be the midwife of the revolution, not the father, [not] to bring it about, but simply to ease it when it occurs. During the period I was in the Communist Party war between the US and Soviet Russia was unthinkable. On the contrary, Party members were among the hardest workers in support of the American war effort. The example set during the period of the leadership of EARL BROWDER and the Communist Political Association seemed to bear out the belief that the US and Soviet Russia could get along with each other.[3]

It has been claimed by some that Communists entered government service during the first years of Roosevelt's administration as part of a plot to infiltrate the newly established New Deal agencies and carry out the goals of the Party and the objectives of the Soviet Union.[4] Was this the case or was their employment as much a reflection of the vast number of new jobs, with good salaries and promotion opportunities during this period of mass unemployment, that opened up for young professionals sympathetic to the goals of the administration?

From my father's vantage point, it was the latter. As far as he knew, he was not recruited for any job by the Communist Party: "To my knowledge the CP never arranged for me to get any job," he told the FBI. He did believe it possible, however, "that because I was a CP member, people who were in a position to make jobs available knew of me."[5] Based on my father's testimony and the testimony of others, historian Earl Latham has concluded that Communists in government *did* systematically bring in their comrades but to some extent this was a simple patronage operation. On the other hand, having established an underground network, "it did not take long for the party to realize it could make use of its members in Washington to gather information."[6]

James Gorham, with whom my father formed the secret group at the Wheeler Committee, also testified before HUAC. His testimony provided a snapshot of the Communist Party's plans for the New York professionals making their way to Washington, D.C. Upon arrival in the capital, these young Communists would receive instructions as to how they were expected to behave as Party functionaries: "They [CP authorities] stated that there was . . . an open party, which did not include Government employees, and there was another party organization [in which] . . . the groups in one unit would have one person in the unit who would meet with similar individuals from other units, who in turn would have one person forming liaison to a higher unit, and the purpose of this was to prevent discovery or detection."[7]

My father's HUAC testimony makes clear that the secret unit at Wheeler was different from the more typical groups of open Communists. Dad and the other members did not hold membership cards or use pseudonyms to conceal their Party participation; most were already known to one another. The group collected dues and distributed Communist Party literature to its members. Though one of the principal objectives was to do union work, there was no union among the employees of the Wheeler Committee when my father arrived there, and, as far as he could remember, there was still no union there at the time he left. According to his recollection, there was no Communist functionary providing guidance as to the activities of the group at that time.[8]

As leader of the group at Wheeler, my father met on a regular basis at "section meetings" with eight heads of secret Communist units at other government agencies. The unit heads served as a kind of steering or policy committee, which had as its goal, as my father understood it, to promote the development of unions among government employees. In the case of already existing unions that were "not sufficiently militant and aggressive," the goal was to promote union activity and "to develop something parallel to unionism outside the Government."[9]

It's not hard for me to imagine my father, after a long day at work, sitting comfortably on a colleague's living room sofa somewhere. He's listening to his comrades hold forth on the country's economic woes or the implications of the actions of the Wheeler Committee and its charge to investigate railroads. I see him clearly, shirtsleeves rolled up, tie askew, suit jacket thrown haphazardly over the back of a chair by his side. He reaches for his pipe, dips its bowl carefully into the soft leather pouch he carried with him everywhere. He lights up, puffs, and breathes in the aroma of his favorite tobacco. I see him deep in thought.

When my father joined the staff of the NLRB in the fall of 1937, the new agency was an exhilarating place for a young left-winger, certainly for my father, who found the goals of the Wagner Act consistent with his own values and the Party's labor objectives. He was happy and engaged working in an environment where, as one of his bosses, Thomas Emerson, has explained, a "sense of mission, a sense of active struggle against opposition and a sense of accomplishment" were shared by all who worked there.[10]

In this early period at the NLRB, there were a significant number of Communists on staff, particularly in the office of board secretary Nat Witt and in the Review Division. I was, of course, anxious to know how the Communists functioned at the NLRB and the extent of their influence on the policies and procedures of the board. My father's HUAC hearing testimony provided some insight.

The secret group that my father led at the NLRB did not have the formal organizational structure that normally characterized other Communist groups. My father did not recall it even having the usual three officers: the group head, an educational director, and a secretary/treasurer to collect dues. This group was, in fact, even more secretive than groups functioning in other government agencies. Communist Party officials determined that members working at the NLRB should be protected, even more stringently than usual, from possible exposure. Toward this end, the Party no longer instructed my father to meet with other unit leaders as he had done previously.[11]

In forming the unit at the NLRB, it was my father's understanding that "the interest of the Communist Party was to have a group working in a professional area in which the party was enthusiastically in sympathy with the program of the Government."[12] Thus the Communists that my father led there discussed "Communist Party issues, the line in relation to what was going on in Washington, and the like." Group members analyzed good and bad solutions to questions relating to their work and to the procedures and decisions of the board. These people were told, and they told themselves, that to be a good Communist was to be a good employee of the board and of the government. "I think that we thought we were doing a patriotic duty by participating in the enforcement of the Wagner Act," my father told HUAC, "and we were zealous in the belief that it was a good thing." My father's unit tried to meet fortnightly but didn't always achieve this goal. At meetings, dues were paid which would later be passed on to the group's higher authority contact.[13]

Much of my father's testimony concerning the underground unit at the NLRB was corroborated by former member Mortimer Riemer. Riemer testified that the group to which he belonged at the NLRB was highly secret. He remembered meeting irregularly with seven or eight others (a subsection of the whole group), perhaps once a week or maybe once every two weeks, at someone's home. He confirmed that members did not carry membership cards or use pseudonyms and that dues were collected according to a "graduated scale based upon income," usually a percentage of one's take-home pay.

Riemer described the activities of the secret group as follows:

> [W]hen I first became a member, it was primarily and almost exclusively devoted to a study of Marxist literature . . . to discuss, analyze, and report on various pieces of Communist Party doctrine or literature. . . . There was also . . . political discussion of events then taking place in the United States.
>
> [T]he Communist Party had voluminous publications, leaflets, pamphlets, and what not. They would be distributed at meetings. You would take them home and read them, and burn them after you read them, and come back and discuss them.
>
> At no time did I ever participate in any intrigue or conspiracy against my Government.[14]

How could my father not realize, I wondered, that something requiring this level of secrecy was bound to be problematic? How was it that he was willing to take the risk that his participation entailed? I know that by the time I was a teenager, my father had developed an aversion to any organization requiring secrecy among its members. I remember how desperately I wanted and needed to join a sorority in high school and how strongly he opposed my doing so. It was the fall of 1956. I was a sophomore, still recovering from the trauma of our family's difficulties, and I wanted more than anything to pledge Gamma Rho. Membership in this elite social group at Western High School promised acceptance and social standing for me among my peers. Balancing his own disapproval with my intense need to belong, my father did, reluctantly, allow me to join and I became the first Jewish member in this organization's history. As time passed, however, and I experienced the cruelty of the sorority's black-ball system and the brutality of its unsupervised bull sessions, I came to have my own strongly held objections to secret groups.

Although most of the people named by my father cited the Fifth Amendment, one cooperative witness was eager to speak and to deny joining the Communist Party. This witness, who had been a review attorney at the NLRB, described in some detail my father's attempts to recruit him, which, in his case, did not work:

> Fuchs at that time told me he felt that I was doing good work with the Board, was a good lawyer, but that I did not know anything about labor theory. . . . Fuchs . . . mentioned to me that he felt that I should learn something about the labor movement . . . , that he personally believed in communism, and felt that Communist theory and Marxist theory tied together the labor movement . . . and the Labor Board. . . . He said to me that he would like to have me devote a few evenings to discussing these things with him. . . . I told him that I was not interested . . . [but] he kept pounding away at this problem that he could be very helpful to me at the Board, if only I learned something, and I did not have the background and I was actually pretty naive about labor problems. This kept up over . . . 4 or 5 weeks.[15]

Ultimately, the reluctant recruit did agree to attend a few meetings where, he testified, the primary activity was discussion of current NLRB decisions and NLRB cases. By his own account, and that of my father, this individual was resistant to pressure from my father and his colleagues, in spite of the promise of advancement in the agency if he would only learn something about labor theory. It soon became clear that he did not want anything to do with this "sinister" group. "Within a few days . . . Fuchs came up to me at the Board and said that we are holding no more meetings, 'and as far as you are concerned, there are no more meetings or discussions.'"[16]

This was Dad as a younger man—self-assured, charismatic, and unyielding. I recognized him, not from my own experience but from the picture my research was painting for me. He was confident, insistent, well informed, but with a narrow frame of reference. I could see him in the role of group leader, defending the Hitler/Stalin pact or the "misunderstandings" of the Moscow trials. The fact that he had been completely taken in by the propaganda illustrated for me the power of the Party to elicit his loyalty and obedience, even when the logic of the Party line failed to square with his basic values and experience.

A second cooperative witness also admitted attending group meetings but denied having joined the Party. "In this group I was never given a membership card of any kind, never took an oath or went through any formality of joining," he explained.[17] A Quaker interested in "the advancement of peace among individuals and nations," the witness said he participated in the group because he'd been told its sole function was to discuss, study, and research Communist theory:

> I was much disturbed about the threat of a world war. . . . I knew that Fuchs felt as I did about this, and I concluded from what he told me that this group was sincerely interested in specific measures to discourage aggression in Europe. Because of my interest in peace and also because of my desire to learn something about Communist theories from discussion with intelligent people, I told Fuchs in the late fall of 1938 that I would join this group.
>
> The discussions frequently developed into heated arguments about world and national issues and principles of politics, economics, et cetera. . . . I found the discussions interesting.
>
> The people whom I met . . . seemed like decent, intelligent people, who were interested in discussing current affairs, and in peace. I would be very much surprised if any thought of overthrow of the Government, or of espionage, ever entered the minds of those whom I met.[18]

This witness pointed to the "extreme and heated arguments" in the group as a reason he did not realize the group's true nature. "It did not seem to me like a Communist Party group," the witness told HUAC, "in that there was no discipline, and no requirement of conformity. Many of the things that were told to the group by 'Mike' were strongly disputed by the others."[19]

"Mike," the group's contact through my father to Party authority, was economist Victor Perlo. In the beginning, Perlo's real identity was not known to members of the group, nor had they met him personally. Apparently, all was not smooth between the group and its contact. Serious conflicts arose between group members and Perlo, particularly over the Party's insistence that the group remain extremely inconspicuous and avoid public protests. My father sided with his colleagues, being eager himself to take part in public demonstrations, and so it was not surprising that his explanation of the Party's opposition did not satisfy them. After a while, Perlo appeared in person and appealed to them to accept the Party's position. Finally, unable to persuade the group of the Party's point of view, Perlo gave up and instead the unit was put in touch with Arthur Stein, my father's original contact. Group members *did* then begin to participate in mass organizations such as the Lawyers' Guild and, as in my father's case, the Washington Committee for Democratic Action, both viewed by the government as Communist front organizations.[20]

In his testimony before HUAC, my father stressed the point that, at least at that time and in his experience, the directives of the Party higher-ups did not always prevail and, in fact, Communist groups differed one from another in terms of the degree to which each group was democratic in its decision-making process. "I have seen [Communist Party] line changes that come like a bolt of lightning, and I have seen also situations in which a group, persistently arguing with the boss, finally has its way."[21] In saying this, my father was challenging the view held by many in the anti-Communist establishment, that all Communists displayed what historian Ellen Schrecker refers to as "robotlike obedience to party discipline,"[22] which made them all potential agents for the Soviet Union.

In my father's view, the primary significance of the Communist presence on the staff at the NLRB was their radical commitment to the Wagner Act and to the "literal enforcement of an expressed policy."[23] To the more zealous members of the staff, the act was inviolate, "like it's handed down by God, this Act is right and you know what it means."[24] On the other hand, according to Dad, members of his group were allowed to join the local NLRB union "on the theory that everyone ought to belong to a union if there was one."[25] And, in fact, members of his group sometimes used the union to raise issues that were "not strictly trade unionism and some of which were political and perhaps even international in context."[26]

From my research, I was learning that my father had been a willing participant in the operation of the Party. Though he dismissed the idea that Communist theory influenced the work of the NLRB staff, it is clear that political discussion concerning the Soviet policies did take place. "[I]t was said of me," my father once told an interviewer, "that if people had doubts about the correctness of the policies of the Soviet Union, they would come into my office . . . and they would emerge refreshed and reassured."[27]

Furthermore, there were a number of more doctrinaire Communists at the NLRB, people such as secretary of the board Nat Witt and board member Edwin S. Smith, who had enormous influence on the actions of the board, particularly as a result of their close affiliation with then general counsel for the Congress of Industrial Organizations (CIO), Lee Pressman, also a Communist. There seemed to be a thin line between the zeal of the pro-labor staff at the board, and the possibly inappropriate manipulation of the board by Communists at the highest levels of the agency.[28]

In 1942 my father began to reassess his employment situation. It was time, he decided, to leave the NLRB. The agency was no longer the vital organization it had been, no longer the agent of change in the unions' struggle for power. The focus and direction of the board had changed. Dad had just survived two investigations; he was eager to move on.[29]

When, at the urging of his colleague Allan Rosenberg, my father joined the staff of the Division of Reconstruction and Reoccupation at the Board of Economic Warfare (BEW) in the fall of 1942, his assignment involved doing "rudimentary research for a project which at that time didn't have any immediately foreseeable future."[30] Because the job held little interest for him, he remained at the BEW for only one month and did not become affiliated with any Communist unit there.

An opportunity now presented itself in my father's chosen field, labor law. Dad accepted an offer to become the first Dispute Director at the National War Labor Board regional office opening up in Denver. We moved there and he immediately reconnected with colleagues he had known in Washington. Together, they formed a new Communist group, which functioned much like the group at the NLRB except that now Party spouses were invited to join, my mother among them.[31]

Phil Reno, one of my father's former colleagues, had been influential in the staffing of the new Denver regional board. According to my father, Reno was the group's contact with the higher authority, the local Communist Party office.

A photo from that time shows my parents at a meeting. Everyone is still wearing work clothes. Someone is reading aloud to the group as the others listen attentively. Dad sits stiffly while Mom rests comfortably, her head on his shoulder, her feet tucked behind her. I can see the closeness between them even as they focus on the serious business at hand.

My parents attending a Communist group meeting, date unknown.

During his time at NWLB a change began to develop in my father's attitude toward the Party. He testified later, in fact, that the Denver experience "marked the beginning of the diminution of activity and interest" relating to membership in the Communist Party.[32]

We left Denver at the end of 1945, when the NWLB expired, and Dad returned to the National Labor Relations Board in Washington. My father attended a couple of meetings with his former Communist group there, but by mid-1946 he had quit the Party altogether. He had recently become convinced that the Communist Party in the United States was under the "direction and direct control" of Soviet Russia. It was impossible for him now, particularly after the breakup of the alliance between the two nations, to be loyal to the United States government and to the Communist Party at the same time. In his words, "[I had] serious doubts . . . as to whether the Communist Party was all that I had thought it to be."[33]

After returning to the NLRB, my father was named solicitor to the board and served in that capacity for two more years. He assumed that the board considered him a "reformed Communist" when they hired him. He believed that board members knew he had been a Communist but had severed his relationship with

the Party, which was the case. His employers did not ask him about his former membership.[34] In November 1948, shortly before Whittaker Chambers's and
Elizabeth Bentley's public testimonies before Congress, my father left the NLRB
for good.

After reviewing my father's testimony, I was reinforced in my conviction that he
was telling the truth by the combined weight of his driving need to confess his
"mistake" publicly, his articulate and detailed explanations of his actions, and the
absence of defensiveness or evasiveness in his responses to questions. Most poignant for me was the account of his struggle with the secrecy and subterfuge in
which he had participated: "I regret that I was gullible enough to become part of a
semi-secret movement and to lie about my party membership, adopting the communist thesis of ends justifying means. It seems to me that secrecy begets deception and that deception tends to lead to worse offenses. I deny that people may be
lied to for their own good, and I reject the substitution of party 'discipline' for individual moral responsibility."[35]

When my father and mother made the difficult decision to quit the Party, they
left behind a whole way of life: a political orientation, a belief system, a social network. It was a devastating loss.

I turned seven that winter. In spite of my parents' distress and preoccupation, they took pains to make my birthday a special one. As a rare treat, my father
took me to lunch with him and to visit the Mellon Art Gallery. I wore a new out-
fit that day—a skirt and top, red plaid and gray, that I could wear inside-out in
any combination—four new outfits in one. I was thrilled to be going alone with
my father on this outing and was awed by the exhibit of paintings. I was most impressed by Renoir's famous *A Girl with a Watering Can*.

One more memory of that day with my father comes to mind. I recall him telling me how pleased he was that Harry Truman had beaten Thomas E. Dewey in
the recent presidential election. "We're Democrats," my father said. "We're happy
that Truman has won." The way he said it made me feel proud to be on the winning side.

15

"But What about Your Mother?"

For years I thought of the "troubles" as something that had been the result of my father's membership in the Communist Party, my father's participation in secret Communist groups in the government, and his involvement with HUAC and the FBI. Though I knew my mother had also been a member of the Party, I simply did not think of her as having been a key player in the events that led up to our crisis in 1955. Her role, as I saw it, had been as my father's loyal partner, his supporter, the person standing by him, holding down the fort.

But one day I was challenged in that view by a friend: "You've written about your father," my friend said, "his background, his career, his political orientation. But what about your mother? What was her attraction to Communism? What was *her* part in your story?"

Like my father's parents, my maternal grandparents, Arthur and Laura Wise Rice, were assimilated Jews who had emigrated from Central Europe. He was born in Vienna, Austria, she in Kassa, Hungary. They met in New York and married in 1896. By the time my mother came along, my grandparents were well enough established to move from Manhattan into a large home in a fashionable neighborhood in Far Rockaway, Long Island. Frances Regina Rice was born on June 29, 1907. Helen, her only sibling, came eight years later.

I never knew my mother's father, who died in 1942, but my widowed grandmother, whom we called Nona, was an important and colorful figure in my life. Nona was a diminutive woman with long snow-white hair twisted neatly on top of her head. Proper and self-possessed, she dressed modestly from head to toe in somber, respectable navy blue.

Though tiny in stature, my grandmother was a woman of ample spirit and drive. She was opinionated and outspoken and had no difficulty asserting her personality and will; in that way she was a woman ahead of her time. Pity the poor drivers making their way down Fifth Avenue near 34th Street, around the corner

My mother, Frances Rice, at one year old, with her mother, Laura Wise Rice, 1908.

from the room Nona rented in the old Gregorian Hotel, because when she decided to cross Fifth Avenue, she would march out into the middle of the street—all five feet, two inches of her—and hold up her hand to signal the cars to stop and let her pass. They would not dare deny her.

Despite having only an eighth-grade education, Nona had many impressive accomplishments to her credit: she spoke five languages and was a voracious reader and a superb cook and gardener. Over the years, she made a name for herself as a respected neckwear designer, supervised the construction of several homes on Long Island, and, in later years, invested successfully in the stock market.

Accomplished and worldly though she was in the business arena, Nona was not a nurturing mother. She was reserved to the point of coldness, holding back the emotional support her daughter craved. As a little girl, Frances was obedient, well mannered, and self-directed. More interested in books than in friends or possessions, she excelled in school and ultimately earned my grandmother's admiration for her academic achievements.

It was my mother's father, a soft-spoken Victorian gentleman who didn't have a mean bone in his body, who gave her unambiguous love and support. Though not as ambitious or as assertive as my grandmother, my grandfather Arthur also earned a handsome living as the manager of my great-aunt Jo's lucrative dress business, J. Wise, Inc.[1] In those early days, Mom had no interest in fashion. She often told me later, however, that she regretted not having appreciated shopping trips to J. Wise. There, seated in a luxurious waiting room, she and her mother would choose from a wide variety of fine (and fancy) dresses specially selected and fitted for them by their own personal salespeople.

As my mother reached adulthood, her relationship with her parents became strained; they were staunch Republicans and could not understand or support her Progressive views. Visits, marred by unpleasant arguments, became infrequent.

It was not until my mother had children of her own that she reestablished a comfortable relationship with my grandmother. We sometimes traveled to New York to see Nona and visit with my aunt Helen and her family in Cedarhurst, Long Island. The road trip from D.C. to New York took six hours then. Because I suffered from relentless motion sickness, those six hours seemed never-ending. Finally, usually at night, I'd experience the thrill I'd been waiting for, the drive through the dark and cavernous Midtown Tunnel and out into dynamic New York City, which I loved.

I looked forward to those visits, especially at holiday time, as I was always amazed by my grandmother's knowledge and competence. Though Nona had little interest in me (she had trouble remembering my name, usually addressing me as "Helen-Frances-Katie-Peggy"), Dad was clearly a favorite. She treated his visits as occasions for celebration. On Thanksgiving, Nona would grace us with her baking. I can still smell her Sacher- and linzertortes served at the end of our holiday meal. For "Herbie" she would also make her specialty, apple strudel. She and Helen would spend what seemed like hours preparing the dough by hand, stretching it until it took on its perfect tissue-thin consistency.

Nona's trips to Washington were also a treat. Waiting for her arrival at Union Station, our mouths would water as we anticipated the big box of layered Barricini chocolates she would bring—I liked the fondant-filled, round chocolates best—

Peter and me, ages 5 and 2, 1944.

My mother and me, age eight, in Cedarhurst, Long Island, summer 1950.

and the package of New York cold cuts, which always included the exotic prosciutto.

Following her mother's example—displaying her intelligence, drive, and audacity and assuming her right to succeed—my mother grew up to become her own person, never believing that opportunities for women were limited. When it came time to attend college, my mother chose Mount Holyoke, where women were encouraged to compete and excel; she was graduated cum laude in 1927 with a B.A. in economics. At the end of her college years, my mother won a Patrick Memorial Scholarship for Social Betterment, which gave her the opportunity to study for a

My father on a visit to my mother's family in Cedarhurst, Long Island, summer 1950.

year at the London School of Economics and the Office of the Ministry of Labour before returning home to New York University Law School (J.D. 1931) and a series of jobs in the field of economic research.[2]

Like Nona, my mother was tough, self-assured, determined—always a woman with a mission. Her interest in Progressive causes led her to apply her training and experience in economics and the law to a career in the New Deal government in Washington. For nine years, beginning in September 1933, she worked in the Bureau of Labor Statistics (BLS) at the Labor Department, finally becoming chief of the Section on Cost of Living Indexes.

My mother's years at the Labor Department were almost completely lost to me; she never talked about them. I had to rely on what I could glean from books on the New Deal and interviews with people who knew her then. Reading *The Roosevelt I Knew* by Frances Perkins, Franklin Delano Roosevelt's secretary of labor, helped me to understand why my mother chose to dedicate her considerable energy to the Labor Department. Perkins describes the president's earliest vision of a "new deal" as a program (or more precisely an attitude) in which "the forgotten man, the little man, the man nobody knew much about, was going to be dealt better cards to play with." The president and secretary shared the goal of bettering the economic lives of ordinary people who had been the desperate victims of the Great Depression.[3] Clearly, these were my mother's goals as well.

"Frances was very good at what she did," 1940s friend and neighbor Harry Magdoff[4] told me when I interviewed him in 1998. "Your mother knew her economics. Her area was the Cost of Living Index. The question was *what are you measuring?* Different weights were assigned to different prices. People buy differently and therefore it was necessary to have an adjustable weighing system, a cost of living index that reflected patterns of buying. Frances was willing to take the time and trouble to analyze the data so that the index could be adjustable in a meaningful way. Others were not willing to do the work necessary to make these adjustments."[5] This was not actually political, Harry explained, not really "left," except to the extent that the index took into account workers' buying patterns in the analysis.[6]

"I was impressed," Harry said, "that when, on a few occasions, Frances and I drove downtown together in the morning, all she talked about were economic issues."

"I shouldn't say this," Harry's wife, Beadie Magdoff, interrupted. "I shouldn't tell you this, but I did not like Frances. If she thought you were wrong about something, she would shake her finger in your face and lecture you. All the men thought she was so smart."

"It's just that she really knew her economics," Harry said.[7]

In 1935 or '36—I have not been able to establish exactly when, nor by whom she was recruited—my mother joined the Communist Party. While at the BLS, she belonged to an underground Communist group composed of people on the staff at the Labor Department; for part of that time she was its leader, and, in that capacity, she met regularly with other leaders of secret government Communist Party units. As part of her work with the Party (1936–42), my mother was encouraged to attend meetings at the Agriculture Department to "assist" the "'little people,' clerks, stenographers, etc., in their CP work."[8]

Louise Hollander, a lifelong family friend and neighbor, told me she remembered meeting my mother through her husband, Ed Hollander, a Labor Department economist who helped found the liberal, anti-Communist organization Americans for Democratic Action. "Ed used to send people to her," Louise told me. "'Call Fran Rice,' he would tell them. 'She knows everything there is to know about the Cost of Living Index.'"

"I met your mother in the League of Women Shoppers,"[9] Louise explained, "an organization started in New York by Evelyn Preston, with the goal of using women's buying power to organize workers; it was workers backing workers, promoting decent working conditions, for laundry workers, for example. Many of the members were wives of New Dealers. Your mother was the chair of the Living Standards Committee of the League. She was always unusually straightforward and refreshing. No stuff about her. I think of your mother as one of the most wonderful people I have ever known. She saw things the way they were and acted on them.

"I remember the Nazi-Soviet Pact of 1939," Louise continued. "There was a Board Meeting of the League of Women Shoppers. We talked about the pact. Fran and a couple of the others said, 'Of course there's an escape clause [that the Russians could use to get out of the Pact when the time was right].'[10] It was then that it became perfectly clear to me that she was a Communist sympathizer."[11]

When the pact was signed, and American Communists found themselves instructed to cease all anti-Nazi activities, members resigned en masse. Not so my parents. My father would later say that the harsh reality of the situation continued to elude him during that time; the Party's hold on him was just that strong. It was not until the close of the war that he became convinced that the Soviets were dictating the activities of the American Party.[12]

"It shocked me to think of your mother and father going along with the Party line," Louise told me. "I couldn't understand how such caring, intelligent people could have let themselves be hoodwinked. They were savvy people; we could not believe how they could have been so naive. Others [Communists or Communist sympathizers] we knew were not very astute, not very sophisticated."[13]

I found this surprising as well. How, indeed, could my parents have continued to defend the decision to back the pact when so many were leaving the Party because of it? By doing so, it seems to me now, they clearly had decided to accept the rigid Party line like the one Elizabeth Bentley attributed to her mentor, Jacob Golos: "[The signing of the pact] means that we may have to twist and turn and do seemingly contradictory things, but we never lose sight of our final goal. . . . The Soviet Union is the only Communist country in the world, and as such she is a strong force in our world movement. She must be preserved at all costs if our hope for a Communist world is to come true. . . . [S]he is surrounded by a vicious group of capitalist nations waiting to pounce on her and crush her. . . . if she hadn't signed that pact, Hitler would most certainly have attacked her."[14]

"We saw less of your parents during those years," Louise said. "They avoided left-wingers who were not Communists.

"I had mixed feelings about your father's decision to name names," she said. "On the one hand I thought it was brave in a way. I didn't agree with the people who thought he was selling out. It was a terrible time for all liberals. Your mother never spoke with me about this, though we remained friends until she died."[15]

My mother left government service in 1942 when the family relocated to Denver but remained a member of the Communist Party until 1946. Years later she would tell me she had developed an aversion to the fields of economics and the law. She never did tell me why.

Throughout my childhood I viewed my parents as inseparable—a devoted couple. I can remember, as a very young child, being jealous of their closeness, the fact that they had each other to talk to at night and I was alone. My parents' relationship was grounded in deep affection and solid friendship, but their strongest bond was in the political and intellectual life they shared. From the beginning, my mother took pride in deferring to my father. She served him first at dinner, always asked his opinion, listened to him talk for hours, and indulged him in childish whims. But it was *she* who was the force behind the union, she who wielded the power. It was my mother who made most of the decisions that defined their everyday lives.

At the time they married, my parents were busy with their careers and their time-consuming participation in regular Party meetings. Nevertheless, they soon began thinking about having a family. This idea appealed particularly to my father, who had lost a stillborn son in his first marriage. On February 23, 1939, Peter was born, and they moved to a house on Cathedral Avenue Northwest, just off the Potomac River. My parents told me Peter was a jolly, sweet baby, easy to care for, responsive, and fun. Right away, my parents hired a series of day nurses to care for him at home. From what I can gather, though his time with them was limited, Peter brought deep pleasure to my parents' busy lives.

My birth followed almost three years later, on December 31, 1941, shortly after Pearl Harbor and the United States' entry into the Second World War. My parents often bragged that my birth qualified them for the $600 tax deduction that year—my claim to fame.

Frequently, a second child adds exponentially to the complexity of the lives of parents. This was certainly true in the case of my birth, as I was born with a congenital cataract, a ptosis (drooping eyelid), and a fussy disposition. I would need several surgeries—the first at one year of age, the second at three—and would not be able to tolerate, at age two, the patch the doctors placed over my good right eye to help strengthen the left one, which wandered aimlessly. I whined and cried incessantly. My mother told me later that when she looked into my face and saw my wandering eye, she was filled with guilt, anxiety, and frustration. Uncomfortable by nature with mothering, these complications added to her sense of insecurity as a parent.

If my mother found caring for two preschool-age children challenging, she didn't find it easier as we got older. Mom was impatient with my brother and responded with ambivalence to my frequent bouts of unhappiness, my hypersensitivity, and my need for attention. Sometimes she was warm and caring; no one could be more reassuring. More often, though, she was impatient, critical, and overbearing. I never knew what to expect. Fed up with my whining and fussing, and not knowing what to do to stop it, she would scream at me: "Keep it up, why don't you. You'll see. I'll give you something *really* to cry about."

Sometimes, after an argument, I would go into my room and cry for hours, wishing my mother would come in, make up, and comfort me. But she never came.

"She's doing this just to annoy me," my mother would say to my father. "I'm going to ignore her."

Finally, I would cry myself to sleep.

Mom couldn't get the hang of parenting even though she brought to the task the same determination she'd brought to all the other ventures in her life. We kids didn't do what she needed and expected us to do. Peter wouldn't pick up his room; I wouldn't stop whining. No doubt she loved us; she would spare no expense or effort to provide us with the best medical care available, the best cultural opportunities money could buy, or anything else for that matter. But she just didn't understand how we worked, what we needed. To make things worse, she was a master of the putdown. Whenever our behavior challenged her, she would berate us. With each demeaning verbal blow in my direction—"Will you never learn?"—I shrank deeper into a chronic suppressed state of self-doubt. I'll always be a disappointment to her, I thought. I'm not smart enough, not well read enough, not together enough to satisfy her expectations. Why doesn't she look up from her book when I come into the room?

I'm not sure if it was the grief of losing her identity as a left-wing activist or the pressures of parenthood or both that caused my mother to become depressed. When I was seven, my father, impatient with her moodiness, urged her to get some help. For five years my mother saw a psychoanalyst several times a week. This experience gave her life-changing insights into the emotional needs of children and relationships and ultimately contributed to healthier and more satisfying interactions between us. She became more patient with us, more apt to explain feelings than to lash out. She began to involve herself in activities relating to our schooling, even serving as president of our elementary school PTA. Though she had no prior experience in education, she brought energy, commitment, and competence to this phase of her life, ultimately earning a master's degree in human relations and moving on to a highly successful second career in special education.

In spite of the improvement in our relationship over the years, my mother and I argued endlessly during my late adolescence. I resented her overpowering personality and lack of tact and had no healthy way to deal with this. It was not until her last ten to fifteen years, after both of us had been in therapy, that my mother

Peter and me, just after my senior year in high school, August 1959.

and I established a trusting relationship, two caring adults sharing news about our lives, both of us grateful we ended up that way.

Thinking back over what I remembered and what I had discovered about my mother's life, I realized how little I knew about the nature and extent of her experience in the Communist Party. Was there more I could find out?

In July 1997, I wrote to the FBI to obtain my mother's file. In the meantime, it was my father's file that led me into the next stage of my journey.

16

Too Close for Comfort

When in 1996 I finally received my father's FBI file, I attacked it with an urgency I didn't anticipate, hungry for information about his experience as a Communist and his involvement in secret Communist cells while working for the U.S. Government.

The file is rife with blacked-out names. The story the file tells (an only sometimes reliable one, even without the redacted text) interrupts itself at every turn and had to be pieced together. The first time I read it, I skimmed over what was not complete, sometimes leafing through multiple pages, able to make out only one or two legible sentences per page. Some pages were missing altogether. I glossed over the more alarming entries, not yet ready to take them in: "Inasmuch as the subject was a member of a secret CP group and an associate of Soviet espionage agents and has refused to discuss his activities and associations, the WFO [Washington Field Office] considers him to be a potential risk to the security of the United States."[1] I glossed over them at first, and then, upon a second reading, felt more as if I was looking at the text of a spy novel: the FBI gone crazy, spinning its hyperbolic tale of intrigue, implicating people by association like the citizens of Salem. "Reliable and confidential informants have advised that FUCHS was a known contact of three individuals who associated with an admitted Soviet Espionage Agent who operated in Washington D.C. from 1941 to 1944."[2] *"I saw Sarah Good with the Devil! I saw Goody Osburn with the Devil! I saw Bridget Bishop with the Devil!"*[3]

Eventually, my denial and cynicism were replaced by an anxious, trapped feeling. Thrown back to the hysteria of the 1950s, to the memory of the threat of the Russians "taking over the world," "controlling our thoughts and actions," or worse, unleashing the hydrogen bomb to produce a "nuclear winter,"[4] a niggling question rose once more into my consciousness: Might my parents really have been involved with people who were spying for the Russians? The idea had a surreal and ominous feel.

Thinking about it now, I'm reminded of the panic elicited in me by the movie *East/West,* how troubled I felt while watching it.

In the stirring early scenes of the film, Russian émigrés aboard a ship headed for Odessa, repatriating to the Soviet Union after the end of the Second World War, celebrate their pending return to the homeland. Full of hope for a bright future, the protagonist, a physician who travels with his French-born wife and child, leads the others in a toast and song of jubilation. Their Russian host welcomes them: "You will soon return back in the homeland," he tells them. "You left her thirty years ago but she never left you. Now she needs you. The Soviet government opens its doors to you regardless of past events." The passengers eat and drink; they dance. They're going home.

A loudspeaker marks the ship's arrival: "Dear compatriots. . . . Welcome to our Soviet homeland, to the victorious nation where, guided by Comrade Stalin, wise among the wise, all people live as one family, united and happy." As the passengers look on, an old man steps from the gangplank and kisses the ground beneath his feet. He has, at last, returned home, his son by his side. With pride and anticipation, the old man and his son give their names to the waiting official. Then, much to the horror of the waiting group, the official separates the old man from his boy, sending each to an undisclosed destination. The frightened son panics and tries to run but is gunned down. The physician and his young family have been lured into a trap from which there is no escape.

I squirmed in my seat as I watched this film, my heart racing. Terror colored my view: the images of cruel separation from loved ones, of losing the freedom to live as one pleased.

I read and reread the text of my father's HUAC hearing. Elizabeth Bentley is mentioned as the informer who named U.S. Government officials she claimed had spied for the Soviets before and during the Second World War. Why had HUAC chairman Francis Walter told the *Washington Star* that my father's testimony in 1955 would be "the biggest of its kind since the Elizabeth Bentley and Whittaker Chambers disclosures in the late 1940s"?[5] Who was Elizabeth Bentley and what was my parents' connection to her and to the people she implicated?

My questions led me to the University of Michigan Graduate Library where I read congressional records on microfiche and old *Washington Post* articles that detailed Elizabeth Bentley's 1948 HUAC testimony. Dubbed by the press "The Blond Spy Queen," Bentley testified that between 1941 and 1944, as a member of the Communist underground, she had been asked by her lover, Russian agent and

American Communist Party official Jacob Golos, "to take charge of individuals and groups who were employed in the United States Government and in position to furnish information . . . political, military, whatever they could lay their hands on."[6] Golos had asked her to meet with his sources, collect their dues, "calm their fears, and flatter their egos." Ultimately, he had instructed her to carry information from them to him in New York.

In her testimony, Bentley described two spy rings, one headed by Nathan Gregory Silvermaster, formerly with the Board of Economic Warfare, and the other by Victor Perlo, then a War Production Board official. Perlo was the man known as "Mike" who functioned as my father's contact with the "constituted Party authority" when Dad was the leader of a secret Communist group at the National Labor Relations Board.

I was dismayed to learn that Perlo and several of my parents' friends and former colleagues were named by Bentley as having been members of a spy ring: Harold Glasser, the neighbor who moved into my family's house on Cathedral Avenue when we moved to Denver during the war; Allan Rosenberg, the neighbor who established the secret Communist group at the NLRB with my father; and Harry Magdoff and Irving Kaplan, both friends and neighbors in the Palisades section of northwest Washington.

Bentley told the Committee that she had met with Victor Perlo, Edward Fitzgerald, and Harry Magdoff in March of 1944, and they and others had agreed to provide her with data from their government jobs. I noted with interest that she said none of the members of either espionage ring took money for their services, except for expenses incurred on trips to New York to deliver information.[7]

When the news of Bentley's accusations became public, my father was a few months away from quitting government service. Now it made sense that Bentley's August 1948 disclosures would have influenced his decision to leave his position at the National Labor Relations Board.

I wondered what my parents' reactions were to what they read in the *Post* the week the Bentley story broke. Did they dismiss this set of allegations as yet one more example of the anti-Communist crusade of the political Right? Might they have downplayed the threat of espionage, as President Truman did, believing it to have been blown out of proportion, a red herring, an effort on the part of the Republicans to embarrass the Truman administration and assure the future of their own political careers? Were my parents shocked by the allegations that people they knew personally had been spying for the Russians? After all, my father flatly denied in his HUAC testimony having made available any information designed for Communist Party uses or having observed or learned of anyone doing so.[8] Were my parents alarmed at the thought of how far some of their friends and colleagues may have been willing to go for the cause? Or did they read what they already knew to be true?

I called my brother, Peter, and told him of my shock, my feeling that our parents may have been closer to real danger and intrigue than we had realized.

"Do you remember these people named by Bentley, friends and colleagues in Washington in the '40s?" I asked Peter. Peter is older than I, his memory better. He remembered Irving Kaplan ("Kappy") vaguely, remembered playing in Kappy's backyard on Sherrier Place. And Harry Magdoff. We both remembered a photo of Peter with Harry's son Michael, posing together in 1941, two contented toddlers.

"Did you know, back in the days of the troubles, that these friends had been accused of spying for the Soviets?" I asked. He didn't remember knowing about that then.

I became fixated on learning all I could about Soviet espionage on the part of committed members of the American Communist Party. It was one thing if people gathered in groups to read Communist literature and share ideas and political goals, as my father's testimony indicated. It was quite another, it seemed to me, if some of these people were handing over secret government data to the Russians even if, as I was beginning to understand, they were motivated by idealism.

As part of my search, I read everything I could get my hands on about the famous Whittaker Chambers/Alger Hiss case, in which Chambers, a senior editor at *Time* magazine and an admitted former courier for the Russians, accused Alger Hiss, then president of the Carnegie Endowment for International Peace and a former State Department official, of having committed espionage on behalf of the Soviets.[9] In a dramatic twist, Chambers pulled copies of State Department documents out of a pumpkin patch on his Maryland farm in order to substantiate his claim. To this day historians still fuss over the "Pumpkin Papers"; they continue to argue about whether or not Hiss was guilty of espionage.

Thinking he might shed some light on my quest, I contacted Allen Weinstein, author of *Perjury*, the definitive book on the Hiss/Chambers case. Weinstein led me to the newly released Venona documents, secret cables transmitted between Moscow and the American Communists helping the Soviet cause. The cables were decrypted in 1948 but were not released to the American public until the mid-1990s. I was stunned to see in these cables references to my parents' friends and colleagues with the code names "Raider," "Ruble," "Ted," "Kant," "Sid," and "Tino," and to read of specific activities attributed to them. If the information contained within the Venona documents was accurate, many of Bentley's claims appeared to be corroborated.[10]

I consumed books and articles about Julius and Ethel Rosenberg. I wondered why the Rosenberg case had not come into my mind when Dad first talked about going before HUAC; the case was almost an obsession with me now. In retrospect, it should have seemed natural that I'd think of the Rosenbergs then. I didn't and I now see why. My mother's offhand remark about Ethel Rosenberg's execution on the day it happened—a statement of fact, not an invitation for discussion—is evidence of how ardently my parents were trying to push that scary time from their consciousness; the topic was not discussed in our home. Perhaps, to have made that association would have been too terrifying for me at the time.

Evidence began to appear (particularly from the Venona decrypts) to indicate that Julius Rosenberg, while not guilty of giving over the secrets of the bomb, had been the leader of a group of men who knowingly provided scientific and technical data to Moscow.[11]

It was difficult for me to adjust to the overwhelming evidence that Julius Rosenberg had worked for the Russians. This case had elicited such strong emotions in me once I emerged from my denial: fear connected with the Rosenbergs' execution and my own realization that I, too, could have lost my parents in such a way; trust in the couple's innocence; indignation at the wrong done them by our government. I identified so strongly with the sons they left behind. Later, I experienced uncertainty as to what really happened, then shock at learning of the new disclosures, and, finally, disillusionment.

I read Robert Meeropol's book *An Execution in the Family* and met him at a talk he gave at the University of Michigan Residential College; I wept throughout his speech. (There but for the grace of God go I, I thought.) Though anguished by the dredging up of old feelings, I was pleased that Robbie Meeropol, while defending his parents' actions as supporting "the cause" against American imperialism, finally acknowledged that his father might have given information to the Russians that wasn't his to give. I was grateful and relieved to hear the more balanced view he presented—no longer an equivocation. Robbie's book is a gift to those of us who struggle to learn the truth.

By 1998, I had reviewed my father's documents, including his HUAC testimony and his FBI file. Challenged by a friend's questions about my *mother's* experience in the Party, I had written for her FBI file and was then waiting to receive it. Meanwhile, I made a point to revisit the trunk in my brother's basement in Washington that still housed some of my parents' papers. Maybe I had missed something the first time around.

Opening the trunk, I gathered up old books, notebooks, and papers. I wondered how my mother and father picked the things they chose to save: a *Life* magazine photo spread on members of FDR's cabinet; a letter from my father's best friend, Teddy Drachman, and his wife, Gracie (songwriter Frankie Loesser's younger sister), expressing humor and amazement at Dad's first wife Rita's choice of a new husband; newspaper and magazine articles, a journal and correspondence chronicling my parents' troubles. My father's HUAC testimony was tucked among these papers along with my mother's thesis on labor in Mussolini's Italy and her curriculum vitae, which included all of her employment from the time she was graduated from Mount Holyoke College in 1927 until she started working for the Special Education Department in Prince George's County, Maryland, in the late 1950s.

Why did they save these things and not others? Had my father planned to write a book someday about his HUAC experience, or was he merely saving "evidence" to defend his actions? (The journal turned out to be helpful in this regard on numerous occasions, when his word was challenged by American University's administration.)

Would my father have been horrified to know that I was writing this book or might he have been pleased that, after his death, it was I who tried to find and write the truth?

But I *had* missed something the first time around. My mother's resume revealed information that I found disconcerting. In 1942, she left the Bureau of Labor Statistics to take a job at the War Production Board (where Edward Fitzgerald, Irving Kaplan, and Harry Magdoff were, or had been, and Victor Perlo was about to arrive); she made this move at exactly the same time my father left the National Labor Relations Board to go to the Board of Economic Warfare (where Greg Silvermaster[12] and Allan Rosenberg were, or had been). And even more disturbing to me, I learned that Edward Fitzgerald, one of those accused by Elizabeth Bentley, was not merely an acquaintance of my parents, but was my mother's *boss* during her brief tenure at the War Production Board, from the end of 1942 until March of 1943. My mother listed Fitzgerald and Kaplan as professional references when she applied for employment in Denver.[13]

Though my father denied any awareness of the Party having helped him get a job, I had to wonder if my parents had been recruited by Party members when he and my mother switched employment at exactly the same time. Still reeling from my discovery that my mother had a close professional relationship with both Fitzgerald and Kaplan, I recalled Elizabeth Bentley's understanding "that it was the general policy of that group [the Silvermaster Group] and also other groups to transfer anyone in what we would call a 'nonproductive' job into a job that would be of more use . . . that in many cases they had conspired to move people into better spots."[14] I remembered her claim that "[w]hat the Russians wanted to know was practically limitless. . . . They sought military data: production figures, performance tests on airplanes, troop strength and allocation, and new experimental developments . . . secret deals between the Americans and the various governments in exile, secret negotiations between the United States and Great Britain, contemplated loans to foreign countries, and other similar material."[15] Jacob Golos, Bentley's mentor and lover, allegedly had told her, "[the fact that the Russians are taking the full brunt of the war] means that we have a difficult task before us. Moscow must be kept completely informed about what is going on behind the scenes in the American government so that she can be prepared to forestall any treachery. That's where we come in. I have received orders to get as many trusted comrades as possible into strategic positions in United States government agencies in Washington, where they will have access to secret and confidential information that can be relayed on to the Soviet Union."[16]

In view of all of this, I was taken aback by the first line in my mother's description of her job responsibilities at the War Production Board: "I direct and control all the procedures on the issuance, collection, tabulation and distribution of WPB [War Production Board] Form 732, a monthly report on plant operations in the war industries."[17]

The work at the WPB was vital to the war effort, it seemed to me. But how important was it really? I learned from James Burnham's book *The Web of Subversion* that Edward Fitzgerald, my mother's boss, received a deferment from the military on the basis that his work at the War Production Board was too valuable to be spared, in particular his responsibility for the "basic information, analyses and reports" contained in the board's periodic survey of manufacturing concerns.[18] I found this information disturbing, as it referred directly to the WPB Form 732 that my mother prepared. This was just too close for comfort.

There are logical (and even probable) reasons why my parents might have sought new employment at the end of 1942. For one thing, my mother may well have been anxious for a new challenge, a change from her old-line office (where she had been for seven years) to this newly formed agency, which, as one friend suggested, "was at the heart of things."[19] Then too, the new job offered a significant raise: $800 in additional annual salary, a considerable difference in 1942. At the same time, my father was eager to change jobs then because the NLRB had ceased to be the vital organization it once was and probably also because the agency was in the throes of an extensive governmental investigation. But I found it troubling to learn that my parents made such moves at exactly the same moment, to agencies through which, according to Bentley, information was being passed on to the Russians. The question remained: If in fact the Party was moving people from job to job, particularly following Germany's attack on the Soviet Union, and if my father and mother were "recruited" as part of this effort to access information of interest to the Party and to the Soviets, how much of this did my parents know at the time?

If they knew what was expected of them and they made a conscious decision to cooperate, that was one thing, difficult as this idea was for me to believe or accept. It was another far more insidious matter if they were manipulated to provide this service, unaware.

Again I shared what I had learned with Peter. He was attentive, interested, a good listener. This was not his search, certainly, not something he would have felt compelled to explore, but he was curious and understanding of my need to know.

"We know Mom to have been strong and feisty," I said to Peter on the phone. "Do you think she might have knowingly provided data from the War Production Board through her boss to the Russians? Might Dad not have known?" I felt my body tense as I thought to myself, Was this a near miss for us? Might we have been at risk of losing our parents, being abandoned by them like the Rosenberg sons? I can imagine the shame we would have endured as teenagers, our parents already outcasts because of their participation in the Communist Party, now regarded as traitors to their country. Do I really want to be writing about this? Do I really want to know? What if I discover something the FBI hadn't learned?

"I suppose it's possible," Peter said, "that Mom was involved in that way. But if she was," he posited, "there's no way Dad would not have known. It's possible she was involved," he said, "but I think it's highly unlikely." I wished I knew for sure.

It seemed serendipitous that shortly after this discussion I learned that Allen Weinstein had a new book coming out, *The Haunted Wood: Soviet Espionage in America—The Stalin Era*. This book, with data pulled from the Venona documents and corroborated by newly released KGB files, would discuss in detail the activities of American Communists alleged to have been spying for the Russians, including my parents' friends and colleagues. I couldn't wait for the book to be published.

In Weinstein's book, the headliners among my parents' associates were Victor Perlo and Harold Glasser. The evidence from the Venona documents and KGB files implicated Victor Perlo as having given over aircraft and other war industries data from his work at the War Production Board. It exposed Glasser as having provided information on many subjects during his tenure at the Treasury Department: wartime and postwar economic and international financial information as well as political, military, and intelligence data.[20]

But what of the three men most closely connected with my parents at the Board of Economic Warfare and the War Production Board in 1942: Rosenberg, Kaplan, and Fitzgerald? Evidence from the Bentley testimony, the cables, and KGB files suggested that these three men had handed over information to her, material they had garnered from their government jobs; Bentley indicated this was the case even at the time my parents knew them.[21] From Allan Rosenberg, she claimed to have received data about the occupation of Germany. She told HUAC that Irving Kaplan provided information from his job at the War Production Board in late 1942 and early 1943; my mother was there then. And she testified that Edward Fitzgerald volunteered to "furnish miscellaneous statistical information coming to his attention as a result of his employment at the War Production Board . . . information concerning production figures" ostensibly gathered from Form 732.[22]

There is no evidence that these people, who were interested in helping the Soviets, intended to subvert U.S. Government policy in the process. Once the Russians took over control of the government "sources" from Elizabeth Bentley in 1944, individuals sharing information became increasingly aware that these data were going directly to the Soviets (if they had not previously known this was the case).

When Elizabeth Bentley defected in 1945, the Russians instructed their American sources to cease and desist; it was the end of an era.

On a trip to D.C., this time to interview John Earl Haynes of the Library of Congress, I took a walk by the Potomac River with my brother, bringing him up to date on what I had learned from the Venona documents and the KGB files.

"How are you defining espionage?" Peter asked, as we walked along the river at the Alexandria Marina. I defined it for him as I was defining it for myself, using the *Webster's* dictionary definition: "1) The use of spies," and "2) The use of spying, especially for military purposes." It has also been defined as the "unauthorized divulgence of government information to agents of a foreign power."[23] I discussed with Peter the perspectives of left-of-center historians like Victor Navasky and Ellen Schrecker, who point out that the government workers who gave secret data away to the Soviets at that time were fiercely idealistic people who did what they did not for money but because of their heartfelt belief that their actions would benefit all of humankind. I told my brother that, from my point of view, their noble motives notwithstanding, these people should have been more aware of the potentially damaging consequences of their actions. At the very least they should have known that their dealings could be interpreted negatively.

I shared my discoveries—my shock, confusion, and fascination—with guests one night at dinner.

One friend, a college professor whose specialty is French history, asked how I would feel if I found out that my father had been spying. My father acted immorally, my friend suggested, by testifying against his friends; it might have been easier for me if I knew he had been a spy. Then I could respect him for having put actions to his deeply felt beliefs and for being consistent by sticking to them. Perhaps then his integrity would still be intact.

My father did not take care of himself, a second friend insisted; he didn't hire a lawyer, didn't take the Fifth, didn't use good judgment. He betrayed his friends and blamed others for the misfortune for which he was primarily responsible. She warned me not to idealize him, not to deny his flaws.

"But he *did* take responsibility for his actions," a third friend insisted. By now, I could see that some of my guests were feeling the need to protect me. "He lived with the guilt from this no-win situation for the rest of his life and went about taking care of his family the best way he knew how."

"And what if you believed in something and that something changed and let you down?" another guest asked. "And what if, to be true to yourself, you had to do something drastically different and distasteful? After all, it's only through moral (and other) struggles that one experiences spiritual growth. Growth doesn't come from easy, right-and-wrong decisions; it's not so much the outcome that leads to growth; it's the struggles themselves."

"You can't be rigid about right and wrong," my psychologist husband offered. "Being consistent when circumstances change is not always the best moral choice. I'm convinced that Peggy's parents no longer believed in the cause that had once been so important to them—on the contrary."

I've got to admit the sting I felt hearing others label my father's actions as weak and immoral. It's not as if I hadn't had such thoughts myself; I had. In fact, I had internalized my father's shame as my own, and I still felt embarrassed sometimes to let people know he had named names or that, desperate for work, he accepted help from HUAC chairman Francis Walter. And yet I understood the reasons for his actions. I appreciated this dinner party for the way the conversation—or argument, as it turned out to be—expressed for me the complexity of my father's moral dilemma.

In a sworn statement in July 1955, my father told the FBI, "I have never engaged in espionage and knew of no one who was engaged in espionage. . . . I wish to assert my undivided and unqualified loyalty to my country, the United States of America. I have never felt any disloyalty to the United States."[24] Although at the NLRB he had regular contact with the Party "higher authority," and although issues relating to the work of the board were discussed, my father testified that he did not "observe or learn of the furnishing of any information to either Victor Perlo or Elizabeth Bentley for transmission to any Communist Party sources." In a sworn statement to the FBI in August 1955, my mother also denied having committed espionage or having known of anyone who had done so.[25]

I didn't doubt that what my parents said to HUAC and the FBI was true. But I still wondered about their close connection to colleagues accused of espionage. What more could I learn?

17

Harry Magdoff

Larger than Life

Given the suffering, hardship and social, political and economic stigma
suffered by the victims of McCarthyism, it is difficult for those of us who
weren't there to claim that McCarthy's victims have any sort of obligation
to put their activities—whatever they were—in context. But unless and
until these witnesses to history tell their tale, we may never know what
happened.
   —Victor Navasky, "Dialectical McCarthyism(s)"

"Gee, Peggy," my Ann Arbor friend Ruth Bardenstein said to me one night, "for such a conventional person you certainly have an interesting background." We were on our way home from an adult Bat Mitzvah class that night, in the spring of 1991. I don't remember what, in particular, caught her attention—my involvement in the Democratic Reform movement in Manhattan amid the Black Power and anti-war crusades? my weekend at Woodstock? my family's HUAC experience? Anyway, it was that night that Ruth told me she had a cousin, Harry Magdoff, a Marxist economist, who had also suffered as a result of the McCarthy Era government witch hunt.

Harry worked for the government in Washington, D.C., during the Second World War, she explained, and in his long career was an economic consultant to people and nations across the globe, including the governments of the Soviet Union and Cuba. In fact, he was employed in government service from the mid-1930s through the '50s, working in the Works Progress Administration at first and later at the War Production Board. Eventually, after a stint in the Department of Commerce, he became one of secretary of commerce Henry Wallace's advisers.

In the late '60s he started editing the *Monthly Review,* an independent Socialist magazine.

"Harry's a wonderful person," Ruth told me, "very accomplished and well respected in his field."

"Well I'll be darned," I said. "Harry Magdoff was a friend of my parents. I still have photos of his son Michael as a toddler, playing with my brother, Peter."

Some years later, when she heard that I was thinking about writing this book, Ruth encouraged me to contact Harry. "I'm sure he'll be happy to talk with you," she said. "And you'll find him an amazing human being with endless fascinating stories to tell."[1]

It took me a long time to get up the courage to write to Harry. When I finally did, I explained that I had not known anything about my parents' experience as Communists until I was thirteen, on the eve of my father's testimony before HUAC. I told him that this had been a traumatizing ordeal, that the family had not talked about it and now I felt compelled to learn what I could.

Months went by with no response. I'd virtually given up hope of hearing from him when one afternoon, an E-mail from Harry popped up on my computer screen. Harry explained that he'd been hesitant to answer me. He did not wish to cause me pain and worried that "going over the old days would stir things up too much." Finally, however, he said he decided "it was only fair that I answer your moving letter.

"We were never intimate friends with your parents," Harry wrote, "but we were friends. They were the life of our social gatherings, full of fun and initiative. Talking with them about serious matters was always of interest. Apart from your father's observations about legal matters, your mother's discussion of the cost-of-living indexes crossed an area of my own work."

Harry wrote that he did not think he had "anything to add to the facts." He said he "knew nothing of [my] parents' politics" other than what he might "surmise from our mutual Left perspective." Nevertheless, he invited me and Michael to come to New York to visit and talk things over with him and his wife, Beadie.[2]

I love Manhattan. Whenever I return to visit, I experience the nostalgia that accompanies happy memories of an earlier adult life: memories of the East Side, the West Side, Midtown, the Village, Harlem. This city still belongs to me.

And so it was on this trip. As Michael and I approached Harry's apartment on West 84th Street in December 1998, I felt buoyed by the city's energy and excited at the prospect of discovering more in my search for the truth. Why did this feel so important?

"Come on in, kids," Beadie called from the kitchen, as her grandson David greeted us at the door. We shook hands; David left. Michael gave Beadie a bouquet of yellow roses and helped her arrange them in a vase.

I'll never forget my first impression of Harry that day. Larger than life, that's how I'd describe him, just as Ruth had said. It was not only his large frame and his ample, imposing face, but also the expansiveness of his gentle voice and his easy, confident, and comfortable manner. Harry greeted me with a big hug that felt like the hug of an old friend, and in fact, his face seemed familiar to me.[3] In addition, some of the expressions he used reminded me of my father, phrases like "on the fence," "in the cards," and "on that score." Over tea, pie, and cheese and crackers, the four of us got to know each other, talking for hours.

Harry and Beadie reminisced. They asked us lots of questions about our lives, our children. I told them about the guilt I carried concerning my father's testimony. I told the Magdoffs I worried they would not want to meet with me. Harry, an attentive and compassionate listener, said he had actually been impressed that I had contacted him and that I was agonizing over this. Most people, he said, would just want to forget it and not try to deal with the feelings. He had done his share of agonizing also. He told me he hadn't known from my letter whether I was aware of the details of my father's testimony, and he did not want to be the one to tell me my father had named names.

Beadie surmised my parents would never have come to visit them. It was fear, she suggested, that had made my father do what he did. "These were terrifying times," Harry reminded us. "Some people held up under the strain better than others. One day you had a job, children, life; the next day you no longer had any income. Some people committed suicide, some had heart attacks." While he was unable to accept what my father did, he said he could never reject the child for the actions of the father. Ultimately, he counseled, "we forgive our parents, just as we forgive our children, because they are ours."

For a time in the 1940s, Harry told us, the Magdoffs and my parents had had close friends in common; these friends lived in the same neighborhood, Palisades in northwest Washington, and were all involved in government service. My parents lived on Cathedral Avenue; Irving "Kappy" and Dorothy Kaplan, the Magdoffs, and the Van Tassels on Sherrier Place; and Artie and Annie Stein on MacArthur Boulevard. The Magdoffs had recently been in touch with the Steins' daughter,

Eleanor, who, according to Harry, had a "nice husband and children." A new-left, activist member of the Weathermen Underground Organization in the 1960s, she had lived underground for over a decade. Eventually, she became an Albany judge. Harry and Beadie remembered my brother, Peter, "a gentle, sweet little boy." They remembered all the kids playing in the Kaplans' yard. Harry commented, "Aren't the kids what we live for?"

The Magdoffs recalled my father with fondness. "Herbert was cute," they agreed. He was generous and helpful with legal advice. He was delightful and fun at parties where, after a couple of drinks, he would often do his favorite shtick, performing the letters of the alphabet with his arms and legs. My mother, Harry said, would join the frivolity; he recalled seeing her at one party standing on the back of a sofa, being silly.[4] I couldn't quite picture this. Beadie, though, let us know in no uncertain terms: she did not like Frances. Frances was "tough and bossy," she said.

Harry told us stories of the "dynamic" New Deal days. "People were committed to a common cause," he said. "We could make a difference." It wasn't relevant, he explained, who was and who wasn't a Communist. In fact, people did not know what each other's politics were. Rather, everyone was of a like mind; they understood what needed to happen. People were not hired because they were Communists. What mattered was whether or not a person could do the job. Harry was offered many different positions over the years; he picked and chose among them according to where the action was and what his interests were. He made it clear to us that he was independent of any party line. He told us that many people were surprised, for example, that he was working for the war effort during the time before Hitler invaded the Soviet Union, when the Communist Party required its members to take the isolationist position toward the war in Europe. He told us that he frequently spoke out about the problems in the Soviet Union's economic policies; he criticized these policies on the occasions he served as an economic consultant to the Soviet government.

Harry did not remember that my mother worked briefly for Harry's colleague and friend Edward Fitzgerald in the Facilities Utilization Division of the War Production Board, a department that Harry himself had started. Although he acknowledged that she might have wanted to work at the WPB because it was near "the center of the action," Harry expressed surprise that my mother would have left the relative security of the Labor Department to come to an agency that would remain in business only as long as the war continued. He had thought of my parents, products of the Depression, as people who would have been anxious about security for themselves and their family. Furthermore, he added, "I didn't know she was that far to the Left."

I asked Harry and Beadie if they remembered hearing about my father's HUAC testimony. Yes, they said. They had heard about it ahead of time, from Kappy. Frances had asked someone to warn them. "Kappy was terribly upset," Harry said. But at least my father had not "spilled all the beans."[5] At the time, I didn't think much about this comment from Harry. It was only much later that the implications of his statement really hit me. Was Harry implying that there were a lot more "beans" to spill? Did my father have important knowledge that he had chosen not to share with the Committee, or had they failed to ask? I know that his intent was to protect others as much as he could without appearing uncooperative.

Kappy Kaplan, Harry said, was one of his very closest friends. He was a gentle man, though his wife, Dorothy, could be "tough." Kappy and Harry had known each other from their work together in Philadelphia. They had a great deal of respect for one another, though they argued and debated constantly. Kappy had wished Harry had been "more connected."

Harry testified before the Senate Subcommittee on Internal Security in 1953, where, like his friend Ed Fitzgerald, he refused to take "immunity." Ed, Harry told us, served six months in jail and ended up a sad and troubled man. Harry lost his job as a professor at Roosevelt University. Ten very difficult years of struggle ensued. Beadie, a teacher, had a principal who supported her so she was able to continue working. Their son Michael's friends were decent to him, but the family suffered terribly. Tragedy hit again later in this period when Michael became ill; he died of leukemia at the age of sixteen.

Ultimately, after ten long years, Harry took a job on Wall Street. Though he "hated every minute of it," Harry made a killing in the stock market. How ironic! He made enough money to retire at age fifty-two, and spend the rest of his working life doing what he wanted to do most, editing the *Monthly Review* and working for the Socialist cause he held so dear.[6]

During the next several years after my visit to Harry, information about the newly released Venona cables and KGB archive files captured the attention of historians of American Communism and, for that matter, the general public. People on both sides of the political spectrum looked to the few still living witnesses to history—those with firsthand knowledge of what really happened—to come forward and help set the record straight.

Historian Ellen Schrecker tried to interview people who had been implicated and were still alive to tell their stories. Some of these people, in her words, "simply refused to talk." Others, such as Harry Magdoff, described by Schrecker as "a highly respected Marxist economist," declined to discuss this matter, not wanting to "reopen old wounds."[7]

Victor Navasky also attempted to speak with Harry Magdoff about the Venona revelations. After the release of the cables, Navasky phoned Harry with the hope of meeting for lunch. The two men had known each other since 1978; their journals, the *Nation* and the *Monthly Review,* had for many years shared office space and there was a tradition of the editors lunching together. According to Navasky, Harry declined the invitation for lunch, saying he was not well and was not interested in talking about this. On the phone, however, Harry acknowledged that his name had been mentioned a couple of times in the decrypted cables, but claimed "he wasn't even there" on the specific occasion mentioned.[8]

When I spoke with Victor Navasky in December 2001, it was obvious that he believed Harry Magdoff may have been falsely accused. Knowing that I had met with Harry in 1998, Navasky challenged me to recontact him to see if he would be willing to discuss this issue with me.

I E-mailed Harry: "So much has been written in the last couple of years and I struggle to keep balanced in my understanding of events in the context of the times. Mainstream historians use the release of the Venona documents as evidence of a 'Red Menace' threat to the country. How have you responded to the inclusion of your name in the documents and in recent books written about them? What would you have people understand about what really went on? Do you not agree that your knowledge, understanding and experience of the period would be invaluable for folks who are trying to look upon it with a proper perspective?" I told Harry I would understand if he did not wish to talk about this; I would respect his desire for privacy. But I told him that if he could find it within himself to share his answers to these questions, I would be a very eager and interested listener. Much to my amazement and in spite of the fact that Beadie, his beloved wife of more than seventy years, was terminally ill, Harry agreed to speak with me again. "We'd be pleased to see you in any event," he wrote, "whether on your 'obsession' or just to say hello."[9] We planned a date to talk, the first week of April 2002, with the understanding that because of Beadie's illness I would need to remain flexible; the visit might have to be canceled at a moment's notice.

I was anxious the week preceding my next visit with Harry in April. Awed by the fact that I was once again meeting with this important historical figure, I was em-

barrassed about asking him to speak with me about spying. I had the sense that my
questions were unimportant in the scheme of things, yet I knew that I was not the
only one interested in his answers. My anxiety became more and more intense as
I made my way from Grand Central Station across to Times Square and onto the
uptown subway to Broadway and West 84th Street. Here was a brilliant, highly accomplished Marxist economist, who had devoted his life to contemplating, analyzing, and critiquing economic theory and practices of governments around the
world. And here I was, preparing to ask him about spies. There was some satisfaction in buying exotic cookies from Zabar's to bring with me, something reassuring and almost soothing about elegant European bakery goods even when I
wouldn't be eating them myself.

Harry had aged terribly in the three years since I'd seen him. He'd lost weight,
had difficulty seeing and hearing, and had recently fallen, causing him problems
walking. Beadie lay in their bedroom at the end of the long hall, attached to an
oxygen machine. She went in and out of consciousness, in and out of pain. Periodically, she would call out for Harry, who tended to her with loving care and patience. No one—not she, he, or the hospice worker helping them out—had slept
during the preceding night.

An unexpected guest had arrived before me. This guest, a dear friend living in
Paris whom Harry seldom saw, was in town only briefly to attend a conference.
Harry signaled me: "We'll talk later; please sit down." Hours went by. Harry's guest
showed no sign of leaving, nor did Harry call an end to her visit. They spoke of complex economic theory, gossiped about their mutual friends, reminisced about their
lives together before the death of her husband, Harry's colleague, leftist French
journalist Daniel Singer (my son's name!). Finally Madame Singer took her leave;
by then I was exhausted and so was Harry. I felt I'd intruded on a private conversation, which I had, though I was the one who had an appointment. Harry urged
me to stay, to have some dinner with him; I suggested we get some rest and meet
again tomorrow.

I returned the next day. Mindful of Harry's sad and stressful situation, I asked
him periodically about his level of comfort. I was aware that this might be my
last chance to visit with him and I took him at his word that he was okay to talk.
I asked him to tell me when he was speaking off the record; he never did. Harry
had accurately interpreted the persistence with which I pursued this topic, what
he teasingly called my "obsession," as an indication of the deep personal meaning it had for me. It was clear that he saw himself as a teacher and was willing to
help me understand. Though he declined to speak about this matter when asked
by Navasky, Schrecker, and others because "it is not important to me and it would

involve talking about other people," he agreed to talk with me because mine was "a personal concern."[10]

Between interruptions we talked. I explained once more my interest in gaining perspective about my parents' experience and particularly the question of the Communist Party's relationship with the Soviet Union. Harry reminded me that in the 1930s anyone with a left perspective who was thinking at all about the issues confronting this country was joining the Communist Party. When I asked if the Party might have requested that its people recruit committed and able Party members to work in the more important government agencies, he again said no, he didn't think so.

Harry spoke at length about some of the jobs he held in the government during the 1930s and '40s. He talked about his first government position, working for David Weintraub (also a good friend of my parents) at the National Research Project of the Works Progress Administration in Philadelphia. There, along with Kappy Kaplan, Edward Fitzgerald, Harold Glasser, and Arthur Stein, he worked on a project called Technological Changes and Production Opportunities. He spoke also of his work as a consultant to Henry Wallace, who, Harry said, had refused to take the position of secretary of commerce unless Harry agreed to be on his staff.

It was toward the end of 1945, Harry explained, that he first noticed changes in the government's attitude toward the Soviets. He began to see ways in which the Cold War was being stimulated by the attitudes and policies of the American government. He noticed, for example, that promises made to the Soviet Union were not fulfilled. Harry did not buy my father's explanation that, in 1946, he quit the Communist Party over the issue of split loyalties. To Harry this sounded like my father's way of "rationalizing his actions."

When I asked about Victor Perlo, Harry said their paths had crossed occasionally over the years. "Perlo was rigid in his personality," Harry told me, "and not careful with how he used data to prove his theories." Perlo came to dinner once, Harry said, but Beadie found him rude and never invited him again. Perlo, according to Harry, remained rigid until the end. He did, however, review Harry's book *The Age of Imperialism*.[11] "He said it was good," Harry commented. "It was."

Harry denied ever having met Elizabeth Bentley or knowing anything about her. "She had me at a meeting when I was still at the Mayo Clinic recovering from gall bladder surgery," he told me. He said he'd read her book, *Out of Bondage*, which he thought was "terrible."

I asked Harry what he thought about the possibility that people he knew had given information to the Russians.

"Like who?" he wanted to know.

"Like Ed Fitzgerald, for example, and Allan Rosenberg."

"Ed? Not Ed," Harry said. "Ed was a very—how should I say—soft, gentle man. He was not high enough to have information of value. Alger Hiss, yes or no, would have had important stuff. Not Ed." Harry was sure the same was true for Allan Rosenberg, whom he knew from the neighborhood.

"Is it possible that people gave information but didn't know where it was going?" I asked. "Might they have thought the information was going only to the Party?"

"Yes," Harry answered. "[John] Abt seems to imply that in his book, true or not, I don't know.[12]

"This question of spying is a difficult thing," Harry said, reminding me that the Soviets did represent the workers' fatherland and that it was important to remember them in terms of the war against Hitler. "In thinking about those who joined the Party and stayed," Harry explained, "one must consider the campaign against fascism. Those who did give information and did not take money for it did so because they were ideologically committed [to the anti-fascism campaign]. The Russians would have asked for as much information as they could get." From Harry's vantage point, historians did "not have independent judgment.

"I know I have been accused of spying," Harry added, cryptically. "Certainly I was very open about my views."

A moment of silence passed. I couldn't bring myself to tell Harry that in my research I'd come upon an entry claiming that FBI agents had followed Harry and Beadie into a movie theater in Manhattan one afternoon in the late 1940s. The movie was *The House on 92nd Street,* a film about Nazi spies. In one scene, a spy unfolds a postage stamp that contains a secret message written on the back. According to the report, the bug caught Beadie asking Harry if this was the kind of thing *he* did.[13]

Once again we were interrupted by Beadie's urgent call for Harry. Again, he went to her bedside, tried to reassure and comfort her. This time, it was time for me to go.

I left Harry's apartment with a mixture of emotions. I was moved and saddened to be witness to the end of the Magdoffs' long and loving life together. I was struck by Harry's sincerity and willingness to talk; he looked me straight in the eye, never hesitated in his responses, and even chose to use the word "spy" when I had chosen other words in asking my questions. Yet my awe was entangled with a feeling of intimidation, and when all was said and done, I ended up with as many questions as I had at the start. I had few, if any, conclusions, only more nuance to contribute to my story.

In a 1998 *Monthly Review* article called "A Note on the *Communist Manifesto*," Harry Magdoff refers to a passage in that document that predicted the global spread of capitalism. The trend described in the *Manifesto* 150 years ago, Harry writes, had been borne out, and with it the tendency of globalization in our times to "widen the gap between a handful of rich nations and the rest of the world. . . . Thus, at the end of centuries of capitalist expansion, here is how things stand: 60 percent of the world's population has 5.3 percent of the world output and income, while more than 83 percent . . . is in the hands of the richest 20 percent."[14]

Harry Magdoff devoted his life to the struggle for social change, change made necessary by the "incredibly uneven . . . distribution of the productive forces from region to region. On the one hand, the miracles of electronics; on the other hand . . . over a billion people . . . [without] access to safe water."[15]

His is still a hard message to ignore.

18

The FBI

Ostensibly a matter of ensuring the loyalty of federal employees, the Communists-in-government issue, as it emerged during the Roosevelt administration, was in reality a partisan stratagem by the New Deal's conservative opponents. They used charges that there were reds in Washington to bolster their allegations that FDR was "hand in glove with the Communist Party."

—Ellen Schrecker, *Many Are the Crimes: McCarthyism in America*

Some have claimed that the McCarthy Era might better have been named after J. Edgar Hoover, the megalomaniac director of the Federal Bureau of Investigation, who played a dominant role in the anti-Communist crusade from its earliest years.[1] Hoover's mandate, to investigate and suppress subversive activities on the part of members of the Communist Party and others on the Left, was enhanced in the 1930s as a consequence of President Roosevelt's animosity toward the people who opposed his foreign policy; the war years saw that mandate strengthened further.[2] It was in the name of national security, for example, that in May 1940 the president overrode the 1937 Supreme Court decision to outlaw wiretapping. The president allowed the FBI to use electronic surveillance of persons suspected of subversive activities against the United States. With each passing year, Hoover felt more and more empowered to expand the business of the FBI, with or without authorization.

The FBI and the intelligence branch of the government were mistrustful of the loyalty of Communists during the war. Militant left-wing unions were among the anti-Left establishment's primary targets.[3] Even more significant in the anti-Communist campaign was the all-out effort to rid the federal government of Communist and other left-wing employees. To "prove" disloyalty, the FBI and HUAC gathered evidence of membership in, or affiliation with, so-called front groups, organizations whose goals were sympathetic to those of the Party.[4]

Hoover, intent on expanding his empire, set out to make and keep the FBI the primary agency in the campaign against subversives in government, often to the exclusion of other agencies involved. Propagating the idea that those who associated with left-wing groups or causes were as dangerous as Communists, he recommended also removing "fellow travelers" from their government posts.[5] In an effort to substantiate the claim that belonging to a particular left-wing organization indicated disloyalty, the FBI added groups to a list of organizations already deemed subversive. Much has been written about the successes and particularly the excesses of J. Edgar Hoover; historians have reported on the often damaging, frequently inaccurate, and distorted reports written by FBI agents over the years. My mother's and father's FBI files from the 1940s list the so-called front organizations to which they belonged. The files also include reports of allegations from anonymous informants.

In early 2001, I set out to find the two FBI agents who interviewed my parents.

THE BOYS: "BOB AND RAY"

I was in the FBI reading room studying the files relating to Nathan Gregory Silvermaster and his associates (known as the Silvermaster Files) when I discovered an organization of former FBI agents. I called the organization and was pleased to find Bob Putnam and Fred Griffith both still alive and on the list of members. These were the two agents who interviewed my parents beginning in 1954 and then, after my father's decision to testify, in 1955 and '56.

The receptionist for the organization agreed to call the two former agents and ask permission for me to contact them. Bob Putnam never responded, but the next day, my son took a message from Fred Griffith, now in his mid-seventies and living in retirement in North Carolina. He said he would be happy to speak with me.

"I remember you, Peggy," Fred Griffith said, "as a bubbly thirteen-year-old. I'm glad to hear from you; I have such fond memories of your parents." To me this phone call, forty-five years after the fact, seemed surreal, a gigantic step back to another world.

Fred explained that in 1954 he had been new to the FBI's Washington Field Office and to his partnership with Bob Putnam. He had come from working in Boston in "domestic intelligence matters"; the bureau had needed him in Washington because of his experience. "We interviewed your parents three or four times a week for nine months," Fred told me.

I asked Fred to talk about what he remembered of those times; he spoke openly, with warmth and clarity. He described my parents as he had known them, a couple who, in the 1930s, had joined the "many people who wanted to right the ills of the world, wide-eyed idealists," but who had later come to have "difficulty with the Party."

"Before they broke," Fred said, "they knew they were being used by people in the Party. They put two and two together."

I asked Fred what he meant by "being used."

"Your parents became uncomfortable with the shifts in the Party line," he explained. "They had been committed in the beginning, ideologically, but changed.

"Herbert was complex and simple at the same time," Fred said. "He had a great sense of humor, loved teaching law. He was very upright, very honest. It was painful for him to talk about his friends. We gave him hundreds of names.[6] I can still remember his pain; it was agonizing for me sometimes. It's not surprising to me that you say he kept a journal; he was organized and fastidious.

"Do you remember that dining room table in your house, with the two leaves?" Fred asked. "I was just telling my wife that your father gave me the plans for that table; he and Arthur Stein made it. I still have those plans.

"I'll always be grateful to your mother," Fred added. "She helped us out of a crisis by finding help for one of our children who was having difficulties at that time."

I asked Fred whether he had found my mother more resistant than my father to talking with the FBI. "No, not at all," Fred answered emphatically. "Your parents were not ideologically convinced, neither of them.

"Frances was the more pragmatic of the two," he told me. "She could really dredge back." Once, he remembered, she commented on the fact that almost all of the people they discussed were Jewish. "The Jewish people were the ones trying to make things right in the world," Fred told me. "The Party took advantage of them. It used them."

I asked Fred if he knew what had happened to any of the people my parents named, besides Gerald Matchett, who, I'd read, had lost his job as a result of my father's HUAC testimony. Fred told me he knew of one woman, named by my parents as a former member of the Party, who had attempted to take her life, afraid to acknowledge her past membership to her disapproving husband. Fred didn't remember her name or any details of her situation. I shudder thinking about this now—I haven't found a way to deal with it. How many more may have suffered?

"Do you think," I asked, "that my father was protecting my mother from testifying because she had things to hide?"

"No. Your mother had a genuine dislike for HUAC. She did not want to testify before that 'horrible' committee."

I asked Fred what he recalled about Garfield Bromley Oxnam, the Methodist bishop and member of the American University Board of Trustees who was critical of HUAC but refused to support my father in his campaign to keep his position at the A.U. law school. "The press had him like a Ping-Pong ball," Fred said, "back and forth with his position."

"What did you know," I asked, "about my parents' friends and acquaintances who were identified in the Venona cables as having given information to the Russians?" Fred said he remembered hearing their names but that he knew nothing of the work of the FBI's "Soviet Section": nothing about the investigations of Americans accused of spying for the Soviets, nothing about the Silvermaster and Perlo groups. "That hadn't come up on my watch," he said. "I am just now reading [about them]." It surprised me that the different units of the FBI had not shared information with each other on this subject.

Fred characterized his relationship with my parents as "unlike anyone would expect working for the bureau."

"How so?" I asked.

"You didn't develop friendships, weren't supposed to get involved with the people you interviewed. We got involved with Frances and Herbert and with what they went through. We won their confidence. They leveled with us; they gave us what they had."[7]

I hadn't known at the time of the extent and depth of the affection that had developed between my parents and the two young agents.[8] My father made frequent references in his journal to "Bob and Ray" (after comedians Bob Elliott and Ray Goulding) or "the boys," as he affectionately called them. Though my parents considered talking to the FBI far more acceptable than speaking with the HUAC investigators, my folks' relationship with Bob and Fred was unusual and I wondered what made it work. Certainly they found the two young men to be well educated and respectful in contrast to the crass and bumbling HUAC staff. Was their close relationship an example of identifying with the aggressor? I suspect it was more complicated than that.

Even though he had boxed himself into a corner and was forced to testify or risk contempt of Congress and a possible jail sentence, my father was still eager to talk about his own past activities in a movement he no longer could support. Dad became convinced that cooperating with the FBI was, under the circumstances, the best thing to do. Bob Putnam and Fred Griffith had the right combination of personality, skill, and intelligence to win his trust.

Who Was Gibby Needleman?

In April 2000, I received my mother's 138-page FBI file. It made reference to her under twenty-three versions of her name.[9] I had been hopeful that her file might help to answer some of the questions that still hung over my search; it did not.

My mother's file included reports of her connection with organizations considered subversive; a 1942 FBI investigation under the Hatch Act, in which my mother denied membership in the Party; endless pages, many with blacked-out names, of FBI interviews held in 1954 and 1955; and a report of my father's HUAC hearing and the publicity that followed. The file contained a statement, submitted and signed by my mother in 1955, in which she denies ever having been engaged in "espionage or sabotage" and denies knowing of anyone engaged in such activities. The file indicated that my mother and father furnished names of individuals known to them or believed by them to have been members of the Communist Party in Washington and Denver.[10] My parents chose to have their own names concealed in FBI reports written about others. They opted not to testify concerning any information they provided to the FBI.

The focus of the interviews in my mother's file was on identifying people as Communist Party members, not as spies. There were only a couple of brief references to her friendship or business association with people accused of providing privileged information to the Soviets, such as Irving Kaplan and George Silverman.[11] In the record, my mother did not discuss individuals or activities relating to the three months she spent at the War Production Board; there was no evidence of anyone asking her about that. There was one reference to a 1947 FBI memo, the only one in which my mother was implicated: "A Bureau Memorandum dated 8/29/47 indicated that Frances Rice suspected of Soviet espionage activities, was a contact and associate of [BLANK]. Rice was also a known contact of Irving Kaplan, reported CP member who allegedly turned over to those active in Soviet Intelligence operations confidential information which he had obtained through his employment with the War Production Board."[12]

One particular reference, at the very end of my mother's FBI file, caught my attention. This entry referred to a memo from the New York office, "date unknown," which mentioned my mother's relationship with one Gibby Needleman (pronounced "Jibby"), a name I'd never heard before. Apparently, "it was noted" that my mother had had a "personal affair" with Gibby Needleman before she married my father in 1937.[13]

So who was this man with the wonderful name Gibby? Maybe he was still alive; maybe I could find him.

My first clue as to the identity of Gibby Needleman popped up in a book by Robert J. Lamphere, the FBI special counterintelligence agent in charge of the investigation of Soviet espionage in the United States. This clue led me behind the scenes into the cloak-and-dagger world of the FBI. In 1948, Bob Lamphere laid a trap to capture two suspected Soviet spies, Judith Coplon, a clerk at the Justice Department, and her accomplice Valentin Gubitchev. As Lamphere describes in his memoir, *The FBI-KGB War,* he decided to bait a hook for the couple by creating a fake memo that Coplon would be sure to see:

> I prepared a memo that contained enough truth to make it seem important and enough false information to make it imperative for Coplon to grab it and quickly deliver it to [Gubitchev]. The memo was supposed to go from Hoover to a division of the Department of Justice, and would carry a security classification; the subject was the Amtorg Trading Corporation [a legal Soviet trade organization that served also as a cover for Soviet espionage]....
> It summarized some of what we knew about Amtorg and contained the completely false statement that we had placed an informant inside Amtorg and expected that he would soon prove a valuable source for us.[14]

When Lamphere wrote his second memo, he named Amtorg employee Isidore Gibby Needleman as the FBI informant. While the entrapment of Coplon and Gubitchev succeeded after a dramatic subway chase,[15] Gibby would never rid himself of the taint of his fictional association with the FBI, much to his dismay.

According to the FBI, Needleman was born in November 1902 in Kamenst-Podolsk, Russia, and educated at Cornell University and St. John's University law school. He became a United States citizen in 1926 and served as a legal representative of the Amtorg Trading Corporation for a number of years.[16]

Amtorg, located in New York City, did millions of dollars of business. Because it was a legitimate trading institution, it provided a legal way for the Soviets to stay on top of American industrial development and a convenient cover for personnel involved in Soviet espionage operations. A large number of Amtorg employees were members of the American Communist Party, Needleman among them.[17] Lamphere writes, "The wry nature of the Coplon affair was finally symbolized for me by the matter of Isidore Gibby Needleman. In spite of repeated insistence at the [Coplon] trials that Needleman was not and had never been an FBI informant, a cloud hung over him, at least as far as the KGB was concerned. Evidently the KGB could not decide whether I had lied about him or had told the truth, and determined not to leave any doubt about the matter—Needleman was fired from his Amtorg post."[18]

I learned little more of substance about my mother's relationship with Gibby Needleman, but I did discover, from the FBI Silvermaster file, that he had been close to some of her friends. He had, in fact, shared an apartment on West 93rd Street in Manhattan with his wife and Irving Kaplan in December 1946. The FBI surveillance indicated that Harry Magdoff and others suspected of spying made frequent trips to New York and visited the apartment there.[19]

Harry Magdoff confirmed that he had known Gibby Needleman, whom he'd met through their mutual close friend Irving Kaplan. Once Harry had moved to New York, he and Gibby became good friends.

According to Harry, Gibby had been and remained an attorney for the Party until the very end. Harry told me he spoke at Gibby's funeral in the late 1980s. Gibby's son David Needleman had been there, and the grandkids. "Someone from the Party spoke at the funeral," Harry told me, "but said nothing really important."

I mentioned to Harry that Gibby and my mother had been close, early on. "Gibby was a feisty, virile, and courageous person," Harry said. "I can see Frances and Gibby together. That makes sense to me now."[20]

I returned to my mother's FBI file and the reference to her "personal affair" with Gibby Needleman.

"Although it has not been possible to directly question her concerning this activity," the memo read, "it was to be noted she had admitted going with Needleman." I read on and was amused to see my mother's description of her relationship with this man. In a manner that to me captured her often clever, and at the same time dismissive, manner, my mother told the FBI, "I went with him in the way that others with my background and emotional experience tended to go with people of the opposite sex at that time."[21] This comment, I thought, was quintessential Frances!

THE PARDON

After five years out of the limelight, my father reconnected with Bob and Fred in the fall of 1962. Dad told the two agents he was getting older and was concerned about having enough money to support himself in his retirement.[22] He told them he was considering making an appeal to President John F. Kennedy for the restoration of annuity benefits denied him under Public Law 769 (the Hiss Act)[23] because of false statements he had made about past membership in the Communist Party. My father was successful and well liked in his new Judiciary Committee job; his six-month appointment had already stretched to six years. He was confident that Representatives Emanuel Celler, chairman of the Judiciary Committee, and Francis Walter, HUAC chair, would lend their support to his appeal. My father's colleagues on the Anti-Trust Subcommittee staff urged him to act right away, while the two influential congressmen were still in office. Optimism about the appeal was fueled by a new law, a recently passed amendment to the Hiss Act, Public Law 87–299.[24] This new law would allow the president, through an official pardon, to restore benefits in all Hiss Act cases except for those that constituted a threat to the security of the nation.

On September 10, 1962, my father submitted a petition for a presidential pardon, stating that he felt entitled to the annuity retirement because, since 1946, he had "shown himself to be a patriotic citizen," a "law abiding citizen," and "even while a member of the Communist Party had never personally advocated the overthrow of the U.S. government." He promised "further obedience to the country and loyalty to the Constitution of the United States."[25]

In conjunction with his application for clemency, my father made it known how "appreciative" he was of the possibility of having his rights restored. According to the FBI report, he mentioned at that time that he had just experienced "the greatest thrill" of his life when, on March 8, he had "witnessed the commissioning of his son as an ensign in the U.S. Navy at Newport, Rhode Island." He told the FBI agents it was difficult for him to understand how this commission could have occurred while the authorities knew of his own "past history." To him, this was "a wonderful example" of the benefits of "the right to live in a democracy. . ."[26]

On March 7, 1963, J. Edgar Hoover directed the Washington Field Office to conduct an investigation to determine my father's eligibility for a presidential pardon.[27] Criminal checks were conducted on all of the family, Civil Service Commission files reviewed,[28] neighbors interviewed, and employers and colleagues consulted. At that time I was a senior at Colby College. The FBI consulted police and credit records in Waterville and Augusta, Maine. My brother's records in Newport were checked as were those of my parents and my father's two brothers. The report of the investigation reflected contrasting impressions. While a number of my parents' neighbors admitted having "mental reservations" about my father's loyalty, based on his Communist history, all of his employers and colleagues expressed their belief in him as a man of the highest moral character whose extraordinary abilities, unquestioned loyalty, and hard work made him deserving of every consideration.

FBI agents visited five homes in my parents' immediate neighborhood in the spring of 1963. Due to the widespread publicity surrounding my father's case in 1955, all of these neighbors knew the basic facts of my father's HUAC testimony. Disapproving of his participation in the Communist Party and the fact that he had lied about it, some expressed displeasure that a person with such a background would end up with a responsible position in government; this just didn't make sense to them. "[T]oo many people who have taken liberty with their Constitution are being coddled," one neighbor said, "rather than being shut out and deported." All agreed, however, that my parents, whom some characterized as "aloof," had been "good neighbors." After all was said and done, several neighbors suggested that perhaps my father had "suffered enough" and should be forgiven for his past transgressions and allowed to "prove his love for his country." One of them suggested "'that the applicant having sold his soul once will most likely never be in a position to do so again,' [and] therefore should be given another chance to prove himself."[29]

Meanwhile, on the Hill, my father's professional colleagues all expressed their eagerness to provide support to his pardon bid. Calling him "a gifted writer, a dedicated worker, and one of the most important members" of his staff, Congressman Emanuel Celler told the FBI, "They are very fond of Fuchs on the Committee. . . . [H]is work . . . has been exceptionally good. . . . [H]e is very forthright and very kind." Celler claimed to have "no questions whatsoever concerning the applicant's character, associates, reputation and loyalty." Referring to Dad's bid for renewal of his retirement rights, Celler stated "it would be unfair because of his excellent work that he not be entitled to retirement benefits." The congressman said he had "joined with other members of the Committee to recommend to the President of the United States that Fuchs be afforded his rights in order to reap the harvests of his work for the Committee."[30]

Congressman Francis Walter told the FBI that he, too, had written a letter of recommendation on behalf of my father. Like Celler, Representative Walter stated that he had "no question" regarding Dad's loyalty, character, and reputation. Walter said he was positive that my father "did not retain any sympathy toward any subversive organization" and that he was "an honorable man." Others followed suit: Walter's administrative assistant, Congressman Edwin Willis,[31] Congressman William Tuck, and colleagues on the staff of the Judiciary Committee; all voiced their opinion that the facts justified giving executive clemency to my father. One colleague asserted that she believed my father had "suffered more than enough for what he has done, and that to cause further suffering would be an injustice."[32]

Finally, my mother's supervisor, Betty Rieg, director of special education in Prince George's County, Maryland, weighed in, stating that she knew my parents to be "excellent people." She said she was "100 percent sure" of my father's "loyalty to the government of the United States."[33]

On November 8, 1963, President John F. Kennedy granted a full and unconditional pardon to my father. Just two weeks later, on November 22, President Kennedy was gunned down as he drove in his motorcade through the streets of Dallas. Over the years, members of my family of origin, my own family, and my brother's family have all been the recipients of benefits that this pension made possible.

IV

RECKONING

19

Naming Names

They named the names because they thought nobody would remember, but it turned out to be the one thing that nobody can forget.
—Victor Navasky, *Naming Names*

The worst times for me, in this long journey, have been the occasions when I was confronted with the undeniable fact that my father named names. At these times, the reality of this tragic event has overwhelmed me and I've released my shame in a flood of tears. This has been worse for me than learning my parents were Communists, worse than fearing they might be without work or might go to jail, worse than being shunned in the neighborhood. I internalized my father's guilt and grief, and, to some extent, I continue to struggle with these feelings even to this day.

In the very beginning, when my father first explained his difficult situation and the reasons he decided to act as he did, I completely accepted his explanations. He had always been my moral guide and his soul-wrenching candor and sincerity left me with no doubt that he was on the side of right, even when he decided to testify fully before HUAC.

It was not until later that summer, in 1955, several weeks after his decision to cooperate fully, that the deeper implications of his ultimate actions took hold. I was on an outing with our friend Fran Lichtenberg and a bunch of kids. Fran stopped her car in front of a shop; she left us there while she ran a quick errand. Who knows how the subject came up; I can't remember. All I know is that in response to a question, I acknowledged that my father had testified before HUAC. Fran's niece, then in her early twenties, told me she knew all about it. She told me, with disdain, that my father had been weak, he had been unable to withstand the pressure of the contemptible House committee, he had been "broken." She was telling me something I could not ignore, something terrible. Forty years would pass before I allowed myself to think or talk about the humiliation I felt that afternoon.

As I began writing this book, I was regularly reminded of the shame and grief surrounding my father's decision to talk. When I first read his journal, I came upon an entry written in late September 1955, in which he tried to take stock of the events that followed his original appearance before HUAC; he tried to make sense of the nightmare months that followed. I was moved by the anguish he expressed over the possibility that his actions had harmed others, his rage at the university for firing him, and his fear that he might become isolated "from the society of my fellows."[1] I was deeply affected by his determination to rise above the crisis through the love of family and a few close friends. One night I decided to read the journal entry to a couple of friends, hoping to find some relief from the pain my father's words had elicited in me, but I failed to anticipate their reaction. Left-leaning academics, they were clear and emphatic in their assessment that my father had sold out, that his actions were self-serving. He should have known, they said, that his only choice was to take the Fifth. That night, once more overcome with shame, I couldn't sleep. Michael told me he thought their response was "too cynical." At the same time, he was unable to muster sympathy for my distress. Why, he wondered, had I read this to them? Why hadn't I anticipated their response and protected myself?

That same month, it happened again. I was at our synagogue and ran into a colleague of Michael's, a psychoanalyst. He asked me about my book and told me his father had also been a leftie, not a Communist but a "fellow traveler." He told me he remembered his father explaining to him that during the McCarthy Era there had been the "good guys" and the "bad," those who talked and those who did not. His next words cut straight to my heart. "But, you know," he said, "even the Nazi doctors were human beings." Nazi doctors! I cringed at the analogy. Later, alone, I wept.

I've often asked myself, what if things had been different? What if, for example, my father had chosen a different attorney to represent him? I thought about this when I read Evan Thomas's biography of Edward Bennett Williams, Dad's attorney during the time of his troubles. Williams was a famous trial lawyer, known for his ability to get the job done, the man to see for legal assistance, particularly if you needed to get off the blacklist. I was fascinated by this biography, full of the drama of that period. But the more I read, the angrier I became. It galled me to learn that during the McCarthy years, Williams not only represented actors, producers, and screenwriters brought as witnesses before HUAC, but he also assisted Senator Joseph McCarthy, first in a couple of libel suits and later in the 1954 McCarthy censure hearings.[2] Thomas acknowledges that "[b]ecause of his close ties with McCarthy, Williams seemed to be serving two masters, the congressional witch-hunters as well as his clients, in a way that was financially rewarding to him."[3] This was a man for whom the term *conflict of interest* had no meaning.

I do not know to what extent my parents were aware of this conflict of interest. More to the point, I do not know if they knew that *all* of Williams's HUAC clients had named names. One, Martin Berkeley, a screenwriter, actually set the record for the number of people named, between 150 and 162, depending on who was reporting.[4]

Knowing that my father wished *not* to name names, should Ed Williams have declined to take him on, since naming names was the only action Williams ever really counseled?[5] Might my father have been more successful by consulting a different attorney—Joseph Rauh, perhaps? Rauh managed to beat the Committee at its own game in the cases of Lillian Hellman and Arthur Miller. Or he could have chosen Sidney Cohn, who believed that a man should neither have to take the Fifth nor inform. Cohn was successful in making use of what he called a "diminished Fifth," in which a witness denied current membership in the Communist Party but took the Fifth otherwise.

When I think about Williams in relation to my father's case, I feel disappointment and resentment. Realizing that he had a major influence on how the events unfolded, I wonder if he was of any help at all. I wonder if, instead, Williams's indifference to the conflict of interest in his own practice may have contributed to my father's downfall. Perhaps this is unfair. Perhaps, when all was said and done, Dad's need to talk was the overriding reason for his actions; after all, he did say his decisions were his own.[6] In any case, my father never forgave himself for what he did, and I, in turn, carried his guilt for years.

Working through these painful emotions has been a major goal for me, a guiding incentive in the writing process. The desire to confront my shame, to understand it and then let it go, led me to Victor Navasky's definitive book on informing, *Naming Names*. Navasky suggests that the act of informing, for most people, ranks among the basest of human acts, perhaps even alongside of "lying, theft, murder, incest and treason." "The very fact that an informer knows he has betrayed—even if only symbolically—depresses him."[7]

Whittaker Chambers, in his book *Witness,* dramatizes this perception that to be an informer is to perform a despicable act:

> To be an informer . . .
>
> Men shrink from that word and what it stands for as from something lurking and poisonous. Spy is a different breed of word. Espionage is a function of war whether it be waged between nations, classes or parties. Like the soldier, the spy stakes his freedom or his life on the chances of action. Like the soldier, his acts are largely impersonal. He seldom knows whom he cripples or kills. Spy as an epithet is a convention of morale; the enemy's spy is always monstrous; our spy is daring and brave. It must be so since all camps use spies and must while war lasts.
>
> The informer is different, particularly the ex-Communist informer. He risks little. He sits in security and uses his special knowledge to destroy others. He has that special information to give because he knows those others' faces, voices and lives, because he once lived within their confidence, in a shared faith, trusted by them as one of themselves, accepting their friendship, feeling their pleasures and griefs, sitting in their houses, eating at their tables, accepting their kindness, knowing their wives and children. If he had not done these things, he would have no use as an informer.
>
> Because he has that use the police must protect him. He is their creature. When they whistle he fetches a soiled bone of information. . . . He has surrendered his choice. To that extent, though he be free in every other way, the informer is a slave. He is no longer a man. He is free only to the degree in which he understands what he is doing and why he must do it.[8]

It is Navasky's belief that most of the people who named names before the investigating committees knew that what they were doing was wrong; they "shared the revulsion with which our country, our culture, and the entire Judeo-Christian tradition view the informer and the presumption against playing the 'squealer,' the 'fink,' the 'stoolie.'"[9]

I found Navasky's book extremely interesting and helpful. In it, Navasky explores the moral issues involved in the McCarthy Era investigations, what he calls this "episode in collaboration and betrayal American-style." He asks how it came to pass "that scores of otherwise decent individuals were compelled to betray a moral presumption"—the presumption against informing—and whether there were ever extenuating circumstances. He explores the lasting effects of these

deeds, including the "moral outrage and indignation" that has "survived in sur-
rogates who will outlive the original participants." He wonders whether there is
or should be "a statute of limitations on moral crimes."[10]

Navasky's greatest contribution may have been to borrow from 1950s socio-
logical research on social deviance, particularly the work of sociologist Kai Erikson. Using Erikson's research as a base, Navasky suggests that, rather than forums
through which to gather information for legislation, the House and Senate hearings were really rituals, "Degradation Ceremonies" that stigmatized witnesses by
denouncing them as deviants, thereby rendering them unemployable in order to
"neutralize the harmful effects" of their misconduct by blacklisting them.[11]

Kai Erikson's studies of the symptoms of trauma experienced by disaster victims has informed Navasky's understanding and mine of the trauma symptoms
experienced by those blacklisted during the McCarthy Era. Navasky writes, "according to Kai Erikson, first there is numbness of spirit, rage, anxiety, depression,
apathy, insomnia . . . a heightened apprehension about the environment . . . the
very symptoms exhibited by the blacklistees . . . a growing conviction, even, that
the world is no longer a safe place to be."[12]

During his year on the blacklist, my father suffered many of the symptoms
identified by Erikson. The words he left behind in his journal, words like "despair" and "ruin," and the description of his loneliness and isolation certainly reveal his state of mind. His words disclose feelings of extreme loss, exacerbated of
course by equally intense feelings of guilt. "It is more than four months since the
House Committee investigator telephoned me at the Law School, and came to see
me. . . . The intervening time has been a nightmare. . . . I see that I fluctuate between extremes of feeling—between manic optimism and whole despair ('ruin').
As to my first decision to respond fully to the C's [Committee's] demands on me,
too, I have frequent soul searing anguish for people who . . . are to suffer as I do
for . . . idealistic nonconformance."[13]

My father's loss was threefold: loss of employment for having been a Communist, loss of a sense of his own integrity for having betrayed former friends, and
loss of his social milieu as he was ostracized by the far Left for having cooperated
with an "amoral" government body and by the Right for having been a Communist. Few outside of family and close friends were witness to my father's feeling of
defeat. But I see it reflected in the words of Judiciary Committee chairman Manny
Celler, who, in his statement of support for my father's bid for a presidential pardon, told the FBI that "at first Fuchs was diffident . . . he never spoke before being addressed."[14] That sense of defeat was best described by my friend Jim Lich-

tenberg, who remembered that "after the troubles, Herbert seemed to fade like a flower. He just seemed to fade away."[15]

I've come to understand that my own teenage depression, my chronic anxiety, and my dependency on relationships and food were rooted, at least in part, in my own traumatic reaction to the events of this period and my internalization of my father's suffering. Seeing me cry myself to sleep night after night in my tenth-grade year, my mother sent me to a therapist. I didn't stay long as I was unable to speak in those sessions; I sat mute. Now it seems to me only natural that I would be hesitant to speak about my pain when I had been told, only a year or so before, never to "discuss this with anyone." Then, too, hadn't I learned, after the fallout from my father's decision to talk, that it was dangerous to speak out?

What if my father had decided to take the Fifth Amendment? I know he grew to question his decision not to do so,[16] but, in the end, would invoking the Fifth have been the right action for him? Would it have made him feel any better about himself? How would this have made our lives different? My persistent questions led me to review what my father had to say about his decisions at the time and in retrospect, and to wrestle with the moral implications of his actions. Not in order to judge but to understand and, ultimately, to let the matter go.

Toward this end, I began to explore how people confront and resolve the dilemmas of everyday living—how they make tough choices, particularly those decisions that challenge one's basic core values, those that pit right against right.[17]

My review of the facts in my father's case indicates that his decision process, following his departure from the Communist Party and ending with his full disclosure before HUAC, took place during three distinct periods in his crisis:

In the first, 1946, my father had become disillusioned with the Party as a result of a change in the Party line. He was unhappy with what he now considered the Party's manipulation of its members, and had become convinced that he must choose between loyalty to the Party and loyalty to the United States. "In 1946 the world situation had so shifted," he explained ten years later in a letter to Dean Henry P. Brandis Jr., of the Association of American Law Schools, "that continued membership in the Party, with its Soviet connections, seemed inconsistent with loyalty to the United States, and I dropped out. . . . My disillusionment with and falling away from the Party left me a political nullity, with no wish but to live down and forget the past." My father quit the Party in distress. He regretted that he had ever made the decision to join a movement that required its members to conduct their business in secret and to lie about their membership.[18] In his mind, it would have been wrong, at this stage, to reveal his own past participation in the Party and to identify those whom he knew to have been Party members; nobody had asked him to do so and he was sure no harm had come to the nation as a result of his and others' participation in the movement. He was sure that the others, like himself, had seen the error of their ways.

Writing about this period a decade later, in that letter to Dean Brandis, my father said,

> I have been criticized for my silence from 1946 when I dropped out of the Party until 1955 and particularly in 1949, when I came to the University. My break with the movement in which I had spent twelve years was not a painless one, nor was it attended by immediate and total revulsion against my friends who remained in it. They were known to me to be persons like myself, conscientiously motivated by principles in which they thought they believed. As time passed, I consoled myself with the thought and hope that they, too, had put Communism behind them. I desired to excuse neither myself nor them.
>
> My sole present concern about the period of my protracted silence is that I failed to make greater effort to find myself politically, but I believe that had I done so I should still have refrained from volunteering information about my former friends. I confess that I had to be coerced.[19]

Even by his own reckoning, my father was not struggling morally at this time.

The next period encompassed the time in mid-1955 after my father had been approached by the FBI and called to testify before HUAC but before the testimony itself. He had been told that the authorities already knew he had once belonged to the Communist Party. My father decided, at this point, to reveal (confess) his own past in the Communist movement, which he was now convinced was under the direction and control of the Soviet Union.[20] Reflecting on this second stage, Dad later wrote,

> In retrospect, I deplore the Communist Party and my past party membership for both political and moral reasons. Politically, the Party now seems to me always to have been largely an instrument of Soviet foreign policy, though this was not clear to me when I was in it. On the moral side, I regret that I was gullible enough to become part of a semi-secret movement and

to lie about my party membership adopting the communist thesis of ends justifying means. It seems to me that secrecy begets deception and that deception tends to lead to worse offenses. I deny that people may be lied to for their own good, and I reject the substitution of party "discipline" for individual moral responsibility.[21]

My father would refrain from taking the Fifth Amendment. To take the Fifth, he thought, would give the appearance that he had something to hide, and that he was interested in protecting the Communist Party. In his words, "to plead immunity is to lend support to 'organized defiance' and to appear to espouse a cause I had long abandoned."[22] He would also refuse to speak about others; that was out of the question.

This decision was difficult; it was what he called his "first real crucial decision."[23] But I don't see that it presented a moral conflict for him. At the time, he was convinced it was morally right for him to speak about himself; he believed it was right for him to refrain from taking the Fifth; and he knew it was right to refuse to speak about others.

Finally, the third period of the process began after he had testified in executive session, speaking openly about his own Communist activities. Committee members demanded that he testify about others he had known as Communists or risk contempt of Congress; they refused to accept his insistence that his conscience would not allow him to do this. "The Committee declined to respect my reluctance. Lawfully constituted authority was making lawful demands on me. Although I feared that no salutary public purpose was to be served by yielding, I could not rationalize a privilege on my part to defy the law."[24] Though he had desperately hoped it would be successful, my father now realized that his strategy of agreeing to testify about himself but holding out on naming names had failed completely; he later concluded it was naive of him to think he could pull it off.[25] Because he had spoken freely about himself, the immunity option was no longer available to him. What remained was a decision to cooperate fully with the Committee and name names, or refuse to do so and face the prospect of contempt and a prison sentence. This was the most difficult moral dilemma of his lifetime.

Of course, the Left would look at this dilemma surrounding his testimony as a right versus wrong choice. Though they might agree that my father was basically, in Rushworth Kidder's words, "morally fit," meaning that he agonized over his decisions, engaged in "reflective dialogue," and truly cared about the outcome,[26] they would surely conclude that his "ethics muscle" was not strong enough. He should have been true to his conviction, they would certainly say, that to betray old friends was wrong, period. But, to end my exploration with that conclusion, I believe, would be to leave out aspects of my father's personality and experience that add to an understanding of why he did what he did, when he did it.

My father, by this time in his life, had adopted a rigid adherence to telling the truth and obeying the law. This truth telling was already part of his nature, but it was intensified, I believe, by his disillusionment with the Party after the war. Dad had been burned by the Party's deceptions: its endorsement of lying in the service of an agenda that had strayed from its earlier position, and its manipulation of its members to serve in ways that were beyond their original commitment.[27] He was upset when he learned that people he knew had been accused of passing information to the Soviets.

Dad was so let down by this breach, this betrayal, and so upset by his own past participation in practices he now disparaged, that he became almost obsessed with the truth. He believed that trust is essential to sustaining positive and productive human relationships.

I knew my father as a scrupulously honest man, whether filling out an insurance claim or completing an income tax form. He never lied about anything, in my memory, and he imposed his meticulous standards on me. For example, when away from home, some of my friends would telephone their parents to let them know they had arrived safely at their destination. To save money in that pre–cell phone era, these friends would call home "person-to-person" and ask for a phony individual, a name agreed upon with parents ahead of time. This was a way to signal their parents without having to pay the charges. My father would not permit me to do this; he would not allow me to cheat the phone company. Recognizing the depth of his commitment to truth, I decided to explore the question of whether or not my father's decision to talk was one that pit the obligation to tell the truth against loyalty to others. For my father, it was right to tell the truth about his Communist experience, particularly if the Party and its connection to the Soviet Union now posed a threat to the nation; it was right to obey the law of "constituted democratic authority," even if one objected to its methods of inquiry;[28] it was right to use the Fifth Amendment in the way it was meant to be used, in other words, when one was actually at risk of incriminating himself;[29] it was right to reject the practice of lying and the belief that the ends justify the means. The dilemma for him was that *it was also right to refuse to inform.*

Victor Navasky has challenged the principal justifications for naming names.

First, he asks, "Did those who defended their naming names really believe in what they did or is it all after-the-fact rationalization?" His answer: since most informers talked only when the Committee pressured them to do so, "we (and in some cases, they) can never know whether they acted from noble or ignoble motives."[30]

Navasky considers citing a "commitment to 'truth'" inadequate as a defense. In his view, there is no justification for using one's disillusionment and defection from the Party, and one's need to speak the truth about it, as reasons to cooperate with the Committee: "[W]here the higher loyalty is asserted to be an ideological imperative and/or a commitment to 'truth,' the defense seems inadequate not only because so many of the name-namers told less than the whole truth, and because they waited so many years to tell it, but because as many of these people will now freely concede, the congressional committees were obviously an inappropriate forum for the realization of such high ideas."[31]

It seems obvious to me that my father's dilemma about naming names can also be seen as one in which loyalty to family and to current life commitments is pitted against loyalty to former affiliations. I know my father looked at the dilemma in this way. Did he not owe it to his family to stay out of jail? Why should he be a "hero" for something in which he no longer believed? Referring to these considerations when explaining his actions, he quoted from a law school colleague who wrote him urging him to cooperate with the Committee: "Do it for your own sake," the colleague wrote, "the sake of your family, and for the school. . . . You simply *must* come all the way home." My father explained his response: "The University had already come to my defense before I agreed to talk about others. The pressure exerted by Dr. Anderson . . . to 'go all the way' I interpreted partly as a request to render the University's defense of me more palatable to its public and partly as a demand by my present associates . . . that I choose between them and my past."[32]

By the time Dad was faced with this decision, there were several new considerations concerning the needs of his immediate family. First, there was the issue of my mother's being called to testify, particularly in light of my father's experience. Although I'm sure it's true, as Fred Griffith pointed out, that my mother resisted testifying before HUAC because she hated the Committee, it was also the case that she would have been vulnerable—perhaps more vulnerable than my father—in testifying before it. It was she, after all, who had been professionally connected with Edward Fitzgerald and Irving Kaplan, both of whom were believed by the government to have been Soviet agents. My father could honestly say he knew them only socially, not as Communists; my mother would have had to take the Fifth or admit to having had a professional relationship with each of these two men. If both my parents had gone before the Committee and both of them had refused to testify, and if the Committee had followed through with its threat of finding them in contempt of Congress, my parents would have lost two jobs, would have been blacklisted, and, if sent to jail, would have been forced to find homes for my brother and me with friends; we had no extended family nearby.

I know other families experienced such extreme conditions, and worse. This is my attempt to understand, not excuse, my own parents' actions.

Though Victor Navasky has some sympathy for the suffering of those confronted with a decision that pits loyalty to family or other personal commitments against loyalty to principle, he rejects the idea that this represents an ethical justification for informing: "Where the 'higher loyalty' is asserted to be family support or other personal commitments, one must concede that conflict and pain may have accompanied the choice (although to do so is not, of course, to endorse the ethics of the decision)."[33]

Navasky and the Left believe the name-namers had no justification for informing. They take exception to the notion that ex-Communists were justified in naming names because the Communist Party was rigid and oppressive, and because the Communists were misguided or wrong in their continued allegiance to the repressive Stalinist regime. "There was myopia on all sides," Navasky concedes, "but one's victim's inability to distinguish right from wrong is not justification for one's own misdeeds."

Furthermore, Navasky insists, "such justifications ignore the political effect of naming names—of confirming who was and who was not active in left-wing politics, of creating a climate of concern and fear. The effect was to create an exact parallel of McCarthyism: namely, the purging of the cultural apparatus, an exercise in political purification."[34]

Navasky is convinced that, when all is said and done, the chief and overriding rationale for naming names was to save oneself from losing one's job—a pragmatic motive, with no moral, ethical, or political reason for doing so. He drives home his point, dramatically: "Both resisters and informers claim they were acting according to their lights. The difference may be that the former were true to their mistaken convictions, whereas the latter were untrue to their correct ones—they knew better than to condone Stalinism but they also knew better than to cooperate with McCarthyism."[35]

All of this having been said, one thing remains a certainty. For my father, this

painful dilemma was intense and unrelenting. The following excerpt from his letter to Dean Henry Brandis reflects his confusion, after his testimony, about his
moral conflict:

> The decision I made was my own. I can only hope that the injury I caused
> possibly innocent people will not, in the end, outweigh the "service to my
> country" of which members of the House Un-American Activities Com-
> mittee speak. It would be comforting to know with certainty either that
> American communism is so great a menace to our institutions that all for-
> mer Communists ought to be exposed to public censure or, on the other
> hand, that the American communist movement of the 30s and 40s was so
> largely a loyal, if obstreperous opposition that only an unprincipled person
> would inform on his then Communist friends. I do not have the comfort of
> certainty. I am in doubt.[36]

20

Remembering Them

Dad loved to be the center of attention. He was the kind of guy who charmed dinner company with limericks, puns, recitations. At those times, he was winsome and funny and had an irresistible warmth and joie de vivre.

I like to remember my father focused on one of his many pleasures. Perhaps he's playing the banjo mandolin: "Peg-o-My Heart," "Margie," "Bésame Mucho." Or maybe he's reciting Walt Whitman; he loved showing off his cache of crazy poems. This one he recited in rapid-fire fashion: "Once there was an old woman went into the garden to get some cabbage to make an apple pie. Just then a great she-bear comes up and pops his head into the shop. 'What, no soap!' So he died, and she married the barber, and there was present at the wedding the Jicaninies and the Picaninies, and the Grand Panjandrum himself, with a little round button at the top, and they all fell to playing the game of catch as catch can, till the gun powder ran out of the heels of their boots."

Perhaps, wearing his hallmark red baseball cap, he's lost in a blissful reverie while dancing with his toddler granddaughter, Ilana, at our summerhouse in Maine. Or maybe he's entertaining friends at a party, donning goofy hats or "performing" the alphabet by shaping the letters with his arms and legs. Out in the world, my father was serious, even shy and retiring. At times he was depressed, particularly during the period I've been writing about; then you couldn't reach him—he'd be hidden behind a book or a magazine or simply lost in his own private thoughts. But as the center of attention, with close friends, especially after a drink or two, he was witty and engaging.

"Your father always seemed to me to be whimsical, amusing," my friend Devin told me when I called to speak to him about the book. "Hardly the passionate ideologue."[1]

"I remember Herbert as a very cool man," Jim Lichtenberg told me. "When we were little, he seemed happy-go-lucky, seemed to have, as we say in baseball, soft hands: no matter how hard the ball was, he could catch it. I remember him as

My father with my daughter, Ilana, August 1982.

carefree. Much to my parents' horror, we would ride on the running board of his 1940 Plymouth.

"Our mothers would fight like cats," Jim reminded me. "*My* father would try to say something and my mother would accuse him of disloyalty. *Your* father would stay out of these fights, following his own gyroscope—didn't seem to be at the mercy of his emotions like the others."[2]

Dad was particularly fond of children, and I think he found Peter and me fun and amusing. Photos show him with us when we were little, enjoying a neighborhood picnic in the Lichtenbergs' backyard, wading with us in a river in Estes Park in Colorado, relaxing on a rock at Whiteface Mountain in the Adirondacks. He was never involved with our routine care, and was really inept at providing it when it was necessary for him to do so. (Once, he treated an infection on my arm by applying a boiling-hot washcloth to the affected area, exacerbating the problem by causing a second-degree burn!) But it was Dad who played with us. It was he who set up the American Flyer trains in the basement, who built and flew model planes with us, who took us on hikes or read books or sang songs to us at night before we went to sleep. Often he told us stories, some of his own invention. These are happy memories.

In one favorite story, a little girl named Peggy sets out to become a puppy: "'A white scotty [sic] would be nicest,' she thought, 'with short ears and a red tongue and a yippy bark. . . . For next to being a mother, Peggy would like best to be a puppy.'" In this story, told to us one chapter at a time at bedtime, Peggy takes care of her "sick children," her dolls "Mary, Mary Jane, and Mary Ann," before practicing being a puppy by "yipping and wagging" her imaginary tail. Finally, she falls asleep and a little brown man appears, "just one foot tall," who challenges her methods of transforming herself. After playing a tune on his harmonica (Dad transcribes the notes of the tune into the story), the little man declares, "'Nuts and scallions! Just stop trying to wag your almost tail. It won't do any good. If you really want to turn into a scotty pup, you must bring me two clothespins, one acorn, and a dab of peanut butter the size of a half dollar.'" The next night, Peggy dreams she is in a play at school and is reciting "Twinkle, Twinkle, Little Star," only the words come out

> "Tinkle, tinkle, samovar,
> Life preserver motor car,
> Hot potato, oyster fry,
> Orange juice and apple pie."

"Oh dear," she says to herself in the dream, "that doesn't make any sense. It really goes:

> Winkle, pinkle, ha, ha, ha,
> Daddy smokes a big cigar.

Daddy, won't you tell me why?
The little brown man is one foot high?"

The little brown man appears and tells her in verse: "I'm one foot high because you see / It's the very best size in the world for me." He then gathers the supplies she has collected and, "With the acorn for a head and parts of the clothespins for body and legs and a tiny tail, the little brown man carved, and stuck together with peanut butter, a likeness of a very small Scottish terrier . . . just the right size dog for the man."

Each night, Dad would tell us another chapter of the story of the little brown man. Unfortunately, he never finished telling his tale and only a small section was transcribed.[3] But I still remember how delighted we were with his storytelling; through it he conveyed to us his gentleness and love.

My father and mother were intellectual partners, companions, and friends. They liked reading together, going to the movies, and going to dinner in other people's homes. After my brother's and my college tuitions were paid off, my parents allowed themselves to enjoy some of the perks their improved financial status offered. They bought the house in Stonington, Maine, and began to spend summer vacations there. They traveled abroad—to Scandinavia, the Caribbean, and Europe. I was with them on some of these trips and cherish memories of them swimming at Sand Beach in Stonington, dancing together on the balcony of their room at the Grand Hotel in Stockholm, and "jumping up" at Carnivale in Trinidad.

While my father could be childlike and endearing (losing himself in a puzzle or a game while he shut out the mundane things of life), at times he could be childish, petulant, self-centered, and dependent, insisting on having his own way. Nowhere did this manifest itself more than in his relationship with my mother at the end of their life together. As they grew older, my father's Parkinson's rendered him less and less mentally able. My mother became increasingly frustrated with his absent-mindedness, and a discordant dynamic between them intensified. Mom felt the need to have a hand in everything, and if she couldn't, her anxiety and her need to bully surfaced and usually led to conflict. Feeling incompetent to perform the simplest everyday task, Dad would let her take charge. Then, feeling victimized, he would become resentful and would reproach her bitterly.

Unfortunately, in 1984, the year Daniel was born, my parents were abruptly separated when my mother suffered a stroke after open-heart surgery and was no longer able to look after my father at home. Dad went, against his will, to live at the Hebrew Home of Greater Washington. When he was placed in the Hebrew Home my father felt betrayed once again, this time by his mind that had deserted him and by his family who could not take care of him.

Now, as I write, I choose to remember my elderly father in happier times, before my parents were separated by illness and infirmity, when he was still able to enjoy himself through play even though he was losing his sharp mind to senility. I see him vacationing in Maine, deeply contented, walking, painting, and lopping bushes on Herbert's Hill in front of our house.

At the time of Dad's death in May of 1988, our dear friend and former Maine neighbor Bud Estey wrote a eulogy in the form of a "letter to Herbert." In his letter, Bud captured the essence of Dad in those happier days. Bud wrote, "We shall no longer be in our house and you will no longer be in yours. But we know we shall see you, red hat, and walking stick, striding along Route 15 halfway between Deer Isle and Stonington, and we'll wave to each other and you'll refuse a ride because you like to walk and we'll go on our way and you'll go yours. But we shall all of us always be neighbors."

The years immediately following my father's death were difficult for all of us. My mother, whose health continued to deteriorate, had moved into a retirement home in Bethesda and then, ultimately, into the Hebrew Home in Rockville. Though we visited as often as we could and she made every effort to adjust to her new life, my mother was lonely and depressed, having been cut off from the active life she'd loved. Though I knew how unhappy and frustrated she was, I was surprised that my mother sought—and I believe received—comfort from several clergymen who visited the home and from books that dealt with the meaning of life, what she called her "whither books."

Sunday, April 21, 1996. Though not unexpected, Peter's call to me at my home in Ann Arbor came as a shock. "They're giving her less than forty-eight hours," he told me. "She's not eating and she's very weak."

After watching my mother's slow, painful mental and physical decline for so long, I could only feel relief that she was dying. We had been grieving for years as my mother suffered one frightening and debilitating stroke after another, as she lost her keen mind and her physical strength and mobility. I already missed her terribly. Soon, she would be lifted out of her lifeless nursing-home existence and Peter would be spared, finally, the endless burden of seeing to her remaining business details—taxes, hospital bills, the occasional greeting cards—all that was left of my parents' long and active lives. Peter had tended to these tasks with grace and without complaint for twelve years, ever since our parents first became too ill to care for themselves at home.

I booked a morning flight.

It had been only a week since I'd last gone to see my mother at the Hebrew Home. At that time, she had lain motionless, her eyelids closed, her shallow breath labored, a frail reminder of her former self. She could not speak.

I boarded the familiar Northwest flight to Dulles, dreading what I would find when I arrived, worrying about the children I'd left behind. Had I given enough instructions for the care of the kids? I wondered. They would need help with home-work and rides to ballet and soccer. Gritting my teeth, I drove my rented Chevy Cavalier along the airport access road, north on the I-495 Beltway, and up Route 291 to Rockville and the Hebrew Home of Greater Washington. Hang in there, I told myself firmly. You can do this.

Finally, I arrived at the home's newly renovated Wasserman building. Anx-iously, I walked past the withered elderly people sitting in the lobby, their vacuous expressions calling from me the same dread and guilt that always accompanied my visits there. If only I could have eased the pain and boredom of my mother's last years, I thought. If only there had been a better ending.

I walked down the long hall past the paintings by artist Chaim Gross to the ele-vator that would take me, one last time, to my mother on the fourth floor. Nausea, anticipation, relief. What would life be like without her?

In her room, I found Peter resting in the armchair next to my mother's bed, sitting in silence but for the monotonous hum of the oxygen machine. We sat to-gether during the long afternoon, reading and speaking only occasionally. I found comfort in his presence, in his quiet strength. Later, we grabbed a bite at T.G.I. Fri-day's a block away. While Peter went home to get a few hours' sleep, I stayed with my mother through the night, dozing, stretched out on two chairs facing one an-other, a sheet and pillow provided by a nurse.

My mother died on the morning of April 23, 1996. She was eighty-nine years old and, except for the unfortunate infirmity of her last twelve years, she had few regrets. My mother had had a privileged childhood. She had become an accom-plished student and later a committed left-wing government economist. She had been a faithful wife and, though she considered herself poorly equipped for parenthood, a devoted mother and grandmother. But perhaps the thing that ultimately gave her life the most meaning was her twenty-year career as a pioneer special educator in the Prince George's County, Maryland, school system, a career she chose after earning a master's degree in human development in the late 1950s.

It was with the help of two friends, colleagues from Prince George's County, that we arranged a memorial service for her at the Frances Rice Fuchs Special Center, a school named in recognition of my mother's years of service on behalf of handicapped children in the county. Since she had been ill and disabled for so many years, we expected few people to attend.

Peter, his family, and I arrived at the 1950s-style, single-floor elementary school to be greeted warmly by the school principal, the daughter of my mother's former colleague. Touring the school, we walked past walls decorated with colorful cards and paper flowers created by Fuchs Center students who took the time to honor my mother, a woman whom they had never met. My mother's picture hangs in the front hall; a plaque bears her name. One by one, friends and colleagues entered the building and walked past our reception line at the door to the assembly room. More than seventy-five people arrived bearing cards and flowers to pay their respects to my mother and her family. Finally, the time came to begin. Marilyn Colborn, a gifted educator and my mother's loyal friend, delivered a stunning testimonial that set the tone for the afternoon:

> We are all drawn together here today to mourn, to laugh, to tell stories, and bear our personal witness to the life of Frances Fuchs, whom we honor this day. We come from many different places in her life, and from many different times. Yet we are bound together in a shared remembrance of a personal force of character that was brilliant, and passionate, and stubborn, and sweet and far beyond the ordinary.
>
> Frances lived the life of a woman who did it all. Born in a generation and time when most women were doing a full job at home, she had a husband, kids, a house, and an outside job. She was a steamroller intellectual whose credentials were there in gold—a Mount Holyoke graduate, a law degree, a master's degree, and a resume reflecting a highly eclectic array of professional positions.
>
> At the age of 50, when many folks are preparing for that slide into a sub-tropical retirement community, Frances came to work for the Prince George's County School System as assistant supervisor of special education.

She was the chosen one, picked out almost 40 years ago by the visionary special education supervisor, Betty Rieg, to join her in the task of building what became the second largest special education program in the U.S. Two very powerful and very different energies came together to forge what could arguably be called the finest, most innovative and forward thinking system of services for special needs children of its time. It was a national model, visited by people from all over the world, and it rests with honor in the annals of the history of special education.

Frances's management style was in the mode of Lao Tzu, the great Chinese philosopher and founder of Taoism who lived some 600 years before Christ. Lao Tzu, in describing the good leader, said, "A leader is best when people barely know that he exists, not so good when people obey and acclaim him, worst when they despise him. Fail to honor people, they fail to honor you. But of a good leader, who talks little, when his work is done, his aim fulfilled, they will all say, 'We did this ourselves.'"

Well, we all know Frances liked to talk a lot, but she also liked to listen a lot. Fascinated with new ideas, she was a sharp questioner and an avid participant in the forum of the mind. She honored our need to explore and create, while watching and checking us out with the fierce eye of a lion mother. She'd cuff us with her sharp tongue when she thought we needed it, and to earn her respect and regard called upon our always giving our personal best.

As time went by, her pace was slowed by painful knees, but she still exuded this incredible energy and intensity. During the endless rounds of often stultifying meetings, she'd waste not a minute. In her lap, or poking out of a bag would be knitting and the needles would fly as her fingers kept time with the tempo of her thoughts. And when, at 70, she had to retire from the school system, she simply changed jobs, heading off to Catholic University to take on the instruction of the newest generation of budding special education teachers.

Her steel will and indomitable spirit shone through to the last breath of her life. Lying comatose in her nursing home bed, hooked up to an oxygen tank feeding the failing body, through the closing veil she heard her daughter Peggy say that the beloved granddaughters, Peter's [daughters], were flying the red-eye in from Seattle, Washington on Tuesday morning. At 10 a.m., the girls arrived from the airport to her room. Frances knew they were there, faintly acknowledging each girl with her eyes, holding their image for a scant two or three minutes. They had come, and now she could go. There was nothing else to wait for. Her great heart stopped and Frances Fuchs stepped back into eternity . . .

I have little doubt that Frances is here today. She wouldn't want to miss her memorial service. In the East, and in indigenous societies globally, it has been a part of the belief system that we move gradually from our physical death to the next life, just as we move gradually from conception to birth. In Tibet, for many days, the deceased is read to from the Tibetan Book of the Dead, helping him or her to move through the transition.

For Frances, we can tell our stories of her impact on our lives as she moves through her transition. We can share with her and with each other the moments that crystallize in memory, that make us laugh or sigh, or smile with joy. Let us, together, close our eyes, and for the next minute or two, go to our quiet place within and touch that spot where Frances rests. Let us see her surrounded in a golden light, radiant with a divine light that fills our whole mind, and let us be at peace with her there. And then, let us begin to share.[4]

This extraordinary tribute triggered in me a torrent of tears expressing the full force of my grief and pride. Many others wept quietly. One by one, my mother's colleagues rose to remember her—superintendents, teachers, friends. Eagerly, they recalled vivid and usually outrageous incidents that captured the essence of her feisty and daunting personality.

One eloquent, seasoned school administrator recalled interviewing for a job with my mother. Though he had no experience teaching, he had been eager, very enthusiastic, and ready to learn. They spoke for a while and the young man shared with my mother his meager experience and lofty aspirations. When finally the interview came to a close, my mother shook his hand. "You're male," she said. "You're black . . . you're hired!"

Next, another longtime veteran of the schools stood up to speak. Remembering *his* first meeting with Frances, he recalled her secretary ushering him into her office. There he found my mother speaking on the phone to her insurance carrier; it seems that she'd had a fender bender on the way to work. "Go outside," my mother ordered the young candidate. "Look at my car and tell me which bumper I dented." Wanting to make a good impression, the young man left the room and went outside to survey the damage, only to realize, when he reached the parking lot, he didn't know which car belonged to her. She'd failed to mention this important detail, and he had failed to ask!

People spoke of my mother's dedication to the improvement of life for students with special needs; her ability to work within the system while fearlessly opposing the administration when it stood in the way of her staff's goals; her uncanny ability to hire staff with vision, talent, and creativity (though frequently lacking in experience); and her ability to form fiercely loyal personal relationships. All spoke of my mother's deep and lasting influence on their lives and careers. I had not realized the extent of her impact on the lives of so many people.[5]

Finally, her friend and colleague Harriet Lebow, who knew her well personally as well as professionally, rose to speak. "Frances was passionate about the work she loved," she said. "She was competent and committed. But I know how deeply she also cared about her children and grandchildren. Frances spoke constantly about her family, with pride and adoration; she savored the latest events and accomplishments in their busy lives. But it wasn't always easy to be the child of such an energetic, forceful woman. It wasn't easy to walk in her shadow."

I was grateful for Harriet's sensitivity. She was right; it hadn't been easy. But my mother *was* awesome, and she *did* love her job *and* her family.

21

Healing

Old Friends/New Family

[W]ith each additional book I read about the Cold War, I find myself increasingly sympathetic to your father as a tragic but heroic figure. He is like the artist whose work is not appreciated in his own lifetime. He endured the scorn, excoriation and isolation of former colleagues, some of whom were guilty of betraying their own nation in the name of a truly heinous ideology, communism. The righteous indignation of many leftists who failed utterly in the intervening years to condemn the Soviet Union and the socialism that never had a human face, continues to make heroes and martyrs of those who betrayed the nation and villains of men like my uncle who ripped illusion from his eyes and was blinded in the process. Yet he saw communism more clearly than many.

—E-mail communication to me from my cousin Dana Willens, September 4, 2002[1]

"Drive down Geddes Road again, Mom," my son, Daniel, urged, as chunks of ice from frozen branches tapped the roof of our Toyota Camry, creating a serenade of castanets. "I love that sound," Dan said.

It was March 14, 1997, the day after Michigan's second-worst ice storm in history. We were lucky, that late Friday morning, that the frozen streets had begun to thaw and, though ice-encrusted branches crashed to the ground as we passed, major roads were now passable, allowing us to complete our preparations for the celebration that would mark Dan's rite of passage, his Bar Mitzvah. We would be able to deliver flowers to the hotel rooms we'd reserved for our cousins from out of town. Only a few hours earlier, it had been impossible to walk from our house to the garage without slipping; the pavement was a glaze of ice. Now, our car sloshed slowly through monotone darkness, still dodging branches and downed power lines as we carried out our last-minute business. While I shared Dan's excitement and wonderment that his special weekend was beginning with this dramatic act of nature, I worried about the safety and comfort of our traveling guests and wondered how long our neighborhood would be without heat and electricity. Fortunately, the Ann Arbor Crowne Plaza Hotel had not lost power; our Saturday evening dinner-dance would take place as planned and our guests would have a warm place to sleep. We were grateful.

Healing, in this writing adventure, has come in many forms. Usually it has appeared in conversations with people I knew in the traumatic years of my family's troubles, people whom I've now been able to talk with, openly, about my experiences and the feelings that accompanied them. Some such conversations stand out:

There were my talks in the summer and fall of 1996 with Phyllis Fahrney Raynor, whom I hadn't seen in thirty-six years. Phyllis and I had grown up together as neighbors and playmates on 49th Street in Washington. Her family of origin had shunned mine when my father's story appeared on the front pages of the *Post* and the *Star*.[2] In the ensuing years, Phyllis had traveled widely in conjunction with her husband's career as a diplomat, and as a result of her new appreciation for the complexity of the McCarthy Era, she had come to regret her family's rejection of us in the 1950s.[3]

"I've thought about you and your family many times over the years," Phyllis told me in 1996. "I don't feel guilty for the actions of my family at that time; they had limited understanding of the complexity of the situation. But I do want to tell you how sorry I am for the hurt my family caused you."[4] Phyllis and I have renewed our friendship over the past several years on a deeper, more intimate level.

There were the E-mail messages in June of 1997 from my childhood friend Devin Bent. "No one remembers talking to you about your problems with the crisis," Devin wrote. "In a way that is not too surprising. I suspect that all those conversations you had with people (certainly with me) were about their problems. You were everyone's friend and listened to their troubles—no???"

"Perhaps you're right," I replied. "They couldn't know if I didn't tell them."

"The thing that I was trying to do in my last message," Devin wrote back, "was to apologize. I am genuinely sorry that I could understand so much, [the political, social, legal, ethical aspects of all this] but still not as Bill Clinton says 'feel your pain.' I am very sorry about that—I was not a good friend to you when you needed me the most."[5] Devin's words moved me to tears at that time; they still do.

There was the comforting E-mail from my childhood playmate Jim Lichtenberg, lambasting his cousin for insisting that my father had been "broken" by HUAC. Her comments, Jim suggested protectively, had been "totally inappropriate."[6] Jim showed me he was aware of how utterly unprepared I had been to deal with her words. I felt he really cared.

And then there was Harry Magdoff's welcoming hug on my visit to his home in 1998, nostalgia and familiarity from my earliest years.

But none of these encounters has had the healing power or the symbolism of that cold, dark, wonderful weekend in March 1997, when newly united cousins gathered to celebrate the passage of our extended family's youngest member, my son Dan, from childhood to manhood. Images from that magical weekend light my memory.

Cousin Richard Fuchs and his partner, Joseph Malench, are the first guests to arrive at our home Friday evening. They have come from Florida and are more than mindful of the forbidding, yet awe-inspiring, dark gray icy scene that welcomes them to Ann Arbor. Frozen limbs bow deeply across our street, forming a crystal arch. Fallen branches lie scattered across lawns and driveways. Richard brightens the scene with his humor.

Michael, Ilana, Dan, and I walk the several blocks to the Beth Israel Synagogue to attend Friday night Shabbat services. Because of the weather, few people are there. Services that evening are held under a single row of lights at the rear of the sanctuary, powered by a small generator. Rabbi Rob Dobrusin, his two-year-old daughter on his lap, leads the small group in prayer and song, the dim light adding to the peace and serenity of this small, intimate gathering. I am overcome with tenderness and love for Michael and the children.

Dinner is at the home of our close friends Barbara and Barry Nemon. Family members from out of town arrive exhausted and chilled, looking as if they wish they hadn't come, but the atmosphere soon changes to one of celebration as they join us and our closest friends at a beautiful table lit by candlelight. We are all warmed by the heat of the wood-burning stove and enticed by the smell of the sumptuous meal and the genial conversation. I take my cousin Dana by the hand and walk her across the room to meet my brother, Peter. Cousin meeting cousin for the first time.

That night, I enter Dan's bedroom to say good night. Dan is wearing his winter overcoat to keep warm; he's wrapped tightly under woolen blankets. "I can't believe that those people have come all this way to honor me," he says.

Saturday morning, Michael leads the congregation in the Shacharit, the tradi-tional early Sabbath morning service. His beautiful voice floats gently across the sanctuary. Outside the window, the gray-scale winter scene stands as a backdrop to the centuries-old ritual taking place inside. Dan leads the Torah and Musaf services, performing his Haftorah portion and Torah reading with comfort and skill; he does himself proud. Ilana and I and several friends read from the Torah as well; it is a community affair. At the end of his D'var Torah,[7] big brown eyes ablaze with the excitement of the moment, Dan bursts into a broad smile winning the hearts of his doting family and friends, those who have known him his whole life and those who have met him only months before.

That evening we celebrate. Some of our guests, still without heat and electricity in their homes, have taken great pains to get to our party. In a candle-lighting ceremony, Dan honors the special people in his life. Among those important but missing are his four grandparents, all deceased.

We dance to the beat of the DJ—"YMCA," "It's a Family Affair," "The Maca-rena." Dan and his handsome, sophisticated thirteen-year-old friends mix with our older guests on the dance floor. I speak with Dana's son, Scott, who tells me how much our meeting has meant to his mother. "My mother lost three of her fa-vorite cousins in a hurricane when she was only ten," Scott explains. "And now you've come along to fill the void."

I wish my father had had healing experiences in his life. To the best of my knowl-edge, in spite of years of therapy and a brief relationship with a spiritual adviser, and in spite of many happy family occasions in his later life, I believe he did not.

I am sure that my father was aware of people who advocated understanding and compassion as a way of calling a halt to the decades of shame that followed the McCarthy Era. I'm sure he was familiar, for example, with Hollywood screenwriter Dalton Trumbo's "only victims" speech, given at the 1970 Screenwriters Guild ceremony at which he received the prestigious Laurel Award. Trumbo stunned his audience with these now-famous words:

> I presume that over half of our members have no memory of that blacklist because they were children when it began, or not yet born. To them I would say only this: that the blacklist was a time of evil, and that no one on either side who survived it came through untouched by evil. Caught in a situation that had passed beyond the control of mere individuals, each person reacted as his nature, his needs, his convictions, and his particular circumstances

compelled him to. There was bad faith and good, honesty and dishonesty, courage and cowardice, selflessness and opportunism, wisdom and stupidity, good and bad on both sides; and almost every individual involved, no matter where he stood, combined some or all of these antithetical qualities in his own person, in his own acts.

When you who are in your forties or younger look back with curiosity on that dark time, as I think occasionally you should, it will do no good to search for villains or heroes or saints or devils because there were none; there were only victims. Some suffered less than others, some grew and some diminished, but in the final tally we were all victims because almost without exception each of us felt compelled to say things he did not want to say, to do things he did not want to do, to deliver and receive wounds he truly did not want to exchange. That is why none of us—right, left, or center—emerged from that long nightmare without sin.[8]

I know my father was familiar with the philosophy of eminent theologian Reinhold Niebuhr,[9] who believed that sacrificial and forgiving love is the ultimate expression of man's relationship to man. Dad knew about others, like Whittaker Chambers and John Strachey, who believed that our only hope lies "in the rediscovery of spiritual values, the power of redemptive love, the reaffirmation of personal connections and loyalties."[10]

But, unfortunately, neither the eloquent appeal of Dalton Trumbo nor the compassion of Reinhold Niebuhr and other well-known anti-Communists seems to have had a healing influence on my father's regret over having named names. Perhaps if he had been more open with his family and friends about his lingering sorrow, it might have been possible for him to resolve his inner conflicts and forgive himself. Or perhaps, if my father had had an opportunity to speak with one or more of the people he'd named, he could have expressed his remorse and might have received, in return, some human understanding.

When I imagine a healing experience for my father, I remember reading a story told by psychology professor M. Brewster Smith. In March 1953, Smith was called before the Senate Internal Security Subcommittee to testify about his former student membership in the Young Communist League. The professor, who had given the matter a great deal of thought previous to his testimony, was certain he "did not want to be a hero" nor did he "want to be a fink." He decided to "name only the names of open Party members . . . and forget about anybody else who was involved." In the end, Professor Smith was "led into naming one or two additional names," including that of his former wife. Unable to maintain "the posture" that he had originally intended, Professor Smith went away feeling nauseous. "I remember going up to my room in the old Willard Hotel," Smith told interviewer Griffin Fariello, "and retching, as though I was the lowest form of life. It was a miserable feeling."

Smith's testimony was never made public; he ended up repressing the entire episode. Years later, a society of Progressive psychologists asked him to speak at a meeting and comment about McCarthyism. To prepare for his talk, Smith obtained the transcripts of his testimony. When he read them he realized why he had put the experience out of his mind. "I saw the very unheroic role that I had played."

Smith spoke openly about this experience to the psychologists. At the end of his presentation, people came up to him and expressed their appreciation for his candor. "The only ones you hear about," they said, "are the people who were heroic, went to jail or lost their jobs. . . . [A] lot of other people tried to compromise and were hurt. They've just laid low because they felt so badly." One man, who had been fired from Hunter College after taking the Fifth before the McCarran Committee, came up to Smith and expressed gratitude that he "had made a clean breast of the whole experience."[11]

After reading Smith's story, I wept. I couldn't help regretting that my father had had no relief, no forgiveness. If only he had gotten an opportunity to make a clean breast of *his* experience, perhaps he could have had some measure of peace in his later years.

To the best of my knowledge, my father never had a conversation with any of the people he named. Nor had I, except of course for Harry Magdoff, whom Dad identified as a friend, not as a Communist. But in the spring of 2003, I was surprised by an E-mail from a young man by the name of Thai Jones, who'd been given my name by Harry. Thai, as he explained, is the grandson of my parents' friends Artie and Annie Stein, who had lived in our neighborhood on MacArthur Boulevard in the 1940s. My father had identified Arthur Stein as the Party contact who had instructed him to establish a Communist group at the Wheeler Committee, and the man who became the National Labor Relations Board group's liaison with the Party's "higher authority" when Victor Perlo was no longer able to perform that function.

Thai told me he was writing a family history; he asked questions that would help him describe the man who had named his grandfather in 1955. What did my father look like, Thai wanted to know. How did he dress? Did he end up a liberal or did he go all the way to the Right? Why did he do what he did? Because my father's testimony seemed to indicate that Arthur Stein was "high up in the Party," did I think his grandfather had been a spy? Thai and I spoke for quite a while. He asked questions; we talked about the experience of writing; we wished each other luck. I was impressed by the warmth and intelligence of this young man and was intrigued by the timing of our two books: one by the family of the "namer" and the other by the family of the "named."

I took the opportunity to tell Thai that I was sorry if his family had suffered from the actions of my father. Thai didn't think so. His grandfather, he told me, was already in trouble when my father named him. I was moved by Thai's ability to respond to my amends with dignity and grace. He had not been there, of course; he was at this time only twenty-five. But he told me he appreciated what I said. And he would pass my words on to his mother.[12]

As a further step in trying to rid myself of my internalized shame and as a way of considering the ethical implications of publishing my story, I requested a private meeting with Rabbi Rob Dobrusin. Since I had not been an observant Jew from birth and my connection with Judaism has never been what it might be for someone brought up in the faith, I was a bit surprised that I had the desire to do this. But Rabbi Dobrusin is a man of character, insight, and humility, and the wisdom with which he leads our congregation has always touched and inspired me. I had the need to talk to someone I admired and respected; Rabbi Dobrusin fit that description.

I caught the rabbi at a particularly busy time—an afternoon of details in the everyday workings of the congregation. I knew of his full schedule: preparing his Saturday sermon and ministering to his congregants, those mourning the loss of family members, those with serious illnesses, others celebrating family milestones. I felt awkward interrupting his work.

As we sat down and I started to talk about the book and my reasons for seeking him out, I noticed the rabbi's attention wandering, his glance moving to folders on his desk, and I wondered if my hopes for this conversation might have been unrealistic. But as I began telling the details of my story and reviewing the moral and ethical concerns that had plagued me through the years, I saw him lean forward and focus all of his attention on what I was saying. A history buff, Rabbi Dobrusin expressed enthusiasm for my project. His thoughtful questions revealed extensive knowledge about the McCarthy Era. His eyes and his words conveyed compassion toward me and those others who suffered during those difficult times.

The rabbi led me in a discussion of the spiritual issues that my story brought to mind for both of us. We discussed my father's moral decision, acknowledging how difficult this had to have been for him. We talked about the issue of privacy. Certainly this had been of great concern for me, given that my parents (particularly my father) were very private people. Was I justified in writing about them in my story, or was this a disloyal act on my part? In the end, we agreed, I would need to examine my motivation. If my intent to speak the truth, as I have come to understand it, lacks malice, and is rather an attempt on my part to honor my parents' memory, then I should be comfortable with my actions. We discussed my desire to seek and state the truth and the importance of distinguishing right from wrong, of acknowledging mistakes. We spoke of the need to stand up for what we believe.

When it was time for me to go, I thanked the rabbi for speaking with me and made my way outside to Washtenaw Avenue. I took a deep breath and let it out slowly, noticing my shoulders relax, my pace quicken, and my mind suddenly at ease. I began the short walk home acutely aware of the lovely houses that line the side streets of our neighborhood, and the bright colored leaves hanging overhead.

There's nothing like Ann Arbor on a crisp, clear autumn afternoon.

22

Legacy of a False Promise

We who were self-blinded suffer the further pain of shame. Not shame that we joined the fight, which indeed must be renewed and renewed, as long as people are still ill-fed, ill-clothed, ill-housed, and brutally tortured. My shame is in the terms of my joining. I forfeited my most essential freedom, to think for myself. Instead of keeping my wits about me, I gave them over to others, believing big lies and rejecting truths as big as millions starving. No excuse can lighten the knowledge that I used my brain and talent in defense of Stalin.

—Hope Hale Davis, *Great Day Coming: A Memoir of the 1930s*

"The logic was impeccable," writes David S. Landes in *The Wealth and Poverty of Nations*. "[E]xperts would plan, zealots would compete in zeal, technology would tame nature, labor would make free, the benefits would accrue to all. From each according to his ability; to each according to his deserts; and eventually, to each according to his needs."[1] Such was the promise of Communism at its inception in the Soviet Union in the early twentieth century; finally, it was promised, there would be an end to poverty, oppression, and exploitation.[2] But along the way, in the translation of the revolutionary ideal into a social and political movement, "a miscarriage took place."[3] For those who admired the Soviet Union and viewed her experiment with hope and expectation for a positive future for humanity, the later realization that the promise would not be fulfilled led to a disappointment and disillusionment of immeasurable proportions. For formerly committed ex-Communists—even those like my parents, who considered themselves only a little to the left of the New Deal—the letdown was incalculable. "For many," Victor Navasky reminds us, "the . . . red subculture had served as an emotions bank, and when it went under they realized for the first time the extent to which they had invested their lives in it. Since this was a nontransferable investment that could not, as far as anyone could see, be recovered, the loss of community meant that life was irreparably diminished."[4] It meant losing "what alone makes life worth living, and falling back into the outer darkness, where there is wailing and gnashing of teeth."[5]

Communism had had a compelling appeal to my father and mother as it did for so many other American intellectuals during the Popular Front period. Perhaps because of their heightened sensitivity to the promise of change, they became converted, passionately committed, to the cause of working men and women. British political journalist Richard Crossman has characterized the impatience and single-mindedness that often accompanied the intellectual's conversion: "The intellectual in politics is always 'unbalanced,' in the estimation of his colleagues. He peers round the next corner while they keep their eyes on the road, and he risks his faith on unrealized ideas, instead of confining it prudently to humdrum loyalties. He is 'in advance' and, in this sense, an extremist. If history justifies his premonitions, well and good. But if, on the contrary, history takes the other turning, he must either march forward into the dead end, or ignominiously turn back, repudiating ideas which have become part of his personality."[6]

This description fits my parents in their early days with the Party, particularly my mother who, at that time and even in her later years, was always "in advance," at the front of the pack. Quick to learn, impatient, and opinionated, my mother would latch on to a new and compelling idea, usually a very sound one, and then, once committed, would defend it vigorously. My father, I believe, was the more thoughtful and analytical of the two; he was also more of a follower.

The Party offered my parents an answer to the world's economic upheaval. "It . . . promised the backing of a small, disciplined Party and the vast, mysterious strength of the Soviet Union. . . . [I]t gave its members the sort of superiority which allowed them a smug condescension in their dealing with the 'muddle-headed liberals' of the New Deal."[7]

It was not surprising to me that my father and mother felt moved to join the Communist Party in the 1930s,[8] but if, in fact, it was their concern for the underdog status of working people and their determination to defeat fascism that attracted them to Communism, then how was I to understand their decision to remain Communists after it became clear, in 1939, that the Party would betray its antifascist goal and pursue imperialistic ambitions of its own with brutal force and deception? I struggled to comprehend how intelligent people such as my parents could stay involved after the truth became known about the Soviet purges, show trials, and other atrocities. Clearly, they were either in denial, like other American intellectuals—liberal sympathizers as well as committed members of the Party—who continued to defend the Soviets, or they did not take seriously the truth about the Soviet Union and its goals. It was, I believe, the depth of their investment in the promise, and the risk of personal shame, loss, and anger that would result from acknowledging that their beliefs had been unfounded, that caused them to resist, with all the strength of their being, information that did not gel with their strongly held views. Passionate and certain, they just didn't believe what they heard.[9]

But after the war, my parents did begin to have serious doubts about the role played by the Soviet Union in the operation of the American Communist Party. By this point, of course, in the early days of the Cold War, Communism was becoming the single most important issue in the minds of most Americans. Among the many influences in my parents' lives that strengthened their decision to separate them-selves from the Party was the publication in 1949 of *The God That Failed,* a collec-tion of personal stories written by six famous writers who had all been members of the Party or "fellow travelers" and had all eventually broken away. This book had a profound effect on our country's understanding of Communism during the 1950s; it provided the anti-Communist movement with legitimacy and helped to make that point of view a respected political position within the American intel-lectual community.[10]

My mother gave the book to me to read when I was sixteen; she believed it would help me to become familiar with my parents' anti-Communist views. Years later, a parent myself, I could imagine the urgency with which she must have needed me to understand. At sixteen, however, I was too emotionally overwhelmed to read it; I tried countless times. I was not ready to tackle its significance.

When I was finally ready for it, *The God That Failed* was a revelation. I could see why author Arthur Koestler and his editor, Richard Crossman, had chosen for-mer Communists to tell the story of the Communist experience, for, as Koestler suggests, an ex-Communist was, no doubt, the best person to describe what be-ing a Communist was all about;[11] he was well equipped, also, to understand and appreciate the values of Western democracy. "The Devil once lived in Heaven," Koestler says, "'and those who have not met him are unlikely to recognize an an-gel when they see one.'"[12]

I'm sure my mother encouraged me to read this book because she was eager for me to get a sense of the many aspects of her life as a Communist. And so I did, as an adult, when I could handle it.

I came to understand, for example, the exhilaration that many felt when they first joined the Party: "To say that one had 'seen the light' is a poor description of the mental rapture which only the convert knows. . . . The new light seems to pour from all directions across the skull; the whole universe falls into pattern like the stray pieces of a jigsaw puzzle assembled by magic at one stroke. There is now an answer to every question, doubts and conflicts are a matter of the tortured past—a past already remote, when one had lived in dismal ignorance in the tasteless, color-less world of those who *don't know.*"[13]

I marveled at the descriptions of how some Party members accepted mind games in order to justify remaining involved once doubts had appeared,[14] and how others rationalized sharing privileged information with the Party: "a spy was a man who stole military documents or sold secrets of State to a foreign power," Koestler and his comrades told themselves, while "all he had done was to pass on some parlor-gossip to a friend."[15] Self-sacrifice, I read, was the "price of collective redemption" and "[e]very sacrifice was welcomed as a personal contribution." Along the way, I learned that loyalty to the Party grew stronger "not in spite of the dangers and sacrifices involved, but because of them."[16]

For me, *The God That Failed* elucidated much of what had seemed unbeliev-able about life in the Soviet Union during the time my parents were Communists, including the extraordinary Stalin purges and the Moscow trials.[17] This book brought to life the sad, and yet transforming, sense of disillusionment that finally rose to consciousness and caused people to leave the Communist Party, bereft.[18]

As I look back on all I have learned, I am struck by the endless betrayals that have cascaded down from the tyrannical Stalin regime, through the workings of the American Communist Party and the anti-Communist crusade, to my own family's life. As Dalton Trumbo reminded us so eloquently, no one who experi-enced the shameful days of that period in our history escaped unscathed.[19]

McCarthyism wreaked havoc on our nation.[20] Its long reach frightened liber-als as well as radicals. As historian Ellen Schrecker reminds us, "[i]t changed the lives of thousands of people at the same time that it changed the nation's political culture."[21]

The primary hardship was economic. Many who refused to testify, and even some like my father who did, lost their jobs. Dad was lucky to have found work after one year; but his good fortune came at a cost. In order to reenter the work-ing world, he swallowed his pride and accepted help from HUAC, the enemy.

The crusade devastated intellectual life throughout the country. It drastically altered all areas of our government, and by wiping out "the means through which it was possible to offer an alternative vision of the world," it narrowed the debate on American foreign policy and thereby intensified the Cold War.[22]

The personal fallout was brutal. Marriages were destroyed, careers ruined, people jailed; some were deported. Many who became social outcasts developed severe emotional difficulties. They never knew when they might be shunned by close friends, colleagues, even family. Some, feeling helpless, took their own lives. The children of these people suffered with them.

Ultimately, the crusade demolished the Left. It destroyed the Left-labor Popular Front movement "that had stimulated so much social and political change in the 1930s and 1940s." The Communist Party survived, but for all intents and purposes, the American Left vanished. This, in Schrecker's words, resulted in "a world of things that did not happen: reforms that were never implemented, books that were never published, films that were never produced. And questions that were never asked . . . a wide range of political and cultural possibilities that did not materialize . . . a lost moment of opportunity."[23]

While historians argue over the impact of Soviet-dominated Communism and the devastating effects of McCarthyism, some among them credit the liberal anti-Communist community of the 1950s, the political group with which my parents were most closely aligned, as having had the clearest, most balanced view of both. The liberal anti-Communists had been accurate, these analysts suggest, in assessing the threat to our nation posed by Communism and had been successful in developing strategies to contain it.[24] Other critics blame that same political group for not having defended civil liberties and for contributing to an atmosphere that promoted informing through its unwillingness to fight the demagoguery and intimidation of the investigating committees. In the view of many on the Left, this reluctance to actively oppose the investigating committees led to a "moral environment that routinized betrayal." Within this environment, "the informer's particular contribution," claims Victor Navasky, "was to pollute the public well, to poison social life in general, to destroy the very possibility of a community; for the informer operates on the principle of betrayal and a community survives on the principle of trust."[25]

In the final analysis, probably many would agree with Ellen Schrecker on one thing: "[W]hile McCarthyism wiped out the institutional and ideological infrastructure of the Old Left, it created a legacy of a different sort. It showed how effectively political repression could operate within a democratic society. . . . Moreover, the willingness of so many American politicians and community leaders to subscribe to that demonized view of the world and limit political debate in the name of national security set unfortunate precedents."[26] We have suffered, during the George W. Bush years, from this reality.

Historians do not agree about how much damage, if any, was done by the breach of security on the part of Communists in government, but it is clear that by the end of World War II, Soviet spying in the United States had come to an almost total standstill. Some still argue that those who had shared information were only passing gossip to a friend or merely performing their moral obligation to defend the Soviet Union against the threat of the imperialistic Western nations that wished to see its demise. Nevertheless, to most Americans, the actions of these individuals constituted disloyal behavior, a blatant betrayal of our country.

As I have said, learning that some of my parents' friends and colleagues had chosen to share privileged information with the Soviet government was a shocking discovery, particularly when it involved material on arms production and other matters relating to the military during wartime.

By 1948, my parents had at least begun to hear that their friends were accused of having been agents of the Soviet Union; during my father's National Labor Relations Board loyalty hearing, his interviewers questioned him about this. At that time, my father expressed surprise and disbelief that such actions had occurred. In late 1948, my parents read in the news about the testimony of Elizabeth Bentley and Whittaker Chambers.

Though my father and mother were associated with people who have been accused of having committed espionage—in particular Isidore Gibby Needleman, Irving Kaplan, Edward Fitzgerald, and Allan Rosenberg, I have found nothing to implicate my parents.

I believe that neither my father nor my mother personally, knowingly, provided information to the Soviets. For one thing, my parents left the War Production Board and the Board of Economic Warfare just as the espionage was beginning. For another, my father made a big point of telling the truth when he testified before HUAC. Both HUAC and the FBI considered his testimony truthful and reliable. My mother willingly provided information to the FBI, a great deal of information. Given that my parents gave many names to HUAC and the FBI, it seems unlikely they would lie about the level of their own involvement and put themselves at risk of being contradicted by another witness who could demonstrate that the facts were otherwise. And finally, there is no mention of either of my parents in Elizabeth Bentley's testimony; her book, *Out of Bondage;* the testimonies of others; or in any of the books written about Soviet espionage that would indicate that they passed information to the Soviets. There is nothing in their FBI files, beyond their associations with people accused of spying, to indicate that they too had done so.

In July of 2005, a half-century after my father's HUAC testimony and the months of family crisis that followed closely in its wake, the circle for me was closing. Now, as I contemplated what I had learned and as I reflected upon the unfulfilled promise of my parents' Communist past, I had in my hands one last untapped source of information: four executive (nonpublic) sessions of my father's HUAC testimony. These transcripts were made available to me by the National Archives after the required fifty years had passed.

The executive session testimony added few facts to the case, but it did support my belief that my father testified truthfully. Describing Party members' "uniform blanket of denial," he explained in great detail when he had begun and when and why he had continued to lie about his membership in the Communist Party. "I do not condone [the lying]," he said. "I believe [the NLRB loyalty investigation in 1948] was the last time I lied to the Government. I don't condone it at all."[27] "The time for my lying to the Government has ended."[28] "It now seems to me that my ability to continue to live my life with any degree of dignity and with any ability to hold my head up is dependent on my having persuaded this committee that I am telling the truth, and that I have a decent regard for the problems of the United States, and that I am not anti-American or pro-Russian in any degree but really the contrary."[29]

The testimony confirmed my belief that for my father, giving privileged information to the Soviets was unacceptable. While reiterating that he could not believe that any of his associates "was or ever could be a betrayer of this country . . . ," he expressed his conviction that people who had in fact betrayed this country should be "watched and that to the extent they engage in activity which is hostile to the interests of the United States, [they should be] caught, deterred and punished."[30]

When asked whether he had been surprised by the testimony of Elizabeth Bentley, my father insisted he had been shocked by her accusations against people he knew. HUAC chief clerk Thomas Beale challenged my father, asking how it could be possible, considering the "closeness of the association," for my father to have known George Silverman, Irving Kaplan, and Edward Fitzgerald yet not to have known they were engaged in espionage, not even to have known for sure that they were Communists. My father assured the Committee once more that he was speaking the truth. He told them it was not at all surprising that he had not known of his friends' espionage activities. "It seems to me," my father said, "if I were engaged in espionage activities I wouldn't be telling my friends about it."[31]

The Committee pressed my father concerning Irving Kaplan, whom my parents knew well and whom the congressmen had identified as someone who had repeatedly shared privileged information with the Soviets. My father insisted he had never known Kaplan "to do anything comparable to espionage. . . . If I now believe him guilty of it," my father said, "it is because of what I have been reading in the paper. . . . He and I were never revealed to each other in any official way as Communists. He and I never worked together as Communists. . . . He and I were not engaged in any espionage. . . . I was mortally shocked by what I read when the newsbreak first came on him even though we had been relatively close friends."[32]

My parents' political saga started as an exhilarating, passionate adventure; it ended as a nightmare. Unlike my mother, whose courage, perseverance, and tenacity guaranteed that she would ultimately survive and prevail, my father never forgave himself for having lied, for having given over his free will to the Communist Party line; he never recovered from testifying before HUAC and naming names. I believe this experience broke his spirit and changed his life—and mine. I have felt its aftermath in the anxiety and/or paranoia that have gripped me when I have seen my name in a newspaper, when I have had to go to court in connection with my work, or when faced with a difficult decision that has challenged my core values.

In some important ways my father was not a strong man. He did not have the fight in him to do what was necessary to survive the HUAC experience intact. My father's honest and trusting nature—qualities that I cherished in him—turned out to be the same qualities that ultimately led to his undoing; they constituted his fatal flaw. His integrity required him to come clean, but in trusting that he could get away with testifying only about himself, he was naive. He failed to gather adequate support for the challenge that confronted him.[33]

My father's testimony led to a series of betrayals: he was let down by his colleagues at the law school who did not defend him before the American University administration; he was dismissed by the university that promised to keep him on at the school and then fired him; he was misguided by his attorney, Edward Bennett Williams, who should have, in my view, declined to take him as a client in light of the fact that my father was intent on refusing to testify about others; he was deceived by HUAC, which promised no public hearing and no publicity. Betrayed and isolated, my father, in turn, informed on his former friends. In the process of naming names, he ultimately also betrayed himself.

The fact that my parents could not (were afraid to) tell me what was going on in their lives in the years, months, and days preceding the HUAC investigation created and defined in my young life a profound trauma. As Navasky has reminded us, "The progressive-school thinking of the era said, Don't burden the kids with things they can't handle. But the one thing a kid can't handle is not knowing."[34]

Like many other red diaper children, I was lonely and scared. I suffered from intense separation anxiety and grew up with a crippling, amorphous fear that affected my personal and professional life. I lacked the knowledge and awareness necessary to understand these deep unresolved feelings until I started to research and write this book and began to see how the trauma and the paranoia of those years replayed themselves over and over again in my adult life.

But unlike my father, who took the trauma to his grave, I have had a chance to heal through this writing process. Perhaps his struggle itself was the lesson I needed to witness. Right or wrong in his actions, my father's heroic courage was demonstrated in the unending contemplation and questioning of the moral and ethical implications of his acts. Perhaps resolution is not the point, but rather to have fought the internal battle.

When I look back at the legacy my parents left me, I do not end up consumed by the fallout from their difficult ordeal. I emerge grateful for my parents' positive presence. Frances Fuchs was a strong and courageous woman; she modeled a can-do spirit, a commitment to making a difference, a deep love for family. Herbert Fuchs was a man of boundless integrity. This was a good man, a caring man, a man who took living a decent life very much to heart.

Notes

Chapter 1

1. In 1947 a group of motion picture screenwriters and directors were called before HUAC, which was investigating Communist influence in the motion picture industry. The witnesses refused to testify about their political activities and affiliations, choosing to use the First Amendment as their defense with its protection of freedom of speech, rather than the Fifth Amendment with its potentially more reliable protection against self-incrimination. The openly hostile witnesses (who came to be known as "The Hollywood Ten") were cited for contempt of Congress. The case went before a Circuit Court of Appeals judge on June 13, 1949. The judge's decision gave HUAC the power to inquire about a witness's involvement with Communism and the power to "effect criminal punishment" for a witness's failure or refusal to answer questions.

Chapter 3

1. Edward Bennett Williams had a reputation for getting people "off the hook." Included in the long list of famous (and infamous) celebrities represented by Williams over the years are Teamster boss Jimmy Hoffa, Mafia don Frank Costello, fugitive businessman Robert Vesco, junk bond king Michael Milken, L.B.J. aide Bobby Baker, Congressman Adam Clayton Powell, and Texas governor John Connally. Also among his clients—Senator Joseph McCarthy.

2. This meeting was described in a letter from Herbert Fuchs to Professor Clark Byse, Chairman, Association of American Law Schools' Committee on Academic Freedom and Tenure, October 9, 1955, Herbert Fuchs papers.

3. Reflecting upon his experience in the Party some years later, Dad admitted to "a certain amount of intellectual arrogance" on his part and the part of other Party members. "You were always certain you were right. . . . [J]oining the Communist Party gave me a sense of superiority. By joining the Party I became a member of an elite[;] this made me think I was better than any one who was not a Communist Party member . . . Being a . . . member gave me a chance to be a leader, to be appreciated." Washington Field Office (WFO) Interview Report, July 25, 1955, Herbert Fuchs FBI File 101-1169, Federal Bureau of Investigation.

Chapter 4

1. Becky was the daughter of Wilbur Mills, the House Ways and Means Committee chairman, who some years later met with disgrace when he appeared drunk in the middle of one night in the Tidal Basin with a stripper named Fanne Foxe.

2. This subcommittee consisted of Representative Clyde Doyle—(Democrat) of California, Chairman; Representative Harold Velde—(Republican) of Illinois; and Representative Edwin E. Willis—(Democrat) of Louisiana.

3. Phyllis Fahrney Raynor, telephone conversation with the author, fall 1996.

Chapter 5

The epigraph to this chapter is taken from Griffin Fariello, *Red Scare: Memories of the American Inquisition* (New York: Norton, 1995), 25.

1. Herbert Fuchs File, American University Archives, Washington, D.C.

2. Herbert Fuchs's journal, July 10, 1955, Herbert Fuchs papers.

3. *Washington Star,* August 23, 1955, A-1/A-5; Bentley and Chambers, self-proclaimed former Communist couriers, testified repeatedly before HUAC and other investigating committees. Both pointed fingers at numerous government employees, claiming them to be members of the Communist Party and/or members of secret espionage units.

4. Memo from L. B. Nichols to Mr. Tolson, July 14, 1955, Herbert Fuchs FBI File 101-1169, Federal Bureau of Investigation.

5. My father was investigated in 1941 as possibly being in violation of the Hatch Act on the basis of his membership in the Washington Committee for Democratic Action. The Hatch Act of 1941 forbade government employment of any person with membership in any political party or organization that advocates the overthrow of our constitutional form of government. For more information on the Hatch Act, see David Caute, *The Great Fear: The Anti-Communist Purge under Truman and Eisenhower* (New York: Simon and Schuster, 1978), 267.

6. My father was investigated under the provisions of the Executive Order 9835 in 1948 because he knew people whom Elizabeth Bentley had accused of spying. Executive Order 9835, March 25, 1947, was a federal employee loyalty program created by President Truman in response to disclosures of Soviet espionage, pressure from anti-Communist Republican candidates in the 1946 elections, and pressure from the Justice Department to take seriously the Communist threat. Frequently the person accused of disloyalty under this act was unable to know the identity of his accuser and was thus unable to confront him.

7. The McCarran Act (Internal Security Act of 1950) attempted to eliminate the threat of Communism in America by requiring members of the Communist Party and "front" organizations to register with the Subversive Activities Control Board (SACB). The hope was that the resulting publicity would undermine the political effectiveness of the movement. The act gave the government the authority, in a national emergency, to detain anyone suspected of being likely to engage in espionage or sabotage.

8. Memo from the Director to Special Agent in Charge (SAC), WFO, June 17, 1955; memo from L. B. Nichols to Mr. Tolson, July 20, 1955, Herbert Fuchs FBI File 101-1169, Federal Bureau of Investigation. My father would never learn who made charges against him.

9. Memo from A. H. Belmont to L. V. Boardman, Subject: House Committee on Un-

American Activities (HCUA) Name Check Requests, October 7, 1955, Herbert Fuchs FBI File 101-1169, Federal Bureau of Investigation.

10. WFO Memo, July 19, 1955, Herbert Fuchs FBI File 101-1169, Federal Bureau of Investigation.

11. Several letters of support from students are on file in the American University archives. One such letter, which commended the university for its initial support of my father, described him as "an extremely able faculty member" (Katherine M. Greene, July 14, 1955). Another (from P. H. Mayer, LL.B., September 23, 1955) expressed pride in the university's original position of support and described my father as the law school's "most effective instructor . . . a capable and intelligent man." Herbert Fuchs File, American University Archives, Washington, D.C.

12. Herbert Fuchs's journal, July 14, 1955, Herbert Fuchs papers.

13. Jewish religious law directs mourners to observe a private grieving/consoling period, for seven days, in the home of the deceased person. This practice is called "sitting shivah."

14. Herbert Fuchs's journal, July 14, 1955, Herbert Fuchs papers; Report of the American Committee for Cultural Freedom Regarding the Case of Professor Herbert Fuchs, May 1956, Herbert Fuchs papers.

15. Herbert Fuchs's journal, July 15, 1955, Herbert Fuchs papers; Memo from A. H. Belmont to L. V. Boardman, August 19, 1955, Herbert Fuchs FBI File 101-1169.

Chapter 6

The epigraph to this chapter is taken from Victor Navasky, *Naming Names* (New York: Viking, 1980), xv–xvi.

1. WFO Security Matter-C Report, December 8, 1954, Herbert Fuchs FBI File 101-1169, Federal Bureau of Investigation. Based on evidence of past membership and associations in the Communist Party (CP) and my father's refusal to testify, the FBI recommended his name be placed on the Security Index—labeling him an enemy of the state. As a result, all previous sources of information implicating him were interviewed. Memo from SAC to Director, WFO, January 19, 1955, Herbert Fuchs FBI File 101-1169, 4, Federal Bureau of Investigation.

The Security Index was established as a result of the Communist Control Act of 1954, which stripped the CP of its rights and privileges as a legally established organization and gave the government permission to detain suspected members of the CP as well as others thought to be subversive. Later, the FBI determined that my father did not qualify for the Index according to new criteria. "No information has been developed which clearly and unmistakenly discloses the subject as a dangerous individual who would be expected to commit acts inimical to the national defense and public safety of the United States in time of emergency." Memo from SAC to Director, WFO, May 25, 1955, Herbert Fuchs FBI File 101-1169, Federal Bureau of Investigation.

2. WFO Security Matter-C Reports, April 19, 1954, and December 8, 1954, Herbert

Fuchs FBI File 101-1169, Federal Bureau of Investigation. In his famous book *Naming Names,* Victor Navasky points out that informing is considered in our culture to be one of the darkest of human behaviors. An in-depth discussion of naming names as it relates to my father's experience can be found in chapter 19.

3. WFO Security Matter-C Report, April 19, 1954, Herbert Fuchs FBI File 101-1169, Federal Bureau of Investigation.

4. Herbert Fuchs to Dean Henry P. Brandis Jr. (dean of Stanford Law School and chairman of the Association of American Law Schools), Association of American Law Schools, January 27, 1956, Herbert Fuchs papers.

5. Qtd. in Memo from L. B. Nichols to Mr. Tolson, July 14, 1955, Herbert Fuchs FBI File 101-1169, Federal Bureau of Investigation.

6. My thoughts are reconstructed from specific entries in my father's journal from 1954 and 1955, Herbert Fuchs papers.

Chapter 7

1. This entire interaction was reconstructed from my father's detailed journal entry of July 16, 1955, Herbert Fuchs papers.

2. In a letter to Dean Henry P. Brandis Jr. of the Association of American Law Schools, my father indicated that on repeated occasions while speaking with President Anderson, before and after this meeting, he denied he was an atheist, describing himself as an agnostic or theist. Fuchs to Brandis, January 27, 1956, Herbert Fuchs papers.

3. James Rorty, "The Case of Herbert Fuchs" (report prepared for the American Committee for Cultural Freedom), May 1956, Herbert Fuchs papers.

4. Herbert Fuchs's journal, July 16, 1955, Herbert Fuchs papers; L. Brent Bozell, "Special Report: The Firing of Herbert Fuchs," *National Review* 1.10 (January 25, 1956): 13; Gene Higgins, telephone conversation with the author, October 1997.

5. Herbert Fuchs's journal, July 16, 1955, Herbert Fuchs papers.

6. This act was passed by Congress on June 27, 1935, and was signed by President Roosevelt on July 5, 1935.

7. *Chicago Tribune,* July 19, 1955.

Chapter 8

1. References to my father's day-to-day activities during this period are taken from his journal, July–October 1955, Herbert Fuchs papers.

2. *New York Times,* August 16, 1955.

3. *Washington Star* and *Washington Post,* August 23, 1955; *New York Herald Tribune,* September 15, 1955. In November, Senator McCarthy made the following claim: "I have succeeded in uncovering facts which, if true, establish the existence of a currently functioning Communist cell in the NLRB. . . . My information indicates that the National Labor Relations Board is literally honeycombed with individuals identified either as mem-

bers of the Communist Party, or as having had years of constant and close association with known and/or suspected Communists and Soviet agents" (*Washington Star,* November 3, 1955; *New York Times,* November 15, 1955).

4. Herbert Fuchs's journal, September 11, 1955, Herbert Fuchs papers.

5. Ibid., September 12, 1955.

6. Herbert Fuchs to Henry P. Brandis Jr., November 28, 1956, Herbert Fuchs papers.

7. Fuchs to Brandis, January 27, 1956, Herbert Fuchs papers.

8. Dean David R. Bookstaver to Dean Henry P. Brandis Jr., June 11, 1956, Herbert Fuchs File, American University Archives, Washington, D.C.

9. Herbert Fuchs's journal, September 13, 1955, Herbert Fuchs papers; Report of the Committee on Academic Freedom and Tenure of the Association of American Law Schools, II, 2–4, September 14, 1956, Herbert Fuchs papers; Fuchs to Brandis, November 28, 1956, Herbert Fuchs papers; Bozell, "Special Report: The Firing of Herbert Fuchs"; Herbert Fuchs File, American University Archives, Washington, D.C.

10. Rorty, "The Case of Herbert Fuchs"; *Evening Star,* October 29, 1955; Herbert Fuchs's journal, September 28, 1955, Herbert Fuchs papers.

11. *Washington Post,* September 22, 1955.

12. *Washington Star, Washington Post, Washington Daily News, New York Times,* September 23, 1955.

13. *Washington Star* and *Washington Daily News,* September 23, 1955.

14. Herbert Fuchs's journal, October 3, 1955, and October 21, 1955, Herbert Fuchs papers; Rorty, "The Case of Herbert Fuchs"; *Washington Post,* April 22, 1957.

15. "Fuchs Ouster Flayed," *Washington Post,* September 22, 1955; Herbert Fuchs's journal, October 3, 1955, and October 21, 1955, Herbert Fuchs papers; "'AU Pressured into Firing Fuchs,' Red Prober Says: Oxnam Denies Charge Made by Scherer," *Washington Star,* December 14, 1955; "AU President Denies Pressure to Fire Fuchs," *Washington Star,* December 15, 1955; American Committee for Cultural Freedom press release, March 28, 1956, Herbert Fuchs papers.

16. It is clear that some of the faculty were troubled or at least ambivalent about my father's record of repeated lying "under oath and otherwise" and the moral implications of such behavior. Dean David R. Bookstaver to President Hurst Anderson, November 25, 1955, Herbert Fuchs File, American University Archives, Washington, D.C.

17. Herbert Fuchs's journal, September 20, 1955, October 11, 1955, October 15, 1955, and October 21, 1955; letters between Herbert Fuchs and Ed Mooers, September 22, 1955, and September 25, 1955, Herbert Fuchs papers.

18. Because of the risk of being charged with perjury (even for mere misstatements), many witnesses chose to take the Fifth rather than to testify even when they had nothing to hide.

19. Herbert Fuchs's journal, September 28, 1955, Herbert Fuchs papers.

20. *Yente* is a Yiddish word meaning "busybody."

21. Report of the Committee on Academic Freedom and Tenure of the Association of American Law Schools, II, 5, September 14, 1956, Herbert Fuchs papers.

22. *Washington Star,* October 30, 1955.

Chapter 9

The epigraph to this chapter is taken from Navasky, *Naming Names,* 319.

1. Herbert Fuchs's journal, September–November 1955, Herbert Fuchs papers.

2. I have changed the names of this boy and his family.

3. These were get-togethers in which people played instruments and sang folk songs.

4. According to my father's FBI file, one unidentified HUAC member became suspicious of my father: "BLANK from HUAC stated he is becoming suspicious of Fuchs and he is beginning to wonder more and more if Fuchs is not involved far more deeply than he has yet admitted, and in checking his connection with BLANK wondered if Fuchs was not a member of the BLANK espionage group. He has no information to this effect but it is his conjecture." Memo from L. B. Nichols to Mr. Tolson, December 13, 1955, Herbert Fuchs FBI File 101-11691, Federal Bureau of Investigation.

5. Herbert Fuchs's journal, December 6, 1955, Herbert Fuchs papers; Airtel from WFO to Director, et al., Subject: Communist Party USA, District Number 4, IS-C HCUA Investigations, Infiltration of Government Agencies, December 7, 1955, Herbert Fuchs FBI File 101-1169.

6. This song was written by Abel Meeropol, adoptive father of the sons of Julius and Ethel Rosenberg.

7. The Chicago subcommittee consisted of Chairman Francis Walter of Pennsylvania and members Morgan Moulder of Missouri, Edwin Willis of Louisiana, and Gordon Scherer of Ohio.

8. *Investigation of Communist Infiltration of Government—Part I,* Hearing before the Committee on Un-American Activities, HUAC Chairman Francis Walter, House of Representatives, Eighty-fourth Congress, December 13, 1955, 2955–57.

9. Ibid., 2959.

10. Ibid., 2960.

11. Ibid., 2958.

12. Ibid., 2973–74.

13. Ibid., 2980.

14. Ibid., 2988.

15. Ibid., 2992–93.

16. Ibid., 2994–3002.

17. Ibid., 3002–3, 3018.

18. In 1945, Victor Perlo was named by Elizabeth Bentley as the head of a group of government workers later to be known as the Perlo Group whose members had, just prior to and during the Second World War, provided information to the Soviets through Bentley

and her Russian agent and lover, Jacob Golos. Years later, the Venona documents, secret cables between the Soviet government and the American Communists helping its cause, would corroborate many of her claims.

19. *Investigation of Communist Infiltration of Government,* 3006.

20. Ibid., 3008–3010.

21. Ibid., 3016–17.

22. Ibid., 3017–18. In his July 8, 1955, signed statement to the FBI, my father made the following additional comments: "It now appears that I was mistaken. Like others I was told and believed that the objectives of liberalism could best be reached through a disciplined organization. Unfortunately this tended to produce a surrender of the individual conscience to the conscience of the Party." WFO report, July 8, 1955, Herbert Fuchs FBI File 101-1169, Federal Bureau of Investigation.

23. *Evening Star,* December 13, 1955, 1.

24. *Washington Post,* December 14, 1955, 1.

25. *New York Times,* December 14, 1955. That night and the next morning, news articles carried a related story in which Ohio representative and HUAC member Gordon Scherer claimed that Bishop Bromley Oxnam had pressured American University into firing my father because he had testified. In an attempt to substantiate his claim, Mr. Scherer cited Oxnam's recent book, *I Protest,* which Scherer called "a violent attack on this committee." Bishop Oxnam and A.U. President Hurst Anderson categorically denied that Oxnam had attempted to influence the vote of the A.U. Board of Trustees; see figure 10. "AU Pressured into Firing Fuchs Red Prober Says," *Evening Star,* December 14, 1955, 1; "AU President Denies Pressure to Fire Fuchs," *Evening Star,* December 15, 1955, A-1 and A-4.

26. Navasky, *Naming Names,* 321.

Chapter 10

The epigraph to this chapter is taken from Ellen Schrecker, *The Age of McCarthyism: A Brief History with Documents* (New York: Bedford Books, 1994), 82.

1. My father's perceptions of his blacklist crisis are taken from his personal journal and records, September 1955–December 1956, Herbert Fuchs papers.

2. "Tenure and Temperament," *Washington Post,* September 25, 1955.

3. "'Says Dismissal of Ex-Red Stands,'" *New York Herald Tribune,* September 25, 1955.

4. Herbert Fuchs's journal, July 1, 10, 13, 16, 18–21, and 29, 1955; September 11–15, 21, and 28–29, 1955; October 11, 17–18, 20–21, and 23, 1955, Herbert Fuchs papers; Herbert Fuchs to Henry P. Brandis Jr., November 6 and 28, 1955, and January 27, 1956, Herbert Fuchs papers; Henry P. Brandis Jr. to Herbert Fuchs, November 20, 1956, Herbert Fuchs papers; Rorty, "The Case of Herbert Fuchs"; Hurst Anderson to Clark Byse, December 13, 1955, Herbert Fuchs File, American University Archives, Washington, D.C.; Bozell, "Special Report: The Firing of Herbert Fuchs"; "Tenure and Temperament," *Washington Post,*

September 25, 1955; "American U President Calls Fuchs Firing Final," *Washington Post,* September 25, 1955; "The Victim," *New York Post,* January 10, 1956; "U Challenged over Fuchs," *New York Herald Tribune,* March 29, 1956; "Censure of AU on Fuchs Asked," *Washington Star,* April 4, 1956; "College Hit for Firing Former Red," *Labor's Daily,* April 12, 1956; "Moral Dilemma on Campus," *Life,* April 23, 1956.

5. "The Man Who Confessed," *Time,* October 10, 1955.

6. *Washington Post,* September 24, 1955; ACLU Academic Freedom Committee press release, March 15, 1956, Herbert Fuchs papers.

7. Herbert Fuchs's journal and records, 1955–57, Herbert Fuchs papers; Report of the Committee on Academic Freedom and Tenure of the Association of American Law Schools, September 14, 1956, Herbert Fuchs papers.

8. Sol Stein, executive director, American Committee for Cultural Freedom, to Herbert Fuchs, February 1, 1956, Herbert Fuchs papers. After several months' investigation, the ACCF told my father that "there is practically no legal recourse, but a very large area for moral and public complaint in regard to both your dismissal from the University and the quarantine from your students imposed by the University until the expiration of your contract."

9. American Committee for Cultural Freedom (signed by Diana Trilling, chairman, Board of Directors) to members of the American University Board of Trustees, April 17, 1956, Herbert Fuchs papers.

10. Bozell, "Special Report: The Firing of Herbert Fuchs," 13.

11. "Dr. Anderson's Letter," *National Review* 1.10 (January 25, 1956): 15.

12. Herbert Fuchs to Henry P. Brandis Jr., January 27, 1956, Herbert Fuchs papers.

13. Reinhold Niebuhr to Hurst Anderson, March 21, 1956, Herbert Fuchs File, American University Archives, Washington, D.C.

14. "The Fuchs Case," *Cincinnati Enquirer,* September 20, 1955; "The Man Who Confessed," *Time,* October 10, 1955; "Academic Freedom," *Dan Smoot Speaks,* November 25, 1955; "Why No Fuss When a Helpful Ex-Red Professor Is Fired?" *Saturday Evening Post,* December 10, 1955; "Communists at Work," *Washington Star,* December 15, 1955; "The Strange Case of Dr. Fuchs," *Washington Daily News,* December 19, 1955; "The Victim," *New York Post,* January 10, 1956; "The Man Who Didn't," *Commonweal,* April 13, 1956; "Moral Dilemma on Campus," *Life,* April 23, 1956; "The Case of the Fired 'Informer,'" *New Leader,* April 30, 1956; "What Price Forgiveness?" *Washington Post,* May 17, 1956.

15. "Moral Dilemma on Campus," *Life,* April 23, 1956; Bozell, "Special Report: The Firing of Herbert Fuchs."

16. Professor Fred Rodell, Yale University Law School, to the American Committee for Cultural Freedom, March 23, 1956, Herbert Fuchs papers.

17. Draft of letter (never sent) from Herbert Fuchs to Professor Fred Rodell, Yale University Law School, Herbert Fuchs papers.

18. Rorty, "The Case of Herbert Fuchs"; Herbert Fuchs's journal, May 16, 19, and 22, 1956, Herbert Fuchs papers.

19. Herbert Fuchs' journal, June 5, 1956, Herbert Fuchs papers.

20. "American U Firm on Fuchs," *Washington Post,* April 22, 1956.

21. Rorty, "The Case of Herbert Fuchs."

22. Herbert Fuchs's journal, July 10, 1956, Herbert Fuchs papers.

23. Herbert Fuchs's journal, September 28, 1955, Herbert Fuchs papers.

24. Report of the Committee on Academic Freedom and Tenure of the Association of American Law Schools, September 14, 1956, I, 1, Herbert Fuchs papers.

Chapter 12

1. Robert Meeropol and Michael Meeropol, *We Are Your Sons: The Legacy of Ethel and Julius Rosenberg* (Boston: Houghton Mifflin, 1975), 15, 22, 36.

2. Audree Penner, "Shadows of an Execution," *Swarthmore College Bulletin,* February 1995.

3. Walter and Miriam Schneir, *Invitation to an Inquest* (New York: Penguin Books, 1973); Ronald Radosh and Joyce Milton, *The Rosenberg File: A Search for the Truth,* 2nd ed. (New Haven: Yale University Press, 1997).

4. Carl Bernstein, *Loyalties: A Son's Memoir* (New York: Simon and Schuster, 1989), 52.

5. Ibid., 13.

6. This friend's name has been changed.

7. The term *red diaper baby* usually refers to children of past or present members of the Communist Party; it can also refer to the children of others who participated in groups directed or supported by the Party.

8. Kim Chernin, *In My Mother's House* (New York: Harper and Row, 1983).

9. Ann Kimmage, *An Un-American Childhood: A Young Woman's Secret Life behind the Iron Curtain* (University of Georgia Press, 1996).

10. Ibid., xxiv–xxv.

11. Ellen Schrecker, *Many Are the Crimes: McCarthyism in America* (Boston: Little Brown, 1998), 146.

12. Judy Kaplan and Linn Shapiro, eds., *Red Diapers: Growing up in the Communist Left* (Urbana and Chicago: University of Illinois Press, 1998).

13. Ibid., 8.

Chapter 13

1. See Steven Beller, *Vienna and the Jews, 1876–1938: A Cultural History* (Cambridge, England: Cambridge University Press, 1989), chapter 12.

2. The FBI investigated my father in June 1934 in connection with an application for a job at the U.S. Department of Justice: July 24, 1934, Herbert Fuchs FBI NY File 77-400,

Federal Bureau of Investigation. CCNY and NYU Law School transcripts, Herbert Fuchs papers.

3. Richard Fuchs, conversations with the author, September 29, 1996, and July 29, 2001.

4. My father once told a friend that joining the Communist Party was like joining a religion. He told Devin Bent that he joined because all his friends were doing it. Devin also recalls Dad saying that he started smoking because someone had taken him to a smoker at City College. Devin, who was fond of my father (remembering him as the only adult who talked to him "the way one talks to a real person"), was troubled by the fact that my father did not accept responsibility for taking either of these courses of action. Devin had diffi-culty picturing my father as a "dedicated committed social activist," suggesting he either changed drastically over the years or was "never really into it" (Devin Bent, E-mail mes-sages to the author, June 1 and 4, 1997).

5. Dana Fox Willens, telephone conversation with the author, October 9, 1996.

6. In fairness to my uncle Vernon and his wife, Florence, I do remember my uncle reaching out to my parents, particularly during the last years of my father's life when he was living in a nursing home. My mother had a number of conversations with Vernon on the telephone.

7. Vernon and Florence Fox, telephone conversation with the author, October 21, 1996. My aunt sent an article, published in *Jewish Affairs,* in which she denies the existence of anti-Semitism in the Soviet Union: "Amongst the forces working against the establishment of détente and world peace," the article declares, "are those who have spread the canard of 'Soviet anti-Semitism'" (Florence Fox, "Saving Soviet Jews," *Jewish Affairs,* September 1986).

8. As young men, my uncle and several of his friends climbed the George Washington Bridge while it was still under construction. The police had difficulty getting them to come down. The incident made the local news.

9. Vernon Fox, interview with the author, August 22, 1997.

Chapter 14

The epigraph to this chapter is taken from Arthur Koestler, *Arrow in the Blue: An Auto-biography* (New York: Macmillan, 1952), 334.

1. In *Nightmare in Red*, Richard M. Fried suggests that "the Party enticed intellectu-als chiefly by its stalwart anti-fascism" and that the "full employment in the USSR, in con-trast to the breadlines in the U.S., impressed some observers, as did the liberal-sounding 1936 Soviet Constitution" (*Nightmare in Red: The McCarthy Era in Perspective* [New York: Oxford University Press, 1990], 13). Certainly in 1936, the Spanish Civil War was also a strong rallying cry for the enemies of fascism.

2. Reflecting upon his experience in the Party some years later, Dad admitted to "a certain amount of intellectual arrogance" on his part and the part of other Party mem-

bers: "You were always certain you were right. . . . [J]oining the Communist Party gave me a sense of superiority. By joining the Party I became a member of an elite[;] this made me think I was better than any one who was not a Communist Party member. . . . Being a . . . member gave me a chance to be a leader, to be appreciated" (WFO Interview Report, July 24, 1955, Herbert Fuchs FBI File 101-1169, Federal Bureau of Investigation).

3. Interview with WFO agents, June 24, 1955, Herbert Fuchs FBI File 101-1169, Federal Bureau of Investigation. Elizabeth Bentley, in her 1945 HUAC testimony, said the following: "[Overthrowing the government] was not mentioned at all in those days, possibly because that was during Earl Browder's regime . . . they did not come out in the open with any revolutionary program. We were told that the only solution was education [. . .] that people must be taught so that we would finally get a majority of American people to vote that particular regime into power" (*Hearings Regarding Communist Espionage in the U.S. Government,* Hearings before the Committee on Un-American Activities, Congress Committee Hearings, Eightieth Congress [Senate Library, Vol. 1223, 1948], 548).

4. Authors Ralph de Toledano and Victor Lasky claim that "along with other Comintern agents, [Hale Ware] was given the order to begin the systematic creation of Communist cells wherever possible." Ware "was assigned to Washington to direct operations there. The idea was—at first—not espionage but infiltration" (*Seeds of Treason: The True Story of the Hiss-Chambers Tragedy* [New York: Funk and Wagnalls, 1950], 44–45).

5. Interview with WFO agents, June 24, 1955, Herbert Fuchs FBI File 101-1169, Federal Bureau of Investigation.

6. Earl Latham, *The Communist Controversy in Washington: From the New Deal to McCarthy* (Cambridge, MA: Harvard University Press, 1966), 92–94. Allen Weinstein suggests that as the Communist leadership began to take seriously the potential threat to the Soviet Union posed by the Nazis, the Communist Party became more interested in gathering information in the United States (*Perjury: The Hiss-Chambers Case* [New York: Random House, 1978, 1997], 172).

7. *Investigation of Communist Infiltration of Government—Part I,* Hearing before the Committee on Un-American Activities, HUAC Chairman Francis Walter, House of Representatives, Eighty-fourth Congress, December 13, 1955, 3119; qtd. in Latham, *Communist Controversy in Washington,* 126.

8. *Investigation of Communist Infiltration of Government—Part I,* 2964–65. James Gorham's testimony regarding the Wheeler Committee Communist unit corroborated my father's on many points (qtd. in Latham, *Communist Controversy in Washington,* 126–27).

9. *Investigation of Communist Infiltration of Government—Part I,* 2965–66.

10. Thomas Emerson, *Young Lawyer for the New Deal: An Insider's Memoir of the Roosevelt Years* (Savage, MD: Rowman and Littlefield, 1991), 131.

11. *Investigation of Communist Infiltration of Government—Part I,* 2988.

12. Ibid., 3011.

13. Ibid., 2985–86.

14. Ibid., 3027–28, 3038, 3041.

15. Ibid., 3043–55.

16. Ibid., 3053.

17. Ibid., 3063.

18. Ibid., 3063–64. My mother and father were close friends with this witness and his family. There are numerous photos in my parents' photo album of the two families (Herbert Fuchs papers).

19. *Investigation of Communist Infiltration of Government—Part I*, 3066.

20. Historian Earl Latham suggests that for those, like my father, who insisted on involving themselves in mass protests, there appeared not to have been the same rejection of American society as was the case for others who not only joined an illegal organization but were in fact also doing illegal work. Latham points out, "The evident desire of the group to associate actively in public front causes indicates, in some degree, that the absolute alienation from the values of the society, which makes the dedicated revolutionary, did not exist. . . . Fuchs said that the members of the group felt that they were performing a patriotic duty by participating in the enforcement of the Wagner Act, and they were zealous in the belief that it was a good thing" (*The Communist Controversy in Washington*, 144–46). Group members were encouraged to belong to the NLRB Union and to organize other staff employees into it.

21. *Investigation of Communist Infiltration of Government—Part I*, 3004–6.

22. Schrecker, *Many Are the Crimes*, 161.

23. Transcript of interview with Herbert Fuchs by Judith H. Byne, Cornell University School of Industrial and Labor Relations, 1968, 15 (for James A. Gross's history of the NLRB, *The Reshaping of the National Labor Relations Board: National Labor Policy in Transition* [Albany: State University of New York Press, 1981]), Herbert Fuchs papers.

24. Ibid., 22.

25. *Investigation of Communist Infiltration of Government—Part I*, 3004.

26. Ibid., 3013.

27. Transcript of interview with Herbert Fuchs by Byne, 19, Herbert Fuchs papers.

28. Latham, *The Communist Controversy in Washington*, 134, 143. Summarizing the influence of the Communist Party on the policies and procedures of the NLRB, Latham concludes the following: "First, there does not seem to have been a planned and premeditated 'infiltration' of the Federal agencies, certainly not at the start. Second, once the entry into the Federal service by members of the Communist Party took place . . . some members of the party formed in study groups. . . . [T]he aim of these groups seems to have been the promotion of left tendencies in the development of the public policies of the respective agencies. . . . [T]he party groups were not primarily organized for espionage" (150).

29. The two investigations of my father were: the Smith Committee investigation (an investigation of the NLRB with the intent to reorganize the board and strip it of its power

and influence on behalf of labor unions) and an FBI investigation under the Hatch Act (which forbade government employment of anyone who belonged to a political party or organization that advocated the overthrow of the government).

30. *Investigation of Communist Infiltration of Government—Part I,* 2993.

31. Ibid., 3000–3002.

32. House Committee on Un-American Activities Executive Session Transcripts—Herbert Fuchs, June 13, 1955, *National Archives Records of the United States House of Representatives,* 25.

33. WFO Report, July 8, 1955, Herbert Fuchs FBI File 101-1169,Federal Bureau of Investigation.

34. House Committee on Un-American Activities Executive Session Transcripts—Herbert Fuchs, 73.

35. Herbert Fuchs to Henry P. Brandis Jr., January 27, 1956, Herbert Fuchs papers.

Chapter 15

1. A news clipping copyrighted U.P.C. News Service, Inc. (probably from the *New York Times,* in the late 1920s) describes J. Wise, Inc. as "one of the best known firms in the great garment manufacturing industry of New York. . . . [T]here is probably not a dress buyer in the United States who is not familiar with the Wise line. It is sold in every state in the Union" (Frances Rice Fuchs papers).

2. These job experiences included the following: authoring the "Cost of Government in the United States, 1926–27" as a member of the staff of the National Industrial Conference Board; collecting and analyzing material for the volume "Planning and Control of Public Works" with Dr. Leo Wolman at the National Bureau of Economic Research; serving on the National Commission on Law Observance and Enforcement with E. A. Winslow; at the Brookings Institution with Dr. Lewis Lorwin; and on the President's Committee on Social Trends with Dr. O. E. Baker (Frances Rice Fuchs papers, September 13, 1933).

3. Frances Perkins, *The Roosevelt I Knew* (New York: Viking Press, 1946), 166.

4. Harry Magdoff was named by Elizabeth Bentley in 1945 as a member of the so-called Perlo Group. She claimed that this group of U.S. Government employees had provided her with privileged information intended for the Soviets.

5. Harry and Beadie Magdoff, interview with the author, December 28, 1998.

6. "Changes in Cost of Living," July 15, 1935, one of a number of pamphlets prepared by my mother, explains "the results of the methodological revision undertaken" during the preceding year. An article reviewing a study of "Inter-City Differences in the Cost of Living," published by the Works Progress Administration, analyzed "the differences in costs from place to place, emphasizing the particular technique required in pricing the same level of living in different places" (Frances Rice Fuchs papers).

7. Harry and Beadie Magdoff, interview with the author, December 28, 1998; Harry Magdoff, interview with the author, April 5, 2002.

8. Memo from SAC to Director, WFO, October 6, 1955, Frances Rice Fuchs FBI File 101HQ2450, 6, Federal Bureau of Investigation.

9. This organization would later be considered by the FBI to be a Communist front organization because of its core group of leaders (Communists) who met separately from membership meetings to discuss the "correct" position on issues; those leaders would guide the membership to take stands consistent with their point of view.

10. This was the nonaggression pact signed by Joseph Stalin and German foreign minister Joachim von Ribbentrop on August 23, 1939. Hitler's motivation for signing the pact was to free his army from having to fight a two-front war. Stalin, who had been unsuccessful in forming a defensive alliance with Britain, signed the pact hoping this would prevent Nazi Germany from expanding its borders at the expense of the Soviet Union.

11. Louise Hollander, conversation with the author, October 21, 1996.

12. *Investigation of Communist Infiltration of Government—Part I,* 3010.

13. Louise Hollander, conversation with the author, October 21, 1996.

14. Elizabeth Bentley attributed this comment to her mentor Jacob Golos (Bentley, *Out of Bondage: The Story of Elizabeth Bentley* [New York: Devin-Adair, 1951], 106).

15. Louise Hollander, conversation with the author, October 21, 1996.

Chapter 16

1. Memo from SAC to Director, WFO, January 19, 1955, Herbert Fuchs FBI File 101-1169, Federal Bureau of Investigation.

2. Memo number 92077, September 19, 1947, Herbert Fuchs FBI File 101-1169, Federal Bureau of Investigation.

3. Accusation by Abigail in Arthur Miller's *The Crucible,* his play about the Salem witch-hunt.

4. A scenario that predicts dire consequences of repeated nuclear attacks: smoke, soot, and dust blanketing the planet and darkening the skies; dangerous levels of pollutants in the air; freezing temperatures and halted food production, resulting in massive starvation and death.

5. *Washington Star,* August 23, 1955, A-1, A-5.

6. *Hearings Regarding Communist Espionage in the U.S. Government.* Hearings before the Committee of Un-American Activities, U.S. Congress Committee Hearings, Eightieth Congress, Senate Library, Vol. 1223, 1948, 507.

7. *Washington Post,* August 1, 1948, 1, 3.

8. *Investigation of Communist Infiltration of Government—Part I,* 3016.

9. See Elinor Langer, *Josephine Herbst* (Boston: Little, Brown, 1983); Sam Tanenhaus, *Whittaker Chambers: A Biography* (New York: Random House, 1997); Weinstein, *Perjury: The Hiss-Chambers Case.*

10. See Venona cables #588, New York to Moscow, April 29, 1944, National Security Agency, http://www.nsa.gov/public_info/_files/venona/1944/29apr_recruits.pdf; #687,

New York to Moscow, May 13, 1944, http://www.nsa.gov/public_info/_files/venona/1944/ 13may_new_recruits.pdf; #769 and #771, New York to Moscow, May 30, 1944, http://www. nsa.gov/public_info/_files/venona/1944/30may_kgb_ny.pdf.

11. See Venona cables #628, New York to Moscow, May 5, 1944, National Security Agency, http://www.nsa.gov/public_info/_files/venona/1944/5may_new_agent.pdf; #736, New York to Moscow, May 22, 1944, http://www.nsa.gov/public_info/_files/venona/1944/ 22may_spycraft.pdf; #845, New York to Moscow, June 14, 1944, http://www.nsa.gov/ public_info/_files/venona/1944/14jun_rosenberg_spycraft.pdf; #911, New York to Moscow, June 27, 1944, http://www.nsa.gov/public_info/_files/venona/1944/27jun_new_ asset_recruited_rosenberg.pdf; #1053, New York to Moscow, June 26, 1944, http:// www.nsa.gov/public_info/_files/venona/1944/26jul_recruitment_effort_resenberg.pdf; #1251, New York to Moscow, September 2, 1944, http://www.nsa.gov/public_info/_files/ venona/1944/2sept_covername_changes.pdf; #1314, New York to Moscow, September 14, 1944, http://www.nsa.gov/public_info/_files/venona/1944/14sep_gnome_gets_raise. pdf; #1327, New York to Moscow, September 15, 1944, http://www.nsa.gov/public_info/_ files/venona/1944/15sep_specs_robot_aircraft.pdf; #1340, New York to Moscow, September 21, 1944, http://www.nsa.gov/public_info/_files/venona/1944/21sep_recruitment_ by_rosenbergs.pdf; #1491, New York to Moscow, October 22, 1944, http://www.nsa.gov/ public_info/_files/venona/1944/22oct_new_assets.pdf; #1600, New York to Moscow, November 14, 1944, http://www.nsa.gov/public_info/_files/venona/1944/14nov_recruitment_ by_rosenberg.pdf; #1609, New York to Moscow, November 17, 1944, http://www.nsa.gov/ public_info/_files/venona/1944/17nov_resupply_film_cassettes.pdf; #1657, New York to Moscow, November 27, 1944, http://www.nsa.gov/public_info/_files/venona/1944/27nov_ mrs_rosenberg.pdf; #1715, New York to Moscow, December 5, 1944, http://www.nsa. gov/public_info/_files/venona/1944/5dec_various_agents.pdf; #1749-1750, New York to Moscow, December 13, 1944, http://www.nsa.gov/public_info/_files/venona/1944/13dec_ garbled_rqst.pdf; #1773, New York to Moscow, December 16, 1944, http://www.nsa.gov/ public_info/_files/venona/1944/16dec_los_alamos.pdf; #1797, New York to Moscow, December 20, 1944, http://www.nsa.gov/public_info/_files/venona/1944/20dec_new_lab. pdf; #28, New York to Moscow, January 8, 1945, http://www.nsa.gov/public_info/_files/ venona/1945/8jan_victor.pdf; #200, Moscow to New York, March 6, 1945, http://www.nsa. gov/public_info/_files/venona/1945/6mar_liberal_gets_raise.pdf; #3713-15, Washington to Moscow, June 29, 1945, http://www.nsa.gov/public_info/_files/venona/1945/29jun_ victor_perlo_secret_govt_docs.pdf.

12. I have no way of knowing if my father knew Silvermaster or knew about the Silvermaster investigations.

13. Frances Rice Fuchs papers.

14. *Hearings Regarding Communist Espionage in the United States Government,* Hearings before the Committee on Un-American Activities, Eightieth Congress, (Senate Library, Vol. 1221, 1948), 521.

15. Bentley, *Out of Bondage,* 117.

16. Ibid., 99.

17. Frances Rice Fuchs papers.

18. James Burnham, *The Web of Subversion: Underground Networks in the U.S. Government* (New York: John Day, 1954), 13.

19. Harry Magdoff, interview with the author, April 5, 2002.

20. Allen Weinstein and Alexander Vassiliev, *The Haunted Wood: Soviet Espionage in America—The Stalin Era* (New York: Random House, 1999), 208.

21. See Weinstein and Vassiliev, *The Haunted Wood,* 106–7, 229, 261–62; Silvermaster FBI File 65–402, Vol. 6, 220, 54, 58, Federal Bureau of Investigation; Venona cable #1810, New York to Moscow, December 23, 1944, referring to cable #1751-53, New York to Moscow, December 13, 1944, National Security Agency, http://www.nsa.gov/public_info/_files/venona/1944/23dec_foreign_office.pdf.

22. John Earl Haynes and Harvey Klehr, *Venona: Decoding Soviet Espionage in America* (New Haven: Yale University Press, 1999), 123. Elizabeth Bentley FBI File 65-56402, Vol. 82, 1862, 101, 102, and 129.

23. Herbert L. Packer, *Ex-Communist Witnesses: Four Studies in Fact Finding* (Stanford, CA: Stanford University Press, 1962), 8.

24. Confidential report, WFO, July 8, 1955, Herbert Fuchs FBI File 101-1169, 8, Federal Bureau of Investigation.

25. Memo from SAC to Director, WFO, October 6, 1955, Frances Rice Fuchs FBI File 101-HQ-2450, 10, Federal Bureau of Investigation.

Chapter 17

The epigraph to this chapter is taken from Navasky, "Dialectical McCarthyism(s)," *Nation* 27 (July 20, 1998): 30–31.

1. Ruth Bardenstein, conversation with the author, spring 1991.

2. Harry Magdoff, E-mail message to the author, July 1998.

3. I probably did see him once or twice after the war when I would have been old enough to remember.

4. On December 31, 1945, my parents took me along to a New Year's Eve party. I remember it well as we had just returned to Washington from Denver and it was a special day—my fourth birthday. When we arrived at the party, the hostess took me upstairs to a room by myself. I was given a book of nursery rhymes (which I still have) and was left alone to fall asleep. I was furious; I didn't want my parents to leave me alone, didn't like the ham the hostess had given me for dinner, and couldn't fall asleep for all the noise. Much later on the way home, exhausted and enraged, I threw up all over my beautiful new coat.

5. In his testimony before HUAC, my father acknowledged knowing these people socially; he did not mention anything about their work or their politics.

6. Harry and Beadie Magdoff, interview with the author, December 28, 1998.

7. Schrecker, *Many Are the Crimes,* 360.

8. Victor Navasky, interview with the author, December 21, 2001.

9. Harry Magdoff, E-mail message to the author, February 8, 2002.

10. Harry Magdoff, interview with the author, April 4–5, 2002.

11. *The Age of Imperialism: The Economics of U.S. Foreign Policy* (New York: Monthly Review Press, 1969) sold 100,000 copies and was translated into more than a dozen languages (Susan Green, "The Sage of Imperialism," *Monthly Review* [July 25, 2005], http://www.monthlyreview.org/tribute.htm).

12. John Abt acknowledged having been in a secret group, and though he said it was "conceivable that the commentary and analyses we provided to the national Party leadership may have reached the Soviets" because of "regular exchanges of information . . . through the Communist International," he emphatically denied having committed espionage (Abt, *Advocate and Activist: Memoirs of an American Communist Lawyer* [Urbana: University of Illinois Press, 1993], 41–42).

13. Silvermaster FBI File 65-56402, Federal Bureau of Investigation.

14. Harry Magdoff, "A Note on the *Communist Manifesto,*" *Monthly Review* 30.1 (May 1998): 11.

15. Ibid.

Chapter 18

The epigraph to this chapter is taken from Schrecker, *Many Are the Crimes,* 109.

1. After graduating from George Washington University in 1917, Hoover went to work at the Justice Department. Two years later he became the special assistant to attorney general Alexander M. Palmer, who placed him in charge of a new department set up to organize the arrest and deportation of suspected Communists. At the urging of Hoover, Palmer called for the arrest of thousands of suspected Communists and anarchists in raids across the country (the Palmer Raids took place in November 1919). The FBI was established in 1935 with Hoover as its director. For the next almost thirty-seven years, Hoover concentrated on expanding his power and influence as leader of a first-rate crime-fighting organization. He served as director until his death in May of 1972. See Athan G. Theoharis and John Stuart Cox, *The Boss: J. Edgar Hoover and the Great American Inquisition* (Philadelphia: Temple University Press, 1988), and Curt Gentry, *J. Edgar Hoover: The Man and the Secrets* (New York: Norton, 1991).

2. Schrecker, *Many Are the Crimes,* 106.

3. Ibid., 107.

4. Ibid., 108–9.

5. Ibid.

6. At one point Fred said that he and Bob Putnam did not record all of what my parents said. When I pressed him on what he meant by this, in a second phone call, Fred couldn't remember anything being discussed that was off the record. "Frances and Herbert knew

that everything they said was being recorded" (Fred Griffith, telephone conversation with the author, December 30, 2001).

7. Fred Griffith, telephone conversations with the author, February 27 and December 30, 2001.

8. I found it intriguing that there were others who also came to admire the FBI agents with whom they were involved. Like my father, Whittaker Chambers felt isolated during the time he decided to talk; he developed a fondness for the agents who interviewed him: "The agents referred to Chambers, affectionately, as 'Uncle Whit.' His friendly relations with his interrogators lessened the ordeal" (Tanenhaus, *Whittaker Chambers,* 341). Former Russian agent Hede Massing was also pleasantly surprised when she went to the FBI to tell her story: "Two efficient men asked me for some specific information.... There was no coercion, no tricks.... They were intelligent, observant, well-informed—as I could judge by the questions asked—and pleasantly unemotional. They did not underestimate the individual under suspicion, on the contrary, they seemed to respect him and understand him in his own environment. This impressed me indeed. It was most unexpected" (Hede Massing, *This Deception* [New York: Duell, Sloan and Pearce, 1951], 314).

9. Frances Fuchs, Frances Regina Rice Fuchs, Frances Regina Fuchs, Frances Rice Fuchs, Regina Fuchs, Francis Rice Fuchs, Francis Fuchs, Mrs. Francis Fuchs, Mrs. Herbert Fuchs, Mrs. Herb Fuchs, Frances, Frances Regina Rice, Frances R. Rice, Regina Rice, Frances Rice, Francis Rice, Miss Francis Rice, Fran Fuchs, Franny Fuchs, Frannie Fuchs, Mrs. Frances Fuchs, Frances Reiss, Francis Reiss. Frances Rice Fuchs FBI File 101-HQ-2450, Federal Bureau of Investigation.

10. Confidential report, WFO, October 6, 1955, Frances Rice Fuchs FBI File 101-HQ-2450, 3, Federal Bureau of Investigation.

11. Abraham George Silverman was a mathematician and a statistician who worked in numerous government agencies in FDR's administration. He is believed to have been a member of the Silvermaster spy group. My mother, a statistician, knew him, but I don't know when or how well.

12. Bureau memorandum, August 29, 1947, in Summary Report on Frances Rice Fuchs, no date, Frances Rice Fuchs FBI File 101-HQ-2450, 6, Federal Bureau of Investigation.

13. Ibid., 10.

14. Robert J. Lamphere, *The FBI-KGB War: A Special Agent's Story* (Macon, GA: Mercer University Press, 1995), 105.

15. Coplon's convictions were overturned on appeal and she never served a prison sentence (ibid., 122).

16. FBI Silvermaster File 65-56402, Vol. 21, 58.

17. David J. Dallin, *Soviet Espionage* (New Haven: Yale University Press, 1955), 400.

18. Lamphere, *The FBI-KGB War,* 124–25.

19. FBI Silvermaster File 65-56402, Vol. 21, 58.

20. Magdoff, interview with the author, April 5, 2002.

21. Bureau memo, August 29, 1947, in Summary Report on Frances Rice Fuchs, no date, Frances Rice Fuchs FBI File 101-HQ-2450, 10, Federal Bureau of Investigation.

22. Memo from SAC, WFO, Application for Pardon, April 19, 1963, Herbert Fuchs FBI File 101-1169, 3, Federal Bureau of Investigation.

23. Also known as Title 5, U.S. Code 2283B, September 1, 1954, the Hiss Act determined "there shall not be paid any person, who prior to, on, or after, September 1, 1954, knowingly and willfully has made or makes any false, fictitious or fraudulent statements or presentations, or who, prior to, on, or after such date has concealed or conceals any material facts, with respect to his . . . past or present membership in, affiliation or association with, or support of the Communist Party" (Memo from SAC to Director, WFO, March 14, 1963, Herbert Fuchs FBI File 101-1169, 3, Federal Bureau of Investigation).

24. Also known as Title 5, U.S. Code 2285, September 26, 1961.

25. Memo from SAC to Director, WFO, March 14, 1963, Herbert Fuchs FBI File 101-1169, 3, Federal Bureau of Investigation.

26. Ibid., 6.

27. Memo from Director to SAC, WFO, Application for Pardon, March 7, 1963, Herbert Fuchs FBI File 101-1169, Federal Bureau of Investigation. Field officers were instructed to avoid publicity considered potentially injurious to the workings of the Judiciary Committee.

28. SAC Report, Application for Pardon, April 2, 1963, Herbert Fuchs FBI File 101-1169, Federal Bureau of Investigation.

29. SAC Report, Application for Pardon, April 19, 1963, Herbert Fuchs FBI File 101-1169, 6–8, Federal Bureau of Investigation.

30. Ibid., 9. On several occasions, Congressman Celler wrote letters of commendation to my father, thanking him for a job well done. One such letter, from my father's personal papers, follows:

> Dear Herb:
> I want you to know how greatly I appreciate all the effort, the time, and the loyalty you have given this Committee in the matter of the New York Port Authority. The decision of the court reflects the maturity and the thoroughness of your advice and preparation.
> Thank you,
> Sincerely yours,
> Emanuel Celler [signed]

31. Edwin Willis was the chairman of the Anti-Trust Subcommittee on which my father served as counsel.

32. SAC Report, Application for Pardon, April 19, 1963, Herbert Fuchs FBI File 101-1169, 11, 379–83, Federal Bureau of Investigation.

33. Ibid., 11–12.

Chapter 19

The epigraph to this chapter is taken from Navasky, *Naming Names,* 329.

1. Herbert Fuchs's journal, September 28, 1955, Herbert Fuchs papers.

2. During the Army-McCarthy hearings, Williams assisted McCarthy behind the scenes, though not in an official capacity (William K. Klingaman, *Encyclopedia of the McCarthy Era* [New York: Facts on File, 1996], 400–401).

3. Evan Thomas, *Edward Bennett Williams: Ultimate Insider: Legendary Trial Lawyer* (New York: Simon and Schuster, 1991), 71.

4. Fried, *Nightmare in Red,* 154. Fariello, *Red Scare,* 289.

5. Biographer Evan Thomas asks, "If Williams did press Berkeley to name names, is there anything wrong with it? It is perfectly common for lawyers to suggest that their clients finger someone else in order to save their own skin. In cases of white-collar crimes, low-level employees routinely seek immunity from prosecution by offering to testify before a grand jury against their corporate higher-ups. From a legal point of view, there was nothing unethical about Williams' role in the security cases. Still, it recreated an apparent conflict" (*Edward Bennett Williams,* 71).

6. Herbert Fuchs to Dean Henry P. Brandis Jr., Association of American Law Schools, January 27, 1956, Herbert Fuchs papers

7. Navasky, *Naming Names,* x, 375.

8. Whittaker Chambers, *Witness* (Washington, DC: Regnery Publishing, 1952), x, 375.

9. Navasky, *Naming Names,* xiii.

10. Ibid., xv.

11. Ibid., 314.

12. Ibid., 349, 356.

13. Herbert Fuchs's journal, September 28, 1955, Herbert Fuchs papers.

14. SAC Report, Application for Pardon, April 19, 1963, Herbert Fuchs FBI File 101-1169, 9, Federal Bureau of Investigation.

15. Jim Lichtenberg, E-mail message to the author, June 23, 1997.

16. In his journal, my father wrote, "At my appearance in executive session before C. Doyle, Velde and Willis, I made my first and, as it now appears, my only really crucial decision. I declined to take refuge in Constitutional immunity. Perhaps it is important for me to reconsider that decision—from which much of the present stems" (Herbert Fuchs's journal, September 28, 1955, Herbert Fuchs papers).

17. See Rushworth M. Kidder, *How Good People Make Tough Choices: Resolving the Dilemmas of Ethical Living* (New York: Morrow, 1995).

18. Fuchs to Brandis, January 27, 1956, Herbert Fuchs papers.

19. Ibid.

20. *Investigation of Communist Infiltration of Government—Part I,* Hearing before the Committee on Un-American Activities, HUAC Chairman Francis Walter, House of Representatives, Eighty-fourth Congress, December 13, 1955, 3010.

21. Fuchs to Brandis, January 27, 1956, Herbert Fuchs papers.

22. Herbert Fuchs's journal, September 28, 1955, Herbert Fuchs papers.

23. Ibid.

24. Fuchs to Brandis, January 27, 1956, Herbert Fuchs papers.

25. Ibid.

26. Kidder, *How Good People Make Tough Choices,* 76.

27. Herbert Fuchs's journal, September 28, 1955, Herbert Fuchs papers.

28. Ibid.

29. Ibid.

30. Navasky, *Naming Names,* 279.

31. Ibid., 306.

32. Fuchs to Brandis, January 27, 1956, Herbert Fuchs papers.

33. Navasky, *Naming Names,* 312.

34. Ibid., 312–13.

35. Ibid., 313.

36. Fuchs to Brandis, January 27, 1956, Herbert Fuchs papers.

Chapter 20

1. Devin Bent, telephone conversation with the author, May 29, 1997.

2. Jim Lichtenberg, E-mail message to the author, June 3, 1997.

3. Herbert Fuchs papers.

4. Marilyn Colborn, tribute at Frances Fuchs Memorial, Frances Fuchs Special Center, Beltsville, MD, April 26, 1996.

5. My mother received numerous awards during her tenure in Prince George's County, including the William S. Schmidt Annual Award from Prince George's County Association of Personnel Workers, an award as one of the ten outstanding educators of the year in 1977, and the annual Prince George's County Special Olympics dedicated to Frances R. Fuchs.

Chapter 21

1. My cousin Dana Willens stands out among all of my friends and relatives as the person most supportive of my father's actions during his HUAC experience. Dana, whose parents remained loyal to the Soviet Union until their last days, and who is well read and interested in the history of the Cold War, believes that the American Communists were misguided, at the very least, and that many of them betrayed their country by providing information to the Soviet Union.

2. I believe it was Phyllis's father, Earl Fahrney, who told the FBI in 1963 that it had been "difficult for him to feel friendly" toward my parents, and there had been a "continuous mental reservation . . . as to the applicant's loyalty to the Government of the United States" (SAC Report, Application for Pardon, April 19, 1963, Herbert Fuchs FBI File 101-1169, 8, Federal Bureau of Investigation). Though no name was connected with this quote, I identified Mr. Fahrney through the description of the relationship between the two families.

3. Ironically, in the 1970s, Phyllis experienced firsthand the effects of restricted life in a tightly controlled Communist society. She and her husband lived for three years in a house that she knows to have been bugged by the East German government.

4. Phyllis Fahrney Raynor, telephone conversation with the author, fall 1996.

5. Devin Bent, E-mail messages to the author, June 1 and 4, 1997.

6. Jim Lichtenberg, E-mail message to the author, June 26, 1997.

7. This is a short talk, in English, in which the Bar Mitzvah boy discusses some aspects of that Sabbath's readings from the Torah and relates them to his own life.

8. Helen Manfull, ed., *Additional Dialogue: Letters of Dalton Trumbo, 1942–1962* (New York: M. Evans, 1970), 569–70, as cited in Navasky, *Naming Names,* 387–88.

9. Niebuhr was among the theologians and philosophers who came to my father's defense in 1956.

10. Strachey, John, *The Strangled Cry* (New York: William Sloan Assoc., 1962), as cited in Navasky, *Naming Names,* 17.

11. Fariello, *Red Scare,* 444–47.

12. Thai Jones, E-mail message to the author, April 11, 2003. Thai's book is a family history; it covers his grandparents' life in the labor movement as well as the experiences of his parents (Eleanor Stein and Jeff Jones) as part of the New Left, including the Weather Underground. Thai's mother and father went underground in the late 1960s and didn't come out until they were arrested in 1981; Thai was born while the family was underground. The movie *Running on Empty* was written with his family as a model; Thai's book is *A Radical Line: From the Labor Movement to the Weather Underground, One Family's Century of Conscience* (New York: Free Press, 2004).

Chapter 22

The epigraph to this chapter is taken from Hope Hale Davis, *Great Day Coming: A Memoir of the 1930s* (South Royalton, VT: Steerforth Press, 1994), 336.

1. David S. Landes, *The Wealth and Poverty of Nations: Why Some Are So Rich and Some So Poor* (New York: Norton, 1999), 495.

2. Many who experienced the newborn U.S.S.R. in the twenties were deeply affected by its transformation from a country with millions of illiterate peasants to a major industrial nation.

3. Theodore Draper, *American Communism and Soviet Russia: The Formative Period* (New York: Octagon Books, 1977), 9.

4. Navasky, *Naming Names*, 357.

5. "Arthur Koestler," in *The God That Failed*, ed. Richard H. Crossman, rev. ed. (1949; repr., Washington, D.C.: Regnery Gateway, 1983), 23. For decades historians have argued about the extent of the dangers of Soviet-dominated Communism in our country and the evils of McCarthyism; their conclusions have changed over the years. Liberal scholars of the 1950s saw the Communist Party as closely aligned to and influenced by the Soviet Union, while they recognized that many individuals were motivated by idealism. At that time, people took Soviet espionage seriously and believed that some government officials had spied for the Soviets. Historians of the 1960s and 1970s, influenced by the anti-war and new left movements, did an about-face; their analysis held the United States accountable for the Cold War and maintained that Alger Hiss and Julius Rosenberg were innocent victims of the anti-Communist witch hunt. During the 1980s and 1990s, as more and more information surfaced from the Venona transcripts and the Soviet files, mainstream historians began characterizing the Party as an espionage wing of the Soviet government. See David Oshinsky, "McCarthy, Still Unredeemable," *New York Times*, November 7, 1996.

6. Crossman, introduction, *God That Failed*, 3.

7. de Toledano and Lasky, *Seeds of Treason*, 42–43.

8. Richard Crossman describes the appeal of Communism over liberalism as follows: "The intellectual attraction of Marxism was that it exploded liberal fallacies. . . . It taught the bitter truth that progress is not automatic, that boom and slump are inherent in capitalism, that social injustice and racial discrimination are not cured merely by the passage of time, and that power politics cannot be 'abolished,' but only used for good or bad ends" (introduction, *God That Failed*, 5).

9. Hede Massing explains: "For the intellectual with a conscience, it is easy to become a 'trusted soldier of the revolution.' Once he is incorporated and a functionary of the quasi-religious brotherhood, he lives in what seemed to be an elevated world. The rules are strict. It takes a long time to be detached enough to see whom you are serving. And then it takes more courage to break than it takes to join. The step to renounce the brotherhood of men . . . is very difficult. To leave the warmth, the safety and friendship that have been given you is a tragedy" (*This Deception*, 333).

10. Norman Podhoretz, foreword to Crossman, *God That Failed*, vi.

11. Ibid., xi.

12. Qtd. in Podhoretz, foreword to Crossman, *God That Failed*, vi–vii.

13. "Arthur Koestler," in Crossman, *God That Failed*, 23.

14. Koestler describes learning to "distrust" his "mechanistic preoccupation with facts," as he came to view the world "in the light of dialectic interpretation": "It was a satisfactory and indeed blissful state; once you had assimilated the technique you were no longer disturbed by facts; they automatically took on the proper color and fell into their proper place. Both morally and logically the Party was infallible: morally, because its aims were right, that is, in accord with the Dialectic of History, and these aims justified all means;

logically, because the Party was the vanguard of the Proletariat, and the Proletariat the embodiment of the active principle in History" (ibid., 34).

15. Ibid., 38.

16. "Ignazio Silone," in Crossman, *God That Failed,* 99.

17. "Andre Gide," in Crossman, *God That Failed,* 175–95; "Louis Fischer," in Crossman, 196–228. Even among those who understood that Stalin was a tyrant, there were thousands of Soviet citizens who looked upon this man with awe. He was to them the father of the Soviet Union, the man who had brought their nation into the twentieth century as a major world power.

18. As Ignazio Silone explains, "The truth is this: the day I left the Communist Party was a very sad one for me, it was like a day of deep mourning, the mourning for my lost youth. And I come from a district where mourning is worn longer than elsewhere. It is not easy to free oneself from an experience as intense as that of the underground organization of the Communist Party. Something of it remains and leaves a mark on the character which lasts all one's life" (Crossman, 113).

19. Trumbo quoted in Navasky, *Naming Names,* 387–88.

20. See Schrecker, *Many Are the Crimes* 360–86.

21. Ibid., 360.

22. Ibid., 373.

23. Ibid., 369. For a rebuttal of Schrecker's analysis, see John Earl Haynes and Harvey Klehr, *In Denial: Historians, Communism and Espionage* (San Francisco: Encounter Books, 2003), 227 ff.

24. American political journalist Jacob Weisberg sees it this way: "The one group that basically got Communism right back then is the . . . liberal anti-Communists. . . . It was liberal foreign-policy thinkers like Paul Nitze and George Kennan who devised the Truman Doctrine and containment, successful strategies for resisting the spread of Communism at the outset of the cold war. And it was liberal intellectuals like Arthur Schlesinger Jr. and Reinhold Niebuhr who developed the most useful understanding of the Communist threat. In his classic 1949 statement 'The Vital Center,' Schlesinger argued that while communism was certainly a danger to America, it wasn't much of a threat *in* America. The way to answer it, he wrote, was not by banning and prosecuting Communism, but through the Constitutional methods of 'debate, identification and exposure.' There were some things liberal anti-Communists of the 1950's didn't know, namely the extent of Soviet penetration of the United States government during the war years. Yet the new evidence confirms their larger picture. . . . The Truman administration, accused of sheltering spies, in fact rooted them out of the government" (Weisberg, "Cold War without End," *New York Times Magazine,* November 28, 1999, 157).

25. Navasky, *Naming Names,* 347.

26. Schrecker, *Many Are the Crimes,* 413.

27. House Committee on Un-American Activities Executive Session Transcripts—

Herbert Fuchs, June 13, 1955, Records of the United States House of Representatives, National Archives 70–72, 75.

28. Ibid., 40. My father told HUAC that his testimony offered "an opportunity, one which I did not seek but which reluctantly I must face, of being as candid as I am able to be with the United States in the personality of this subcommittee and to tell the truth as I now recall it with as little discoloration as I am capable of about myself" (ibid.)

29. Ibid., 117.

30. Ibid., 35.

31. House Committee on Un-American Activities Executive Session Transcripts—Herbert Fuchs, July 22, 1955, Records of the United States House of Representatives, National Archives, 190.

32. House Committee on Un-American Activities Executive Session Transcripts—Herbert Fuchs, June 13, 1955, 78–79. My father told the Committee that after he heard the accusations against Kaplan, he had become afraid to associate with his old friend. Ultimately Kaplan was told that my father felt this way, and Kaplan stopped attempting to visit my parents socially. At no time after Kaplan's trouble first hit the news, or even before, did my father discuss with him any aspect of the accusations against him.

33. My father's journal indicates that several people, including Bishop Oxnam, felt that Dad had not asserted himself enough to plead his case effectively (Herbert Fuchs's journal, Herbert Fuchs papers).

34. Navasky, *Naming Names,* 364.

Index